The Roman Villa
Villa Urbana

UNIVERSITY MUSEUM MONOGRAPH 101
SYMPOSIUM SERIES 9

First Williams Symposium on Classical Architecture held at
the University of Pennsylvania, Philadelphia, April 21–22, 1990

The Roman Villa
Villa Urbana

Alfred Frazer (†), editor
with contributions by Lisa Fentress, Chrystina Häuber, Adolf Hoffmann,
Ann Kuttner, Hans Lauter, Guy Metraux, Richard Neudecker,
and Andrew Wallace-Hadrill

Published by
The University Museum
University of Pennsylvania
Philadelphia
1998

Design, editing, production
   Publications Department, University of Pennsylvania Museum

Printing
   Science Press
   Ephrata, PA

Library of Congress Cataloging-in-Publication Data


```
Williams Symposium on Classical Architecture (1st : 1990 :
University of Pennsylvania, Philadelphia)
    The Roman villa : villa urbana / Alfred Frazer, editor ; with
contributions by Lisa Fentress ... [et al.] ; First Williams
Symposium on Classical Architecture held at the University of
Pennsylvania, Philadelphia, April 21-22, 1990.
    p. cm. --  (University Museum monograph ; 101) (University
Museum symposium series ; v. 9)
  Includes bibliographical references.
  ISBN 0-92-417159-6 (cloth)
  1. Architecture, Domestic--Rome. 2. Architecture and
society--Rome. I. Frazer, Alfred. II. Title. III. Series. IV.
Series: University Museum symposium series ; v. 9
  NA324 .W56 1990
  728.8'0937--ddc21
                                                   98-25363
                                                      CIP
```

Table of Contents

INTRODUCTION

Alfred Frazer (†)

It was an honor to be asked by the Department of the History of Art at the University of Pennsylvania to organize the first Williams Symposium on Classical Architecture, especially because it and subsequent symposia are made possible through the generosity of an old friend, Charles K. Williams, who has significantly contributed to our knowledge of the architecture of the Roman period in Greece. When asked to suggest a theme for the inaugural symposium, one that would be distinctly Roman in its address, I proposed that of the *villa urbana*, a defining element of Roman civilization, both as artifact and as social, economic, and cultural institution. This topic was enthusiastically accepted by the department, and I would like to express my gratitude to its faculty and staff, most particularly to its chairman, Professor Renata Holod, for generously helping me in the preparation of the symposium. At the same time, I wish to thank sincerely all the speakers for agreeing to participate, in some cases at considerable sacrifice, and for the thoughtful preparation of their contributions.

The *villa urbana*, the country house with the amenities of a city mansion set in a suburban or rural landscape, is a phenomenon widely documented not only in the archaeological record but also in Latin literature. Indeed, prior to the 19th century and the rise of careful archaeological inquiries, the principal mode of cultural transmission was literary. There were the Roman authors on agriculture, Cato, Varro, and Columella, the authority on architecture, Vitruvius, and the pastoral and bucolic works of Vergil and Horace. But most important of all for the transmission of the villa ideal were Cicero and the younger Pliny.

In a famous passage from one of the letters of the younger Pliny (*Letters* II, 17), written in the early second century of our era, he describes one of two villas that he owns and delights in. It is an example of the honorable literary genre *ekphrasis*, in which he presents an artful description of a work of architecture. Yet Pliny's description is not an empty literary exercise, but a deeply felt and revealing exposition of his appreciation of a villa that he has caused to be built. He takes his reader through it lovingly, beginning at its entrance and proceeding, beadlike, through each successive capsule of space until he reaches the villa's innermost recesses, rehearsing along the way the special delights of each part. He then turns and directs his gaze along the path he has traversed, back to the front door and on to the vast natural world beyond.

Here is the radiant face of a *plaissance* set in gardens and orchards that mediate between a great house and ripening fields and verdant woodlands. As in the case of most human enterprises, however, we confront an ambivalent phenomenon in the Roman villa. It touched two strata in Roman society: the ruling elite—the senatorial and equestrian orders—and their slaves, both the domestic servants, members of the *familia*, with their diverse skills, and the agricultural slaves who dwelt apart and worked separately under the supervision of overseers. In the course of time, and with the avenues of social mobility available in Roman society, new people including freedmen acquired both villas and the style of life appropriate to them, including slaves of their own.

This is the darker side of the Roman villa, made up of domestic and agricultural slavery, the patronizing of the *familia*, and the sweating of those chained or regimented into drones who plowed, cultivated and harvested the fields and upon whose unrecompensed and involuntary labor the pastoral superstructure was erected. The delights of the villa as a rural sanctuary were those enjoyed only by the villa owner, his wife, his family, and his friends. This Roman model has had a long effect. We still encounter both faces in Thomas Jefferson's Monticello, whose architecture and ingenious devices for pleasure and profit easily out-do Varro, and yet whose economic base, albeit somewhat shamefacedly, rests on the same Varronian foundation of chattel slavery.

To Americans, the parallel between the Roman villa and the plantation of the ante-bellum South may seem immediately striking, and it has often been drawn. Both were centered on "great houses" and based economically on chattel slavery devoted, often, to monoculture. And indeed, the Roman parallel was often involved by apologists for slavery in the American South. But the analogy is flawed. The Roman villa was enmeshed in a cultural nexus with city life and civic responsibilities. The American plantation was isolated and autonomous to a degree no Roman villa was. Both the villa and the plantation were the sites of great hospitality, but in our South hospitality was offered to other plantation owners desperate for a little sociability; in Roman villas the guests, although also villa owners, were seeking respite from the highly developed city life unknown to American landholders.

A better analogy might be with the merchant and ecclesiastical princes of Italy in the 15th and 16th centuries, where villas often occupied sites near or even in those of ancient Roman villas. These were, like their antique counterparts, linked to a vibrant and powerful urban center, be it Florence or Rome. And for this reason, if for no other, Renaissance villas shared a cultural life with their ancient paradigm unknown to plantations of the American South.

But perhaps the best post-Antique analogy is with the great country houses of England's 18th-century "Augustan Age." As in ancient Italy, power lay in the hands of an elite, who stood with one foot in Whitehall and the other in a great country estate. The culture of the country house was one with that of the metropolis—the best of the city, enjoyed in the best of countrysides. The economy of the English country life was not based on slavery, but something quite close to it. Through enclosure and exclusion, yeomen and peasants were prevented from exploiting public lands in a fashion not terribly different from that which in Roman Italy reduced a small freeholder to a state of rural serfdom or to an urban proletariat on welfare—the price paid for the assemblage of lands for great villas.

It is all too easy to examine an esthetic or cultural ideal without considering the human cost in pain and misery upon which it is built; it is equally easy simply to point a tendentious finger of scorn and reprobation at an institution whose makers were unaware of the moral cost of their enterprise. Neither judgmental attitude gets us very far in assessing the nature and significance of the villa phenomenon in the late Roman Republic and the early Empire, as they do not take into consideration the Roman perception of the situation. Slavery as a social institution was a given, even before the Roman conquest of the East prodigiously increased the number of available slaves. This being so, the great influx of slave labor during and after this period, rather than presenting a human, moral problem, presented to the Roman ruling class a straightforward economic opportunity.

In times past it has been only the life of the *dominus* and *domina*, and the physical setting of their life,

that has attracted the passion of scholars, artists, and most importantly those members of privileged elites who wished to re-create for their enjoyment something resembling their idea of a Roman villa. In the second half of this century we have recognized the two sides to the coin of the Roman *villa urbana*, but recognition is less important than understanding. And attempting to understand the villa phenomenon is a formidable, many-sided problem.

Our difficulty today in comprehending the phenomenon of the villa as it existed in ancient Roman society is surely the result of our modern society's almost complete divorce from the land. In Western countries we confront the paradox of an agriculture of unparalleled productivity that is the work of a minute fraction of our population. The "Man with a Hoe," still a potent symbol in 19th-century Europe and North America, has been replaced by that of the tractor and the harvester.

Wielders of power, intellectuals, and members of the working class are brothers and sisters alike in their lack of experience of the soil either directly or spiritually. Agrarian metaphors scarcely exist in our contemporary modes of discourse. We have no shared agricultural folk wisdom or folklore to which we have daily recourse. In their place we have agribusiness. Thus, in attempting to understand the essence of the Roman villa and its hold on the allegiances of the ruling class and on the experience of the rural proletariat, we lack the cultural indoctrination gained, as it were, at our grandparents' knees to allow us all-but-instinctively to ask the right questions.

To overcome the barrier imposed by profound, structural changes in a modern society and material culture that set us off even from that of early modern society, as well as that of a culture of some two millennia ago, requires the intensely focused talents and commitments of a broad spectrum of members in the community of classical studies. It is for this reason that the group invited to participate in the Williams Symposium included not only art historians and archaeologists but also Roman social, economic, and cultural historians who employ material evidence in their work.

In addition, I especially wished to introduce Greek issues, as they may relate to the villa phenomenon, into this symposium and its publication. Research has lagged in addressing an important problem, the relationship between Hellenistic culture and the formation of the Roman villa. Why did not Greeks in the Hellenistic centuries retreat to luxurious villas when the elite had the means to do so? And why did Romans, given the windfall profits of Eastern conquests, readily fall to villa life? Did Romans and other Italians have a different response to land and landscape than their Greek and other neighbors to the East? If so, why do some parts of the *de luxe* villas built by Romans have Greek names?

Given that the Roman conquest of the Greek world provided the massive transfer of wealth and the no less massive transfer of human capital in the form of chattel slaves that formed the necessary conditions for the appearance of the *villa urbana* in Latium and Campania, it might be presumed that some of the physical features of the villa appeared in Italy as part of the cultural baggage of Hellenism. It is this presumption that Hans Lauter addresses in his essay. (And, if anyone could enlighten us on the evidence of any random or even systematically employed threads in the Hellenistic world that could have been woven into the fabric of the *villa urbana* in Italy, it is Hans Lauter, who has written so widely and so well on Hellenistic architecture.) Correctly, he points to the monarchic-aristocratic society of Macedonia and its clones in the subsequent Hellenistic kingdoms as a far more likely field to discover such evidence than in the realms of the old Greek *poleis*. And, indeed, he does so in mining the tantalizingly fragmentary archaeological record in Macedonia. Yet we must agree with him that, despite the suggestive stimuli he adduces, the Roman Villa is "a product of the specifically Italic structure of society between the Late Republic and the Empire and is thus not to be paralleled in the differently constructed Greco-Macedonian world."

In seeking *comparanda* for the Roman villa beyond the Greek East, one naturally turns to the high culture of the agriculturally rich society of Greek Sicily. In her paper, Elizabeth Fentress interprets the results of her excavation of a site in the vicinity of Marsala in westernmost Sicily, a villa datable by ceramic evidence in its initial *floruit* to the second century B.C. Although Sicily had long before become Rome's first province, as Fentress shows, the essential "Greekness" of this extensive farmstead with a significant *pars urbana* testifies both to the continuing Hellenic nature of such structures in early Roman Sicily and to the land's native prosperity in the initial phases of Roman hegemony. Although features in the Sicilian estate may find some resonance in Roman villas, what is critically missing is the dialogue between *rus* and *urbs* and the social structure implicit in that dichotomy.

Our view of the ancient Roman villa as both an agricultural estate, centered on a group of utilitarian farm buildings for the storage of tools and crops and for the housing of animals and of a largely servile staff, and, at the same time, as a separate establishment of the landowner and his family, characterized by all the sophisticated splendors of his city dwelling, permits a variety of specialists to concentrate their attention on the phenomenon. The historian of agronomy, as well as the social and economic historian, will focus on the *pars rustica* and the *pars fructuaria*. The cultural, political, and art historians, on the other hand, will concentrate their gaze on the *pars urbana*,

the site of a dramatic encounter between Caesar and Cicero, the melancholy refuge of Tiberius, the pathetic yet luxurious prisons of the two Julias, the repositories of great freights of classical sculpture either haphazardly disposed or displayed in some sensible order. A few examples drawn from the essays in this volume demonstrate not only the variety of the facets of the villa phenomenon but also the variety of skills and perspectives, both methodological and ideological, that can be brought to the topic.

The art-historical contributions to this publication include a paper by Richard Neudecker in which he focuses on the question often raised, especially in recent years, of the sense or senses, if any, that informed the grouping and placement of works of Greek origin in Roman villas of the late Republic and early Empire. Cicero lightly characterized the intimate relation of Greek sculpture to the architecture and planting of his brother Quintus' villa with the following words: "Your gardener won my praise. He has covered everything with ivy, not only the foundation walls, but also the intercolumniations of the *ambulationes* so that the Greek statues seem to be hedge cutters and to be selling their wares" (Ad. Quint. 3.1.5). Taking, as others have before him, the sculptural contents of the *Villa dei Papiri* at Herculaneum as his test case, Neudecker illustrates just such an arrangement (albeit before the ivy has taken root) and arrives at different and more latitudinarian explications than have previous scholars.

Among the contributors who focus on the *pars rustica* and *pars fructuaria* of the villa, Nicholas Purcell directs our attention to the ancient economy, reminding us that it was ever one of potential scarcity, a scarcity that could be mitigated only by assiduous agricultural production and storage—be it that from plow land, pasture, vineyard, orchard, or wood lot. In such a reality, the *pars urbana* was ever supernumerary to the *pars rustica* and the *pars fructuaria* of the villa. The rare examples of the purely non-utilitarian villa are the instances that prove the rule. Their collections of Greek sculpture and elements of architectural conceit pale before those villas that gained their representational values in the display of labor and the fruits of that labor in the produce of vineyards, orchards, fields, barnyards, and market gardens.

In a setting in which food and drink are produced, in sight of farmland, pasture, and vineyard, communal eating and drinking, ever an important ritual in civilized life, assume additional weight. Katherine Dunbabin skillfully examines the phenomenon of the *convivium* in the life of the Roman *villa urbana* and its effects on villa architecture. Millennia of human experience at table lay behind the appearance of the convivium in the life of the Roman privileged, landed elite, and surely some of its more extravagant practices and pleasures derive straight from Hellenistic Greek models. Yet Dunbabin demonstrates significant Roman contributions to the art of the *convivium*, especially, as she is at pains to show, in a change from an inner-directed to an outer-oriented focus from the late Republic to late Antiquity, a change that finds ample architectural documentation in villas around the Mediterranean.

Of all the Roman villas, the emperor Hadrian's villa near Tivoli is the least likely to be interpreted as an instrument of agricultural production and display. Rather it is the supreme example of architectural production and display in the service of Imperial power and personality. It was, as it were, a Roman architectural world's fair. Adolf Hoffmann has concentrated his attention on the conjunction of the Vitruvian triad: the *firmitas* of vaulted construction, the *utilitas* of illumination, ventilation, and prospect and the *venustas* of the classical colonnade as uniquely exemplified in the Villa Hadriana. A study such as Hoffmann's, written a generation ago, would have focused on the structural virtuosity of the *Rohbau of opus caementicium* or on the ambiguously simple, yet complex geometry of the villa's individual parts and pavilions. But Hoffmann's interpretation, without any concession to passing fashion, may be characterized as post-modern and synthetic, rather than analytic. His focus is not on skeleton, a skeleton not only of compressively robust concrete but one acrobatically laced with tensily resilient iron bars, but on the skin of a seemingly serene classical colonnade.

Adducing many types of evidence, John Bodel demonstrates in his paper how often in the Roman world a villa of a man of the educated and propertied classes "was a direct reflection of his character: *qualis villa, talis vita.*" He examines the identification of a villa as a *monumentum* of its owner, especially an owner who built it "from the ground up." Here we may again be reminded of American parallels, such as George Washington and Thomas Jefferson, who are both closely identified with their country seats, Mount Vernon and Monticello, each well-regulated, slave-based estates *more Romano*. Both were buried on their properties; and, not only was Jefferson interred on the grounds of his villa, but most of his descendants have been buried there to this day, long after the title to the property has passed from the family. The Romanness of this, especially in respect to Jefferson, is striking.

Given the admiration felt for Jefferson and for the overall *romanitas* of Washington by American scholars of classical studies, it may be surprising that Roman architecture has not been an area to which these scholars have been much attached. Let us hope that the work presented in this volume, in all its variety, will encourage further research in this field among Americans, and that the whole international community of scholars will be stimulated by it to pursue further the important problems addressed here. The topic of the Roman villa seems particularly suited to this aim in that it is both a key characteristic of Roman culture and one aspect of the culture that has exerted a profound effect on various successor cultures, as it has been received, perceived, interpreted, and misinterpreted, naively or deliberately.

The picture emerging from this symposium, which will hopefully be part of the foundation for future studies, is far from the popular conception of the villa based on Victorian novels and Hollywood scripts, with its rose-embowered arbors supported on marble columns, providing a locus for either Sybaritic entertainments or quieter philosophical discourse, with the smoke-plumed cone of Mount Vesuvius looming ominously in the background. Not that there were not elements of such in the villa phenomenon; but our present view is a far more complex, interesting, and truthful one.

Postscriptum

Alfred Frazer's untimely death has, beyond the personal loss, left a wide and sad gap in the field of Classical architecture. In ways we could not anticipate, this is also reflected in the volume presented here. After an all too long span of editorial uncertainty following Al Frazer's decease, the proceedings of the symposium "The Roman Villa—*Villa Urbana*," held at the University of Pennsylvania in April 1990, appear at last, albeit in a somewhat truncated form.

Several contributors to the symposium could meanwhile arrange for other ways of publishing. They belong to this volume no less:
John Bodel. "Monumental Villas and Villa Monu-

ments." *Journal of Roman Archaeology* 10 (1997):5–35.

Katherine M. D. Dunbabin. "Convivial Spaces: Dining and Entertainment in the Roman Villa." *Journal of Roman Archaeology* 9 (1996):66–80.

Nicholas Purcell. "The Roman Villa and the Landscape of Production." Pp. 151–179 in *Urban Society in Roman Italy*, eds. Tim J. Cornell and Kathryn Lomas. New York: St. Martin's Press, 1995.

We include them, if not in fact, so by heart and thank all our authors for their patience and understanding.

Archaeology and the ruins of architecture live, by their sheer nature, with the challenge of limited evidence, and even in its completest form, the volume could not have done full justice to such an overwhelmingly wide-spanned theme as the phenomenon of the Roman *villa urbana*. Most notably, the aspects of landscape and garden in their intertwining effects with architecture, while addressed here in more than one contribution, are not dealt with separately as they would well deserve (and as they were, indeed, treated in a recent conference on "Gardens of the Roman Empire" organized by Wilhelmina Jashemski and Kathryn Gleason in November 1995 at the University of Pennsylvania). Still, focusing on the architectural aspects of the *villa urbana*, from the specific viewpoints of a variety of distinguished experts in the field, is an enterprise worthy to be documented in its own terms. And it is particularly appropriate for a publication series intended to cover various aspects of the wide-ranging theme "Classical architecture"— limited and, at the same time, focused as each of these aspects will have to be and as Classical architecture itself stands within the context of ancient culture and life.

Alfred Frazer, in his introductory words, expressed the wide implications of the selected theme: the *villa urbana* as a form of lifestyle, shaping and being shaped by, but not restricted to, Roman and ancient life. And Al Frazer himself made clear that his words, spoken at the opening of the symposium and composed here from his notes by Susan Tegtmeyer with the help of Cecil B. Striker, will have to be "written out" and expanded. We nevertheless wanted to let him speak here in his own words, and he might like the idea of being so vividly among us and all interested in his field, Classical architecture.

To Charles K. Williams, colleague and friend of Al Frazer, we are indebted for having made the symposium and this volume possible. His generous, all-inclusive passion for investigating Greek and Roman culture in its architectural remains; for training a generation of new scholars in this field; for reinforcing and, where dead, reviving this discipline's strength; for stressing its specific approaches and role as not another subfield but, exemplified by the pioneering 18th century painters and architects James Stuart and Nicholas Revett, as a vital player in reconstructing and visualizing ancient life—all this lays new ground to what will increasingly gain fuller stature. I am delighted that this enterprise included Al Frazer from the outset and hope that this publication in some way realizes his intentions.

In addition to those already named and the contributing authors, I extend my thanks to Renata Holod, then Chair of the History of Art Department at the University of Pennsylvania; to Michael Meister, the current Chair of our Department; and to Karen B. Vellucci, head of the Publications Office of the University of Pennsylvania Museum for Anthropology and Archaeology. She accepted the complex task of giving final shape to this volume.

March 1996
Lothar Haselberger
Department of the History of Art
University of Pennsylvania

1

VILLA RUSTICA ALIMENTARIA ET ANNONARIA

Guy P. R. Métraux

For William Lloyd MacDonald

The letters of Pliny the Younger give a view of the physical and financial situation of Italian villas in the second century A.D., which is the subject of this chapter, especially the situation of the *partes rusticae* of villas in private (not imperial) ownership (Martin 1967). Pliny invested his letters with an air of circumstantiality—specific occasions may be recorded—but they are primarily letters, of course. When Pliny equates his ability to show *horreum plenum* ("a full granary") in one villa and *scrinium plenum* ("a full bookcase") in another (4.6), he is contrasting physical and mental pursuits without giving higher status to either one, much like his repeated conceit of equating hunting and writing, resulting in a kind of "philosophizing" that is at once a distillation and a watering-down more, of Xenophon than of Plato. In a letter to a friend who was building a villa by the sea, Pliny tells us, somewhat vaguely, that he also is building something on the Larian Lake near Comum. The letter (9.7; published in A.D. 108/9) suggests a design based on the contrasting values of tragedy and comedy, tragedy being represented by a "buskined" villa set high on a rock, comedy by a "slippered" villa just below it on the shore. As always in Pliny's architectural descriptions, his charm, his rhetorical devices, and his customary (and oxymoronic) public intimacy are more prominent than anything convincing in the way of architecture (Bek 1976). Certainly Pliny's conceit works well as a letter, if not as an indication of actual construction, and he says *inveni patrocinium* ("I've found patronage [protection]"), which in context seems to mean that he has permission to build, whether he was doing so or not. The best candidate for such a "tragic" villa buskined on a promontory above a lake is the famous *grotte di Catullo* at Sirmio on the lacus Benacus (Garda): perhaps that is the building he was thinking of, and its four-square silhouette would not have been old, because it must

have been built when he was a child (Wiseman 1987: 313–23, 349–60).

Certainly if Pliny and his friend (or others of their generation and social status) were building villas, they were doing something unusual for the time of their maturity, in the early 2nd century A.D. Little mention of actual construction is found in the other letters: Pliny's villas are *toutes faites* and he inhabits them rather than building them or changing their effects and dispositions. The same is true of his mother-in-law's villas (1.4), which he knew well, and of an old one newly bought by his friend Valerianus (2.15). Only one structure—the Tuscan villa—of the eight or so he owned is described as having been partially finished or brought to finish by himself: *Amo enim, quae maxima ex parte ipse inchoavi aut inchoata percolui* (5.6), and the only addition to Laurentinum was the little *amores mei*, or *diaeta*, a kind of private retreat that he indicates is very small—two tiny living rooms, two bedrooms, a corridor and closet, a furnace room, and a portico (2.17). This annex is the only thing that, in his many villas, he actually asserts to have built himself (*ipse posui*). As the inheritor of his uncle's houses, he probably had no need to build much, even though he loves best what he built himself, however small it was in relation to the "main house" (that is one of the themes of the letter, and I note that his emphasis on *nature* and the multiplicity of views in and from the *amores mei*, or annex of the house, is quite different from the formality and directed axiality of the earlier part, which corresponded, indeed, to an earlier taste). Some of the villas or properties (*praedia, ager, agellum*) that Pliny mentions are in bad condition. Two of them, both that of his wife's grandfather in Campania (6.30) and the little one he bought and gave to his nurse for her retirement, needed repairs to house or plantings (6.3, 6.30). On another that he visited, there was a small monument to his patron, Verginius Rufus, which made him sad because it was unfinished (6.10). On the whole, however, Pliny's absorption with architecture is with villa structures that had been completed before his day. Their charm for him derived from his appreciation of them rather than in his active designing, and in this he was not unusual, for private citizens in Italy, who do not seem, in the second and into the third century, to have built very much in the way of villas at all, or even added on to them to any great degree.

The same impression is gained from descriptions of villas in the generation previous to Pliny's, that of the younger Seneca. L. Annaeus Seneca was no parvenu: he was part of a cosmopolitan and rich aristocracy *d'outre-mer* that happened only newly to have arrived in Rome (by one generation). Yet when he mentions villas, the philosopher's customary suavity and sophistication crack a little, allowing us to see in him a little harmless vulgarity, even some provincialism: Seneca was very interested in gawking at the grand country houses of Roman patricians of previous ages. He did so three times; in letters 51 ("On Baiae and luxury"), 55 ("The villa of Servilius Vatia near Baia"), and 86 ("The villa of Scipio Africanus at Liternum"). In the first two letters, he was content to look at the villas from the outside, but at Liternum he actually got inside and had a little tour.

As with all visits to country houses (including literary ones, such as Elizabeth Bennett's visit to Mr. Darcy's estate "Pemberly, near Lambton in Derbyshire" in Jane Austen's *Pride and Prejudice* [third ed., 1817, chaps. 42–43]), the purpose was (and still may be) to make a moral comment about personalities, moralities, and social habits: the Baian villas are represented as examples of nobility of site and Stoic gaze over picturesque decadence, that of Servilius Vatia of ignoble passive luxury, and that of Scipio Africanus of the contrast between contemporary flashiness and ancient functionality. In the last letter (86), Seneca cites certain bathing establishments in private houses as being new additions of the utmost epicene luxury, corresponding to modern tastes of ignobly rich freedmen *balnea libertinorum*, of whom he disapproved, of course. The superior morality of an out-of-date but architecturally "authentic" thermal technology (as in Scipio's narrow dark bath) is obligatory, and Pliny, writing 30 to 40 years later than Seneca, mitigates the flashiness of his own *balineum* at the Tuscan villa by saying that his cold tub is large and dark (*amplum atque opacum*; 5.6).

In the case of Seneca's letters, however, what has been little remarked is that the villas of aristocrats of the Roman republic—villas at least 150 years old or more by the time Seneca wrote about them in A.D. 64–66—were still on view and in "authentic" condition! This is a rather long time for country houses. Seneca would not have commented on subtle architectural changes to these buildings, but gross and visible ones—such as raw new luxuries or functional additions to add cash-crop utility—he would certainly not have overlooked or missed telling us about. Indeed, he would have been eager to comment on them because that is the point of his letters: morality of the past and decadence of the present as represented in details of architecture, site, and decoration (even the *tectum sordidum* of the villa indicates Stoic discomfort and high-mindedness). Instead, with Seneca as with Pliny, we see villas *toutes faites*, old, and without much modification: it is as if villa construction were a thing of the past, and the landscapes of those country houses virtually complete and capable of being inhabited without change. Pliny tells us about one of his views from his little annex in the Laurentinum: it is of a picturesque landscape of villas, always available and more unchanging, even, than his view of the sea (2.17). In addition, at least once Pliny mentions the fact that the infrastructure of roads linking villas to cities was worn out (4.1). Is the impression that Pliny and Seneca give a mere literary effect, or does it correspond to a historical phenomenon?

Pliny gives us an answer; for all his disengaged attitudes, he is part of the phenomenon, not to say the problem. In a model business letter (3.19) about an estate near Comum, he proposed to buy an adjacent property and to combine it with his own to make a single estate "as useful as it would be delightful" (*quod non minus utile quam voluptuosum posse utraque eadem opera*; the phrase is adapted from Varro 1.4.1). The advantages were as follows: fewer administrative costs, almost the same permanent personnel, and only one villa to care for and equip; the *other* villa could be left "as is" and would need no effort of expense and trouble (*unam villam colere et ornare, alteram tantum tueri*). The productivity of the free or servile personnel would rise, as their work would double, and the carrying costs would go down: it looks like a bargain (on enforced increase of productivity from slave labor, Hopkins 1983: xiv–xv). There were some problems: productivity was low among the existing tenantry (*coloni*), impoverished by the *possessor prior* (*in posterum exhausit*). Pliny himself had no more chained slaves (*vincti*), and he would have to hire contract laborers, who might have been more expensive than *coloni*. But all in all, the price was right (it had recently gone down by 40 percent!), and the variety of terrain was attractive. And what he found most attractive—he mentions it up front—is that the *other* villa could be left "as is" (*alteram tantum tueri*). The phrase does not inspire confidence as to the physical fate of the building, and it alerts archaeologists to pay close attention to the sometimes ephemeral accretions to rural buildings indicating "squatting" and conversion to other uses. As a precocious instance of the causes of the physical decline of Italian villas in the second century, Pliny's letter is a good indicator, and, as we have seen, his other letters convey an assumption of the early second-century *status quo* in the life of villas, quite different from the aggressive constructive enterprises vigorously described and promoted by the agricultural writers of earlier times, especially Columella. Although we have no way of knowing whether he actually carried out his intention to keep the other villa "as is," archaeology and architectural history can here document Pliny's financial decisions, and they can contribute to the history of the Italian inhabited landscape. My question is: what was the physical situation of Italian *villae rusticae* in the second century A.D., and what might have been its cause or context?

Physical Situations of Italian villae rusticae *in the* Second Century *A.D.*

There is a frustrating gap in what we would like to see as a progressive phenomenon amenable to developmental analysis: we desire continuities between early Roman and late Roman villas and, as examples of "Romanization," between early villas in Italy and later ones in the provinces. We also want to find some relation between the early Roman *domus* and villa, expressive of familial dignities, and the late Antique *villa urbana*, influenced by Imperial and hierarchical frigidities. Such may not have been the case, however, and perhaps Statius on villas has not been taken seriously enough when he comments on the discontinuous newness of the modern vulgarities of the luxury villas he describes or satirizes. In fact, the archaeological record frustrates our desire for continuities: it shows that many Italian villas of Republican foundation, built in the late Republic and viable through the first and early 2ndcentury A.D., came to the physical end of their existence in the second half of the second century: in providing typological continuities for late Antique villas of the third-fourth century they are of minimal value or none at all. The precarious status of Republican villas in the High Empire suggests that late Antique villas may have had financial bases that were at least a little different from the earlier ones, thus providing a new context—not one of continuity, but one of modification of status and purpose—for late Roman domestic architecture. In addition, many villas of late Republican foundation exhibit, by the late first century A.D., an "as is" state like that described by Pliny; they are used but not modified or architecturally animated. Later, after about A.D. 150, they show signs of collapse and/or conversion to uses other than their

original ones (though remaining part of agricultural enterprises), in the manner of the physical destiny of the other villa (but not the estate belonging to it) that Pliny was proposing to buy near Comum. That the dates vary in this process of physical desuetude of early villas makes little difference; the pattern is part of a process that may have been locally uneven, but in general, in Italy, the process appears to have been inevitable or ineluctable, in villas of quite different size, agricultural character, and location.

Both well-documented Italian *villae rusticae* and those known on a survey basis exhibit this physical desuetude only after ca. A.D. 150 (cf. Tchernia 1986: 257–71). At Francolise in the *Ager Falernus* north of Capua, the small villa *in agris* called Posto, built in the second century B.C. and modified several times through the Augustan period, was given some *luxe* in the mid-first century A.D. with the addition of a little bath building (Cotton 1979: 38–56). This was the last thing done: after that, the building was used without modification for about 100 years until its roof collapsed shortly after the mid-2nd century (Cotton 1979: 55–56). Nearby, the villa *in montem*, called San Rocco, exhibited the same process on a larger scale: a villa with a *domus* and *villa rustica* was built around 100 B.C. with some significant internal changes and expansions within a generation. Then, about 30 B.C., the whole villa was rebuilt on a much grander scale: a 30-room *villa urbana* incorporating modern plan and décor and pious reuse of certain rooms, separated from a substantial *villa rustica* by a road that also linked the villa with others on the hill (Cotton and Métraux 1985: 1–84; Métraux 1984). The last additions were of brick and of mid-first-century date. In the way of *amoenitas* and *voluptas*, a small and doubtfully decorated *balneum* of four rooms was set into the *domus*. In the way of *utilitas*, the *villa rustica* received some separating and storage basins for its oil factory, and a set of kilns for a tile industry. That was it, until the roofs fell in by A.D. 200: 150 years or so of use without modification, or modifications so minor as to be mere maintenance, with no increase or change in agricultural production or productivity, and no new exercise of architectural or decorative taste. The two Francolise villas had been villas on estates of solid viability for about 150 years, from about 100 B.C. through at least the mid-1st century A.D., if viability of estates is identifiable by periodic rebuilding and substantial additions to the domestic structures on them. After that, they were used "as is" without physical change until the 160s or 170s, after which they collapse as habitations. Of course, use of villas without change does not imply decline for agricultural estates, even if the process terminates in collapse: there may just have been no need to change anything, and archaeologically we cannot tell if the cessation of use after the mid-2nd century was the result of a long process of dismemberment through indifference and natural processes, or if it was a sudden decision, like Pliny's, virtually to cease maintenance. Chekhov provides an instructive example in *The Cherry Orchard* (1904), where Lopahin has bought the Ranevsky estate: the villa was going to disappear under his ownership to be replaced with holiday bungalows, but the estate was to go on to more intense and diverse use. The degradation of the villa may by no means indicate collapse of the agricultural estate's financial desirability—Lopahin didn't think so, at any rate.

The same process of physical desuetude occurred in a slightly different sequence at Settefinestre and other sites near it, where, by Antonine times, the buildings were being used as quarries for building materials or worse. There is perhaps no sharper example of the conversion of a building to other uses than that, and if Pliny's *tantum tueri* can mean that a villa will be used as a quarry, there was no need, in the Roman agricultural economy of late Antonine times, for either barbarians or Barberini (Carandini et al. 1985: I 183–85; II 82–85; Carandini 1988: 221–24). Previously at Settefinestre, the changes to the *partes urbanae* and *partes rusticae* had been lively and various from the foundation of the estate and the construction of the villa in the 2nd century B.C. through the mid-1stst century A.D., but ultimately the biggest structural change of Antonine times was the enclosure of the slaves' quarters by the blocking-up of its exterior doors (Carandini et al. 1985: I 183–84; II 162; Carandini 1988: 219–20). This last action has been interpreted as a response to plague, but it is possible, in my view, that it is an example of the greater enforced productivity of slaves (Hopkins 1983: xiv–xv). There may have been a change from an open slave status to a chain-gang situation housed in the above-ground equivalent of an *ergastulum* (cf. the vincti of Pliny mentioned above; Etienne 1974: 249–66 on varieties of *ergastula*).

Closer to Rome, in the villas beside the via Gabina, at both sites 10 and 11, the incidence of fine pottery denoting residential living virtually ceased by A.D. 180, and that of coarse pottery as of the early 3rd century, with, in the intervening 20–30 years, a low-level use of site 11 as an oil factory. Here, abandonment of these villas of Republican foundation was not sudden, but cessation of "fine" residential habitation did occur, and conversion to sporadic or seasonal (and certainly to purely utilitarian) uses also occurred (Widrig 1987). Other villas in the suburbs of Rome exhibit evidence of abandonment in the second half of the century, for example, the large villa at Corcolle Inferiore and others (*Misurare la terra* 1985: 90–109).

On the other side of the city, the quite remarkable building at Fidenae (Castel Giubileo) shows something of the same pattern. This building, which seems to have been built in late Republican or early Imperial times, was a very large warehouse, or *hor-*

reum, with a small apartment for a manager, a cool-storage *deposito* for wine made at the presses in the building, and a warm-storage for olive oil produced in the adjacent factory. The whole complex had a large communal kitchen and common-rooms for the *rustici* or *servi rustici*. The look of the building—with about 80 percent of its area devoted to storage quite near Rome—has correctly prompted its interpretation as a work-and-storage center of a very large (possibly Imperial) property, rather than a villa as such. If Imperial, it might be expected that the Fidenae establishment would have been inoculated with antibodies to the prevailing disease of desuetude, which was exhibited by villas in private hands. But such was not the case: the Imperial antibodies may have delayed or mitigated, but did not prevent, a process that was pandemic. At Fidenae the pattern of mid-first-century modifications (the construction of an external water tank; Quilici 1976: 312–13) followed by a long use in "as is" condition was the same as at other sites. From occasional finds of tiles, we know that the building's roofs were repaired through the middle of the 2nd century A.D.—more janitorial maintenance of a minimal kind. Then, by the late second century and throughout the third century, very miserable tombs begin to appear along the walls outside the building, and the amount of fine pottery dropped suddenly about A.D. 160–80, even though there is a little revival of *terra sigillata chiara* long after, in the fourth century (Quilici 1976: 274–320). The tombs themselves are not the definitive indicator of disuse (if anything, they are an indicator *of* use) because their presence may only be due to the gradual change of popular habit from cremation to inhumation in the second century. Much more significant, of course, is the drop in the amount of fine pottery. This can indicate two things: that managerial and/or servile residence was transferred elsewhere and that only occasional visits to the building, which continued in some sort of use, were required, or else that the building became unimportant or marginal to some larger agricultural estate, and other buildings took over its function. Both are possible. But because its function had *always* been mainly as a *horreum*, with oil-pressing and wine-making units as well, I emphasize this issue—its desuetude as a *horreum*—rather than its loss of residential amenity, of which it had not had very much anyway. In this I follow Nicolas Purcell, who in his paper wisely warned his colleagues to put their concern with villa *habitation* and its life-styles on hold, and to concentrate on villa production and function. In the case of Fidenae, a significant change toward *disuse* of a large agricultural storage facility in the suburbs of a city of about one million is a change in economic infrastructure that may have been at the root of the residential and *partes rusticae* desuetude of the other villas I have mentioned. It is not as if such facilities were not needed; they were. On the via Gabina, for example, a large *horreum* ultimately replaced a villa (Widrig 1987: 259–60). For these reasons, what happened at Fidenae—the long use of the building "as is," from the mid-1st century through the late second century, with the sharp drop in its fine pottery around A.D. 160–80—turns our attention to issues of storage, transportation of agricultural goods, and physical access to markets in Italian agricultural estates in the second century. By storage, I mean spaces holding more agricultural product—wine and oil, mainly—than the needs of the family and *familia* of the villa itself would warrant: Varro, for example, speaks of storage used both for the villa inhabitants and to hold produce for sale (1.56–69). The question has to be: are there storage, transport and marketing, or market-access problems in Italian *villae rusticae* that had consequences for the physical structures of rural buildings in the second century A.D.?

Certainly it is possible—indeed, probable—that larger storage facilities in the later villas merely imply estates larger than those of the earlier villas. Pliny, after all, might have had to build some extra *horrea* on his own estate when he bought the adjacent property, if ever he did as he proposed (3.19). That said, the issue could be left there, had the question as to the possible causes or context of physical desuetude of Italian villas in the second century A.D. been answered. But there are other issues: there are profound differences between early and late villas with respect to access to storage, transport, markets, and distribution points for agricultural goods; and there are considerations of the competitiveness of produce from Italian estates relative to sea-borne produce from the provinces, with regard to the transport and storage of food near Italian markets. To these two must be added a third: Italian owners of agricultural estates had a fair quantity of ready cash virtually given to them by the government in the early second century, and they did not spend it on their villas. Where might they have spent it, and on what? The questions of transport, storage, markets, and competitiveness (discussed below) are issues of the infrastructure of agricultural estates in Italy. The question of cash (discussed below) is a financial consideration involving choices by villa owners that may have had economic sequellae. Villa owners were faced both with the consequences of their past success in creating a viable productive landscape in central Italy and with the consequences of government schemes constituting a new deal for them.

Storage, Transport, and Markets

I am intentionally asking questions to which the answers, if completely documented, would be a lot longer than can be set out in the compass of this paper: there is documentation of a spatial/statistical nature that will have to be broached elsewhere, but crude temporary answers may in this case be as good as ones proved by the refinements of graphs and comparative time-bars. For example, in comparing the architecture of Republican/early Imperial *villae rusticae* with those of the second–fourth century A.D. in the provinces or in Italy, questions of storage arise at, in, and around villas. Setting aside extreme differences in residential design between such villas, what seems clear is that the builders of late Antique *villae rusticae* exhibit a greater concern for storage facilities than did the builders of late Republican/early Imperial villas. What is at issue is not architectural typology but the increased surface percentages or capacity of storage facilities vis-à-vis residential or other surfaces in late *villae rusticae* over earlier ones. *Mutatis mutandis*, let us allow two comparisons and four buildings to stand in the place of a comprehensive statistical and comparative work-up of many villas.

At the San Rocco villa at Francolise, the structure as completed and in use by the mid-1st century A.D., with an *oletum* and a *figlinum* (phase IIA), had the following distribution: with a total surface of about 1850 m² (including courts/peristyle but excluding exterior porticoes and gardens, open water-tanks, cisterns, and the *hortus*), the *pars urbana* occupied a little more than 50 percent (950 m²), the *villa rustica* a little less than 50 percent (900 m²), and of these, the area available for storage was about 18 percent (300 m²) at most (Cotton and Métraux 1985: 42–84). As with many other villas, at San Rocco it is hard to separate the *pars fructuaria* from the *pars rustica*, and by "storage" I mean rooms not definitely allocated (from the evidence of equipment, doors, etc.) to productive equipment (press room, tile kilns), or rooms allocated to slave/servant residence (the apartment of the *vilicus* and the "Commons"). This is a minimal figure, because attics could have been used as granaries, as at the Villa Rotonda at Vicenza. Still, as a percentage of total surface, the space available for storage of agricultural product in the mid-first century thus represents only a small part of the whole villa at San Rocco. It was on the basis of this allocation of space for storage that the use of the San Rocco villa in "as is" condition began.

In comparison to San Rocco, the villa at Sâo Cucufate near Pax Julia (Beja) in Lusitania presents quite a different distribution of space in its several phases. Its initial construction, completed about A.D. 50 and inhabited until about 120/30, presented a substantial proprietor's residence of some 300 m² (half of it a small courtyard) with a work-and-storage building attached to it of some 240 m². These structures were related to two large barns, one of at least 400 m², the other about half the size, and the barns defined a large courtyard of some 1300 m² in which there was a house for the *vilicus* of about 250 m² (Alarcâo and Mayet 1989: 232–34). The covered surfaces thus were allocated as follows: about 20 percent to the proprietor's residence, 15 percent to that of the *vilicus*, and some 840 m², or 65 percent, to storage and working areas, the greatest amount to storage. In a second phase (*ca.* A.D. 120/30 to *ca.* 350), the proprietor's residence was expanded, though its storage facilities were maintained, and a bath building was added, bringing the residential area to about 600 m². The house of the *vilicus* remained, and the smaller of the barns was modified, with the place of the larger barn being taken by slaves' living quarters. To all of this were added two *horrea* with buttressed walls capable of development on two floors, bringing the total storage area to *ca.* 1000 m². Storage thus continued to represent, in the second century in Lusitania, the largest part of the surface area and of the architectural effort, and it continued to do so in the impressive third phase of the villa (*ca.* A.D. 350–450) when a new residence was built against the walls of the western *horreum* (Alarcâo and Mayet 1989: 234–49). In comparison with the San Rocco villa (with about 18 percent of the area allocated to storage), storage in the provincial and later design of the Sâo Cucufate villa was, at least with respect to allocation of square footage, a much more important issue.

The comparison between San Rocco and Sâo Cucufate in its first two phases is one of "horizontal" storage; another late Antique development is "vertical" storage, in which a major sequence of rooms (including one of basilican shape with an apse) was developed on an upper floor, with the basement or upper floor used for storage. At Sâo Cucufate, such vertical storage was part of the design in its latest phase, *ca.* A.D. 350 (Alarcâo and Mayet 1989); the basement of the apsidal room of the late Antique villa at San Giovanni di Ruoti (Basilicata) could also have been used as a store (Small 1983: 26–28). Something of the same arrangement may have been part of the large, late second-century villa called the Mura di San Stefano, near Anguillara, northwest of Rome, though with storage on the uppermost floor as described by Pliny (2.17; Lyttelton 1980: 60–61). In all of these cases, the residential rooms are, as it were, equated with the amount of surface given over to storage, with a consequent high visibility of the stored goods, resulting in an integration of representational spaces with utilitarian ones, rather than their separation.

If we take another comparative example, the Republican and early Imperial villa of Settefinestre near Cosa and the late Antique villa at Montmaurin, the same conclusion about the greater concern for storage in the later design can be reached. At Settefinestre (again excluding exterior porticoes, open areas, and the gardens), the amount of storage included in the *cella vinaria*, the *lacus*, the *basis villa* with its *cryptoporticus*, and the large and beautiful two-floor *nubi-larium* was about 900 m² from a total of about 4300 m²; thus, about 18–20 percent of the building was allocated to storage, in the manifestation of the building in its most developed stage in Trajanic times (Carandini et al. 1985: I 152, 159, 165, 167, 169–70; II 103–10, 189–208).

The case is different at the late Antique villa at Montmaurin in Aquitania, as it was rebuilt around A.D. 350. The function and motivation of the plans of Montmaurin and Settefinestre, and the quite different allocation of types of representational spaces (*triclinia, balnea*) and other rooms, prompt me to emphasize the architectural discontinuities between the two villas, but apart from those issues, the percentage of space allocated to storage at Montmaurin (barns and *horrea* reused from the older villa, of which about half were equipped with buttressed walls and stairs for a second floor) represented about 30 percent of the building (about 1300 m² of a total *ca.* 4500 m²; Fouet 1969: 59–87). This is a very crude figure, because no machines (if there were any) survived at Montmaurin, and some of this space may have been used as toolsheds and dormitories. Still, Montmaurin in about A.D. 350 had some 30 percent of its area allocated to storage, as opposed to 18–20 percent at Settefinestre in about A.D. 100. Montmaurin also had a storage and market facility at La Hillère, about a kilometer away (see below, p. 10).

Though these are raw figures, which might be more greatly refined (Carandini has convincingly reconstructed the capacities of storage in *cullei* of wine and *modii* of wheat; Carandini et al. 1985: I 166–70), they nonetheless represent the greater practical need, in later villa designs, for storage of all kinds. If I may continue Nicolas Purcell's striking phrase, it is clear that, at some time between late Republican/early Imperial villas and late Antique ones, the "romance of storage" became a very lively love affair, and it resulted in large and numerous offspring in the way of storage capacities in villas, both relative and absolute. My two comparative examples are intended to stand for a more fully documented claim that almost all later Roman villas have greater capacity for storage of agricultural products than did villas of the late Republic/early Empire. What follows is an attempt to provide a context for this change in the design of *villae rusticae*, and it includes the agricultural writers' remarks and assumptions about both storage and transport of produce.

From the evidence of my examples, we cannot be surprised by the differences between the early agricultural writers of the late Republic and early Empire (Cato, Varro, and Columella) and the single late Antique one which we know of (Palladius), when they write about storage in villas and transport of produce. The capacity to store and transport agricultural products was a consideration for all these writers. But while the three early writers differ somewhat among themselves on these topics, they differ very conspicuously from Palladius: something of the differences between early and late villas with respect to storage, and by implication transport, are certainly present in the differences between Cato, Varro, and Columella, on the one hand, and Palladius, on the other. Cato, writing in the second century B.C., is not so concerned with storage capacities in the *villa rustica* except insofar as it is good to have *cellae* for olive oil and wine for the following reasons: "to await price-increase [of produce], and to be both the virtue and the repute of the business" (*uti lubeat caritatem expectare, et rei et virtuti et gloriae erit*; 3.30.2). On both of these very interesting topics he says nothing more at all, and his phrase seems to be a throwaway, put in as an "obligatory" remark with bad-tempered irony. It is an early version of Pliny's *horreum plenum/scrinium plenum* remark, and the reasons are certainly good motivation for storage rooms, if they had been elaborated. Instead, Cato assumes throughout his manual that almost all produce (except that held back as food for the *familia*, as seed stock, fertilizer, or for making tools and grease) will be converted immediately into money, and that all purchases (except for percentages of produce in certain lease or contract arrangements) will be made in cash. A purpose of storage facilities is to await upward fluctuations of price, but, as his remark makes clear, storage also *looks* good, an exterior mark of interior goodness. The rarity of the former, and the relative unimportance of the latter with respect to the actual business of making money, prompted Cato to make this his only general remark on storage. His other remarks on how to build a *torcularium* for oil and a *vasa vinaria* for wine (18–26) make no mention of storage whatsoever; and he does not appear to be making *grand cru*, as the impression he leaves is that, after a 30-day fermentation, his wine containers are sealed to be sent on their way to market. Cato assumed an infrastructure of transportation facilities of mule trains and ox-teams (he gives transport prices at 22.3–4), and he assumed that equipment would be available for ready-money purchase at hardware stores and equipment yards (which he names, with prices, quality assessment, assembly costs of machines, and locations at *loc.cit.* and 135.1–6). Cato also assumed that the local markets for agricultural produce would provide an immediate cash return, allowing the villa owner to buy, in the market towns, all the rope, nails, tree hooks, and so on that he needed. I am not here concerned with either the economics or the finances of Cato's *villae rusticae*. I am concerned only with his allocation of space and his assumptions about the physical character of the farm. For him, storage was of little importance except rarely (for rise in prices) and culturally (for looking good), because he assumed two things: that there was good transport to and from the villa, and that there was al-

ways a ready market off the estate that would provide a cash return. Transport and marketing were no problem for Cato, and he relied on the markets of Cales, Suessa Aurunca, Nola, Pompeii, Venafrum, Casinum, Rome, and so on, both to take his produce off his hands and to provide him with necessities (cf. Carandini 1988: 173).

With Varro, writing in the 20s B.C., the question of storage is a question of proportion: size of estate suggests size of storage. In a phrase that has philosophic and accountancy overtones he says: "Doubtless a larger wine-storage should be built on that estate which has a vineyard, and larger granaries if the estate is cereal-producing" (*Dubium enim non est quin cella vinaria maior sit facienda in eo agro, ubi vineta sint, ampliora ut horrea, si frumentarius ager est*; 1.11.2). Ultimately, for Varro, the question of proportion is overthrown by the special case of high-luxury produce with elaborate architectural and land-use requirements he discusses in his book III (*viz.*, the aviary built for *animi causa* or the simulated "Orphic" forest at Laurentum for boar, 3.5.8–17; 3.13.2–3). These demential and prestigious elaborations are for game raised near the metropolis for immediate transport to cooks of *haute cuisine* and to *fins becs* with a mania for freshness. For our purposes, it is only in book I, where Varro describes *villae rusticae* farther afield, that issues of agricultural storage are raised, and even then only slightly. He mentions working sheds (*nubilaria*; 1.13.5) for grain, but the *instrumentum mutum* of his *vinetum* and *oletum* (1.22) includes *dolia* and their covers in numbers and sizes needed for processing a season's harvest rather than for longer-term storage. Wheat is a little different (he claims that in Greece, Africa, and Spain wheat can be stored for 50 years following special techniques!), but his discussion of its storage is more picturesque than useful in an Italian context (1.57). Even more picturesque is the "natural" décor of the *oropothecon* (fruit house) arranged as a *triclinium* for dining (cf. his own strictures in the introduction of book II!), but the principle of Varro's sense of storage space in *villae rusticae* is basically this: Since no one stores produce except to use it later, little needs to be said on the topic (*Quod nemo fructus condit, nisi ut promat, de eo quoque . . . animadvertenda pauca*; 1.62.1). He is here talking about shelf space for jars of preserved food for the needs of the *familia*. He assumes, like Cato, immediate conversion of produce into money with little or no storage on the estate: he has already said that a good villa is near a road or riverine transport facilities (1.16.6) and near a town or village (1.16.3), and he seems to assume that such will be the case. Indeed, Varro derives the word "villa" from haulage (*vehere*) of produce to and from it (1.2.14); the etymology may be false but no less revealing for his assumptions about the lively and immediate movement of produce off the estate and on its way to market.

Columella, writing a systematic manual in the mid-first century A.D., distinguished the *villa fructuaria* from the *partes urbanae et rusticae*, but he still shared many of Cato's and Varro's assumptions about storage and transport. The *villa fructuaria* that he advocates is a grouping or rationalization of what Varro had described piecemeal: Columella briefly coordinates the granary (*horreum*), the presses and storage jars for oil and wine, the *cortinale* (for boiling wine and making *defrutum*), and the *fumarium* (smoke house) in one building (1.6.9–20), giving an impression that this storage-and-work unit is to hold what the villa inhabitants will use during the year, rather than to store produce destined for market, which is treated elsewhere with an assumption that it will be immediately transported and converted into cash (3.3; Carandini 1988: 235–65; cf. the three-part villa in the Tavogliere Romano in Potter 1987: 102–3). For this reason he has already said that the villa should be close to a city and close to transportation facilities (road and riverine; 1.2–3), but not near a military (paved?) road or a marsh because visitors and bugs are both pests (1.5.6–7). Almost everything else in Columella about storage and preserved stores is derived from the description of Ischomachos' country house in Xenophon's *Oeconomicus*, with the exception that what the Greek writer attributed to the *wife* of the owner, Columella says are to be the duties of the female slave who is the slave manager's companion (cf. Pesando 1987: 83–87; this is indeed an example of the progressive enchattlement of women in antiquity).

Thus the early writers on agriculture—Cato, Varro, and Columella—speak little of large-scale or long-term storage of produce, and agricultural goods, once harvested or processed, are immediately transported and sold. The relative absence of storage facilities in their villa architectures, and their assumption that estates will, as a matter of course, be close enough to transport facilities and markets to generate immediate conversion of *fructus* into *pecunia*, are indicators of the physical situation of villas and infrastructures linking estates to markets in Italy before the 50s A.D. (on this topic, see Corbier 1981: 427–44).

Three or more centuries later, the late Roman writer Palladius made no such assumptions. Granted, Palladius was also using the manuals on architecture by Vitruvius and Faventinus, which the earlier writers had not used, with a resultant elaboration on the architectural parts of the *villa rustica*; but even so, Palladius' manual presents more recipes (instructions about foundations and floors, plans for cisterns, composition of mortars and caulking, etc.) and is more abundant in practical directives than any manual heretofore (Martin 1976: xxxii–xxxix). Cato's sense of proportion, Varro's *utilitas/voluptas* trade-offs, Columella's coordination of buildings—these are all reproduced in various ways by Palladius, but he adds

much practical advice, as if the villa as a moral and a managed environment had become, instead, a purely physical construct. Unlike the others, Palladius does not give the reader alternatives and possibilities; he tells him exactly what to do and when, and he assumes that everything he describes in his manual will be undertaken by the reader, an assumption markedly different from that of the earlier writers. Construction, maintenance, and preparation of storage facilities are described in all months except July, September, and December, and Palladius elaborates on the manufacture of bricks (in May: 6.12) and the stocking of seasoned building-wood (in November: 12.15). August is good for building aqueducts and large cisterns (9.8–12), and far from assuming, as Cato did, that construction would be done by a contractor (price schedules in Cato 14–15), Palladius gives specific instructions on construction in his first book, assuming that the proprietor will be undertaking it himself. Finally, he does not give the complex lists of store-bought equipment (machine parts, rope, baskets, etc.) that Cato had listed together with the most reliable hardware stores to buy them in. His villa is not entirely autonomous—no question of a "manorial" situation—but he writes as if he could rely a lot less on the local landscape of towns and than the earlier writers had. Tellingly, his injunction to the proprietor to organize so that trips to town by the villa personnel are made unnecessary (1.6.2) is taken from Varro (1.16.4), but with this interesting variation: for Varro, it was a question of work productivity (which the distractions of the town would diminish), whereas Palladius says that, at a villa, blacksmiths, carpenters, and potters (*ferrarii, lignarii, doliorum cuparumque factores*) are essential craftsmen to have as part of the permanent personnel so that visits to the market town would be otiose (Martin 1976: 94).

Palladius also makes no assumptions about the transport infrastructure, saying plainly, "An ill-maintained road is as bad for pleasure as for usefulness" (*Viae malitia aeque et voluptatis et utilitatis adversa est*; 1.6.7); the *voluptas/utilitas* idea is copied from Varro, but I emphasize that Palladius puts it negatively, in terms of a *bad* road, whereas the early writers assumed that all roads were useful because usable. More significant are Palladius' instructions on the husbandry and tack of haulage and pack animals (donkeys, oxen, horses; month of March; 4.11–14). These had been specialized activities requiring separate facilities and special pasturage (in Varro's case, at Reate), and for that reason they had not been included in Cato and were mentioned in Varro as a matter of interest only (2.4–8), or with respect to the gigantic prices charged for jacks (2.1.14). It is assumed by both Cato and Varro, and also by Columella (6), that on an agricultural estate the numbers of transport animals will be small, used for carrying things about the estate rather than hauling produce away from it.

Mules for pack trains bringing oil, wine, grain, and other produce from Brundisium and Apulia to the west coast were the objects of training and organization undertaken by specialized *mercatores*. For Varro, this was certainly not done by villa owners (2.6.5), but by Palladius' day it may well have been.

Thus Palladius' geography seems not to be a local one: it is much larger than Cato's, who went from town to town between Nola and Rome (at most 250 km) in the discharge of his duties at his agricultural estates. The increase in agricultural geography had grown already in Varro's and Columella's manuals—they mention Baetica and Africa very frequently—but by Palladius' day, agricultural geography was larger still: he mentions Hispanic and Gallic *agriculteurs* who gave him tips on techniques directly, not from books. Personally, Palladius tells the reader that he had agricultural estates near Naples and in Sardinia (discussion of lemons; 4.10), a farm near Rome (quinces: 3.25), and a fig farm in Italy (4.10), besides having connections in Gaul in the way both of practical knowledge and perhaps of paternity (on Gallic harvester: 7.2; White 1970: 30 and n.56; on paternity: Martin 1976: 207). Sardinia and Gaul were producers of wheat, and villas near Naples and Rome were in good spots to provide fresh produce to the cities: Palladius' estates are farther flung than his predeccessors' had been. His sense of large-scale storage is bigger and more careful because more necessary, and he does not assume that transport of produce is *en place* and so gives directions for husbandry of haulage and pack-train animals, probably to be undertaken by the proprietor himself. For the earlier writers, villas were still oriented toward the local urban centers of production and consumption, whereas Palladius assumes both greater independence and autonomy of villas, and an orientation that is not purely local but that gave the landowners room for commercial maneuver and access to markets that were well beyond merely regional boundaries. The roads may indeed have been worse by Palladius' day, so that compensating for the *malatia viae* by building, storing, and taking on the responsibility for transporting the produce was the more necessary.

Questions of storage and transport are, of course, linked with access to markets, the latter both in the form of regional *nundiae* (scheduled nine-day markets) and also of markets in the economic sense. In Cato's manual and into the first century A.D., villas in Italy seem to have relied on quite local market towns to provide both sorts of markets for villa produce; Cato also relied on the market towns as places to shop for equipment. Villas, of course, always depend on cities and on the transportation facilities between them: the Posto and San Rocco villas were close to the via Appia and near the bridgehead of several roads at Capua, and in the *ager Veientanus* and *ager Cosanus*, villas tended to cluster close to roads, even

though paved roads as such are not an absolute necessity for land transport of agricultural produce (Hopkins 1978: 42–46; Kahane et al. 1968; Potter 1987: 106–9). This is as we might have expected, because it is certainly the geography of nundiae in a smallish, closely connected landscape implied by Cato. His market towns—Nola, Venafrum, Cales, Suessa Aurunca, and so on—are reproduced almost as if he had dictated them to the middleman, who made a calendar of *nundiae* to help him keep track of his business (McMullen 1970: 339–41). This object, a marble plaque dated to about A.D. 50 and found at Pompeii, is a commercial *aide-mémoire*, which, marking the intersections of circles inscribed on it, allowed its user to send goods to the markets held every nine days in the towns between the Bay of Naples and Rome; and it tells us how the agricultural producer or middleman in the Campanian, Falernian, and Latian regions could combine traveling with buying and selling at agricultural markets, and how he estimated the successive market days in a Catonian landscape of productive villas and *nundiae* where the produce was sold. The Francolise villas would have been part of this landscape, being probably in the legal territory of Cales, a *nundia* mentioned in both Cato and the Pompeian calendar (Small 1985: xx).

The picture of good access to viable local markets that absorbed villa produce seems to persist in both Varro and Columella, but by the mid-1st century A.D. some problems may have arisen. None of the agricultural writers mentions a practice heard about in the first century A.D., namely of rich landowners holding *nundiae* on their own private estates. This is attested to first in Suetonius' life of Claudius for the early A.D. 40s, where it is mentioned in relation to the modest and unassuming politeness of the then-new emperor, who asked permission of the Senate to hold such markets. Where these markets of Claudius took place is not known. More specifically and later, Pliny the Younger in a letter (5.4) mentions that a landowner called Sollers, a man of praetorian rank who had an estate near Vicetia (modern Vicenza), requested permission of the Senate to hold a market on his estate, and that his request was opposed by representatives from the town of Vicetia who presumably wished to retain their own market in the forum of Vicetia as the central locale for buying and selling agricultural produce (Forlati Tamaro et al. 1956: 102). Why Sollers wished to bypass the local market is not clear (Pliny's letter is not about this as such). But the fact that he was opposed by representatives of the town indicates a fact about how *nundiae* were regulated: it was a matter of state concern. For example, on the local level of the seven-man Senate of the town of Casae in Byzacium in Africa, during the reign of Hadrian, one Lucilius Africanus, *vir clarissimus*, was permitted to establish a market on his estate. It was to be a twice-monthly market, on the fourth day before the Nones and the twelfth day before the Kalends of every month (CIL VIII.2 11451, CIL VIII.5 23246). The bypassing of municipal *nundiae* in market towns by rich men, and their holding *nundiae* on their estates on a regular basis, may indicate either that the local market had declined and become inadequate for some reason or that some disadvantage in sending villa produce to the town could be mitigated by selling from the estate. It may also indicate that estates of great size (such as Claudius', presumably) were selling produce in such quantities that brokers were willing to deal directly with the estate agents at the villas, bypassing the *nundia* in the local market town. All three are possible, and they indicate some problem of access to markets and/or some problem in using market towns as *entrepôts* for produce in quantities beyond the needs of the local *macellum*. Producing food may not have been the difficulty: getting produce sold in efficient ways may have begun to pose problems.

The issue of villas and markets can be illustrated if we return briefly to the two Francolise villas and Montmaurin. Of course, these villas are in quite different regions, but while the *location* of the Francolise villas in their small Catonian landscape of good roads (the via Appia) near well-established market towns is perhaps predictable, the location of the Montmaurin villa in the fourth century was not set up in the same way, being far from a town and on no major road. Montmaurin, in its newly large manifestation of about A.D. 350, was sited on the walls of an earlier, smaller villa (Fouet 1969: 46–91). But about 1000 m away, at a bend in the river Save, the Montmaurin villa seems to have generated a mixed-use annex conveniently close to its *horrea* and perhaps even on the estate itself: the complex of buildings at La Hillère. This site, which stood at the junction, or at least on the path, of tracks suitable for cart haulage and pack trains, combined a large *mansio*, or "caravansary," with a market building, dormitories, and a small shrine with bathing facilities (Labrousse 1966; Fouet 1972; on the tracks, Fouet 1969: 297–301). While La Hillère could well have been a commercial business-in-common undertaken by several proprietors in the region, the facilities there must, I think, be seen as an indispensable and permanent component of the productive part of the estate. Among other things, they are the architectural expression of access to transportation and commercial marketing of agricultural goods, and the place to shop for hardware, for the landowners of the area. La Hillère was the equivalent of Cato's Venafrum and Suessa Aurunca, and the difference between Cato and the owner of Montmaurin is measured by the difference between going to "Lucius Tunnius' equipment yard" at Casinum to buy rope at quotable prices, and going to the *mansio* at La Hillère to bargain for tree hooks brought in the panniers of an itinerant tradesman. For owners of villas, substitutes, and alternatives, by no means ineffective ones, could be found for market towns.

Here I broach a problem that I can document through examples only. On the one hand, there is no particularly good evidence of a general, regional, or even local decline of market towns in Italy in the 2nd century A.D.; I am, however, unaware of any detailed study of the topic, as opposed to the study of their origins. The expansion of estates, the construction of villas, the growth of towns, and the urbanization of Italy in the late Republic are obviously related phenomena that have been intensively studied (cf. Gabba 1972; 1977; Brunt 1971: 294–301). But for the 2nd century A.D., the end or decline of the phenomena (estates, villas, towns, urbanization, and their relationship) has not been studied synoptically. I am not claiming a generalized decline of Italian market towns in the second century, even though it might be predictable from what we know of Italian villas. Regional surveys do exist and indicate a decline, though it is not yet possible to document it architecturally and in detail (Dyson 1978; 1981; Wilson 1985: 321–23). For example, market buildings—that is, *macella*, or urban buildings specifically designed and built for the sale of agricultural produce of various kinds to the inhabitants of a town or city—continued in use if well established, were renovated if they were old, and continued to be built if needed in Italy in the second century. In Campania, after the earthquake of A.D. 62, the *macella* of Pompeii and Puteoli were rebuilt, and as a recent survey of the building type shows, the *macella* of towns in the interior and mountainous parts of central Italy were either built or renovated, some of them along the new trans-Appenine *via Traiana*, with increasing frequency in the second century (De Ruyt 1983: 256–59). The *macella* were for daily urban use as an adjunct to scheduled *nundiae*, but the physical evidence indicates, if anything, the viability of marketing resources for villa produce at that time. Of course, municipal *macella* were just that—points of market access for local consumers and producers of food. They were certainly not *entrepôts* where the produce of several estates could be combined as a big commercial consignment and transported by land, river, or sea to some larger metropolitan or regional market, or abroad. The continuance of municipal *macella* thus does not in itself indicate continuance of the town as an *entrepôt*, and it is with this that I am concerned.

It may be that, by the second century, smaller towns such as Cosa or Formiae, which during the late Republic and early Empire may have functioned efficiently as *entrepôts* and lading points for the wine trade, were losing the business. Places such as Puteoli and Ostia, which had corporations of transport brokers and business groups for the import and export of comestibles, may have been more competitive

(D'Arms 1974; 1976; 1981: 121–71; De Robertis 1971: II 235–410; Meiggs 1973: 277–311; Rougé 1966: 107–74). Such places, with their concentrated and extensive infrastructure of such things as *horrea*, docks, specialized brokers, and bottomry-insurance agents, may have been more efficient and more attractive as places to send produce than local market towns, particularly for exportable produce (Rougé 1966: 177–322, 345–60; Schlippschuch 1974: 11–39). Of course, it is precisely in those places that Italian produce would have had to compete with imports from the provinces in terms of both price and availability, but this may not yet have been a consideration in the late first and early second century. Much more study is needed, however, on the physical and financial situation of agricultural market towns in the second century before anything can be said about how their situation related to that of the villas in their *retroterre*, or how it related to the *entrepôts*. Some relationship between villas in "as is" condition and the economic state of the local market town is likely, though a causal relationship need not be supposed.

Indices of some decline in at least one town do exist, at Cosa, where the decline and depopulation of the municipality of occurred as early as the mid-1st century B.C., and increasingly after that, at times when the villas were still viable (Rathbone 1981; Carlsen 1984: 55–56). The continuance of the villas at a time when the local market town was in bad shape indicates that agricultural producers had found access to markets farther afield than merely local or regional, and the importance of the Italian wine-export trade in this period has been abundantly documented (see, e.g., Tchernia 1983; 1986; Carandini 1981; Purcell 1985; *Misurare la terra* 1985: 180–94; Carandini 1980a; Garnsey and Saller 1987: 59–63; Hesnard 1980). Cosa may have worked well as an *entrepôt* for export through the 1st century, but it must at some point have lost out to larger, more concentrated, and more efficient centers of distribution and export. Its decline, and the decline of other places like it, may even have precipitated a change in habits of how wine was readied for market (cf. Tchernia 1980: 310–12; Garnsey and Saller 1987: 59–63). It may be significant, in this respect, that donors of private liberality in the small towns of Italy had switched, by the mid-2nd century, from giving buildings and shows (gladiatorial and theatrical: the usual liberality of the first and early second century) to giving food and money: the cost was the same or greater, but the populace of a declining market town might have needed more in the way of relief from hunger than in the way of architectural grandeur or pleasure (Mrozek 1987: 27–32). Charity describes the needs of its recipients rather accurately, and culture or pleasure was, by mid-Antonine times, not one of them. Food and money for the short term were.

Markets, of course, have something to do with rela-

tive prices for agricultural goods, and ultimately with the competitiveness of Italian wine, oil, and wheat vis-à-vis provincial imports of such goods. It was the latter that had prompted the creation and development of the great port-*entrepôts* and dock buildings—both the human organization and the architectural assemblage of storage, transport, and distribution services—at Puteoli, Ostia, and on the Tiber-side at Rome (Rougé 1966: 107–74; Pavis d'Escurac 1976: 203–39; D'Arms 1974; 1976; 1981: 149–71; Rickman 1980b; *Misurare la terra* 1985: 162–71). In part because of them, on all scores of storage, transport, and distribution, produce from Sardinia, Gaul, Egypt, and Africa came ultimately to undercut the cost of the same produce from Italy. As implied by Columella in the preface (20) of his first book, there were also social and legal advantages to engaging in the transport and distribution of goods (Rougé 1966: 177–322; Pavis d'Escurac 1976: 204–20; on prices, Duncan-Jones 1982: 367–69). Transport costs by land from Italian towns to Rome were higher than those of seaborne transport from Egypt, and Egyptian costs of production may have been lower as well, though the efficiencies of scale in transport seem to have been the main factor. The figures may somewhat exaggerate the difference of transport costs between Italy and the provinces, but only somewhat, and the difference may indeed have had to do with the physical and financial situation of Italian villas by the late 1st century and into the 2nd (Martin 1971: 278–86). All agricultural writers, and Pliny as well, emphasized the need to have many villas, to have them in differing climatic and geographical locations, and to have, within a single estate, a variety of plantings and produce (the "*villa perfecta*"; Carandini et al. 1985: I 107–37; Carandini 1988: 19–108). The purpose of this multiplicity was to maintain the potential to offset one year's failure with success elsewhere, good return on one estate compensating for blight, hail, or mud slides on another. All the writers urge the villa proprietor to hedge his bets in this way, because temporary disappointments always occur. What could not be survived was long-term competition by competitors who had real cost advantages and access to markets just as good as, or better than, Italian producers, and for whom climate and geography were not merely peninsular considerations but Mediterranean-wide (Garnsey 1983; 1988).

Thus these issues of storage, transport, and markets are at some point crucial to the history of Italian villas and villas elsewhere in the empire, and we may expect that they had direct and indirect effects on villa structures themselves. Resolving them in some way, and accommodating themselves to competition, would have been a serious task for Italian villa owners; finding resources to help in the resolution and accommodation would have been a priority for proprietors. I am still concerned here only with the ar-

chitectural and habitational consequences of these issues in the Italian countryside, and I suggest that the
use "as is" of villas in the second century was due to a
deviation of resources and money away from the estate and toward storage of produce *extra villam*, close
to the large markets of the *entrepôts* (Puteoli, Ostia,
Rome), which had taken over the functions provided
before by market towns and by *mercatores, negotiatores,
diffusores*, and other middlemen (on these, Schlippschuch 1974: 86–108; D'Arms 1981: 149–71; Garnsey
1983: 188–30; on the laws of commercial *collegiae*, De
Robertis 1971: II 235–410). Besides the costs, the actual transport of produce itself may have become
problematic in Italy, perhaps because *mercatores* of
land-transport systems found they could make better,
easier money by joining the business *collegiae* of seaborne enterprises. However, my suggestion, which is
based on the circumstantial witness of agricultural
manuals and the archaeological evidence cited a-
bove, leads to another question: what *were* the resources of villa owners in the late 1st/early 2nd century A.D., beyond the normal resources of profit from
the produce of their estates? Did they have access to
special help in overcoming their problems, problems
that were going to affect their villas' physical and financial status? The answer is yes, and it brings us to
the question of the *alimenta* schemes in Italy, and to
the possible indirect effects of the annonarian legisla-
tion on Italian villas in the High Empire. The *alimenta* gave cash, and the *annona* had given an indirect
advantage, to Italian villa owners.

Italian Villas and the Alimenta and the Annona

The *alimenta* scheme, instituted officially in the
reign of Nerva and expanded under Trajan, made
Italian *agriculteurs* mortgagees of the government by
scheduling their estates as surety for loans. This was a
financial new deal for agriculture, in the sense that
the mortgage system was widely instituted throughout central Italy, that it was not subject to individual
choice (it may in fact have been compulsory; Garnsey
1968: 377–81), and that it was more or less uniformly
applied. Its target appears to have been the wide
range of middle- and upper-level estates, which were
put under perpetual obligation of interest payment
(Duncan-Jones 1990: 121–42). The principal of the
loans did not need to be repaid or amortized, and
the interest rate was low with respect to the sum of
the loan, and low with respect to the total declared
value of the estates: financially, the loans had more
the air of subsidies to property owners, even though
they were a species of transfer payment from rich to

poor. It can be noted that, although the loans were
made to individuals, it was the estates that were under obligation, because most often, in the two inscriptions that list the obligations from the towns of
Veleia and Ligures Baebiani, the individual mortgagees were owners of many estates, some not in the territory of the towns handling the mortgage schemes.
What the *alimenta* system was for is not clear: ostensi-
bly, it was to provide local towns with a permanent
and annually paid charitable cash fund with which to
support orphans, widows, and poor families of the
communities (the number was usually fixed: at Veleia
it was 300; Veyne 1957: 105). The charitable intent
(for which the effects and the official expressions of
gratitude were outlined in inscriptions offered by
groups of its beneficiaries throughout Italy) is patent
and constitutes good reasons for the scheme
(Ruggiero 1895: I 404–5, 408; Duncan-Jones 1964:
124–25,146). The real reasons may have been otherwise, and, to be sure, they have been debated. In part
the *alimenta* funds may have been intended to ensure
continued efforts at procreation of boys, who were
more heavily subsidized, and for longer, than girls,
among the class of people who would provide army
recruits. The government may also have wished to
counteract a falling birthrate (Duncan-Jones 1982:
288–319; Garnsey 1988: 67–68, 252). It has been
claimed that, given the extremely advantageous
terms, the charitable intent was merely a cover for an
overt grant of money and patronage to middle- and
upper-level landowners (cf. Duncan-Jones 1982: 295
n. 5). The obligation to undertake such loans has
also been interpreted as a means of equalizing the
municipal obligations—euergetistic or liturgical in
character—between local members of town councils
or freedmen groups (*ordo decurionum or Augustalium*)
and those owners who either did not, or could not,
belong to the *ordines* (e.g., female proprietors); questions still remain as to whom and at what status the
alimenta loans were applicable (Veyne 1958: 218–19;
Duncan-Jones 1964: 130–35; cf. Garnsey 1968:
368–77).

The *alimenta*, while centrally promoted by the *fiscus*
and endowed with regional *praefecti* and *procuratores*,
were locally set up and administered, with the result
that their appearance in Italy was not quite uniform
(Pflaum 1960–61: III 1033, 1037–38, 1041; 1982:
114). The scheme appears to have been an idea of
the administration of Nerva, but it was promoted by,
and was always associated with, Trajan's administration; there is some evidence of its continuance
throughout Italy and its extension by the Antonine
emperors and the Severi. The charitable value of the
scheme may have been undercut by inflation in the
third century (Duncan-Jones 1964: 142–44). The
main moment in the administrative and financial history of the *alimenta*—the moment at which large
amounts of cash were made available for estates in

Italy—was in the reign of Trajan, early in the second century.

In whatever way we interpret the *alimenta*, their result was to put cash directly into the hands of owners of Italian villas, the same owners who at the time were ceasing to animate their properties in any significant way architecturally or technologically. The *alimenta* loans had no physical effect on villas, and they arrived at a time when, for some 20–40 years, little building had been going on, and when, in another generation or two, the villas would begin to be abandoned, converted, or quarried. The owners of the Francolise villas, in the legal territory of Cales, must have received *alimenta* loans: they were villas on the type of middle-level estate that were the objects of the scheme. The loans thus came at just the time that Pliny, the owner of the type of upper-level estates included in the scheme, was proposing to keep the other villa in "as is" condition: whatever the intention of the *alimenta*, the cash was certainly not used either for *voluptas* of the *partes urbanae* or for *utilitas* in *partes rusticae*. This was perhaps to be expected, because the annual and perpetual obligations incurred by the terms of the loans depressed the values of Italian estates, at least according to Pliny, whose intentions were euergetistic in favor of poor children at Comum, for whom he set up a private *alimenta*. He writes (7.18) that he put an estate he owned under obligation to pay annually a rent (*vectigal*) of HS 30,000 to the town, declaring the value of the estate at HS 500,000, which was much lower than its real value. The obligation being based on a low valuation, and the return on the estate being greater than the annual rent, the measure allowed him (or a later proprietor) both to continue to profit from the estate and to continue the charity. Still, he considered that the value of the estate had been diminished by at least as great an amount as the low valuation he had professed it to have (Duncan-Jones 1982: 298–300, 306). In this respect, as well as in respect to the other estate he was proposing to buy (which had recently dropped 40 percent in value, from HS 5 million to HS 3 million; 3.19), if this other estate indeed represented one that had an obligation to an *alimenta* scheme, then the decline in value of Italian estates and villas was significant. We have no way of knowing if the other estate was charged with an *alimenta* loan, and complaining about declines in real estate values was possibly an obligatory topic of moaning at Pliny's social level. Still, Pliny was genuinely concerned with the profitable management of his estates, and declines in their values would have prompted him to think of the physical conditions in which he kept his villas. Perhaps, in view of the decline of estate values that his own alimentary scheme, and also the official ones, seems to have caused, his proposal to keep the other villa "as is" is understandable. Euergetism for the poor (whether voluntary or compulsory) of the Italian *municipia* may have reinforced the physical desuetude of Italian *villae rusticae* in their environs.

Some examples can give an impression of the range and scale of the sums involved in the *alimenta*. At Veleia, near Placentia, the emperor Trajan put on deposit with the town a sum of HS 1,116,000 to be disbursed as loans to some 47 landowners professing to own estates ranging in value from HS 50,000 to over 1,000,000 (Pachtère 1920: 98–115). Veleia was only one, and by no means a larger one (or the largest), of the many dozens of towns that received such loans (Duncan-Jones 1964: 146; 1982: 337–41). At Ligures Baebiani, near Beneventum, one Gn. Marcius Rufinus owned the following *fundi*: the Marcian farm, the Satrian farm, the Julian, the Avillian, the Vitellian, the Nasennian, and the Marcellian farms, the Curian and Satrian farms in an outlying village, the Albian farm and its outbuildings (also in another district), and the Caesian farm in the Beneventanum (Veyne 1957: 86; 1958: 211–12). Rufinus must either have bought or have inherited previously purchased estates: to own all those farms out of natural inheritance, he would have had to have been the sole living heir of no fewer than 11 families that had all died out in his lifetime; this seems improbable. On the other hand, the range of sizes and values of his estates, and their dispersion, seems to argue against anything like the rapid latifundization that Carandini has posited for this period.

Rufinus professed a total value of HS 466,000 for all his estates and received a loan in the amount of HS 42,440 (about 8 percent of the value of his properties) at a very low annual interest of HS 1,061, or about 3 percent. The total value of his properties would not have qualified him even minimally to be a knight at Rome, even though one of his descendants became an imperial official in the reign of Septimius Severus (Veyne 1958: 212). He was only one of many thousand estimated to be much richer or poorer villa owners throughout Italy. The sums for the whole *alimenta* schemes throughout Italy cannot, then, have been insignificant; their distribution was widespread and thorough, and the individual loans advantageous, even though the global outlay represented a small part of the total imperial budget (Duncan-Jones 1982: 318 n. 4).

What did owners of Italian villas do with the money? Certainly nothing in the way of architectural additions to their villas that are archaeologically recuperable or recordable. Investing in slaves is a possibility, even though Pliny in the letter cited above indicated that there were problems in finding a servile workforce for the estate he was proposing to buy. Investing in machines or methods to generate higher productivity is also possible, depending on which side of the debate about technological advance in Roman times one wishes to stand (Kiechle 1969;

Carandini 1988: 235–65; cf. Finley 1980: 62 and, for a specific earlier example, Cotton and Métraux 1985: 72–73); but investment in agricultural "research and development" would not be possible to prove. One answer is that the mortgagees took the money and let it out at current rates of interest higher than the ones they had to pay, though whether this could have been effectively done anywhere except in Rome or other *metropoleis* is apparently doubtful, and there is also no drop in interest rates at the time of the *alimenta* loans to indicate any large flow of money into private banks (Duncan-Jones 1982: 299–300).

Another resource of Italian *agriculteurs* in the second century was the *cura annonae*, or, better, the indirect and unintended advantages that the administration and organization of the food supply of the capital had on Italian farmers. There is no place here to speculate on the direct effects in Italy of the organization, history, or development of the *annona*: supplying the food dole for the part of the population (the *plebs frumentaria*) qualified to receive it and providing grain at low prices, as well as provisioning the Imperial administration and the army, were matters ensured by imports from abroad anyway, and the annonarian prefects as a matter of policy were reluctant to intervene in the commercial markets for grain, wine, oil, and meat (Berchem 1939: 69–83; Rougé 1966: 459–90; Pavis d'Escurac 1976: 253–66; Casson 1980: 28–29; Garnsey 1988: 126–28). In addition, while a comparative history of prices between the annonarian province of Africa and Italy has been outlined, it does not concern agricultural produce (Duncan-Jones 1982: 357–60), and while the prices per *modius* of wheat in different parts of the empire is known, specific figures for the second century A.D. do not help in elucidating the architectural decisions of Italian villa owners. We do know that by A.D. 153, the prices for "ordinary" wine at Rome had increased by about 200 percent over what they had been a century earlier in Pompeii and Herculaneum: the evidence indicates both that prices increased absolutely over time and that prices for agricultural produce were relatively higher in Rome than in small towns, a circumstance would have been of equal advantage to either Italian or Gallic (or other) *viticulteurs* (Duncan-Jones 1982: 364–65).

Complaining about the high costs of living in Rome is an obligatory theme in Latin satirical poetry. Studies comparing wheat and flour prices in Italy and the east point out the relative advantage that farmers near *metropoleis* had: they could get significantly better prices for produce in big cities, and particularly in Rome, than they could in small towns (Jasny 1944; Duncan-Jones 1982: 345–47). The effect of annonarian measures and of provincial imports on Italian agricultural producers, which has been assumed by many scholars to have been disastrous, may have been less disastrous than has been thought

(Garnsey 1988: 190–91 n. 23). Columella was assuming profitability in Italy in the mid-1st century A.D., and much later Palladius still spoke highly of Italian villas. At Settefinestre, the piggery, large and well designed, was an addition to the *pars rustica*, probably as a means of ensuring financial participation in a resolutely Italian market for pork, an important peninsular contribution both to the diet in general and to the *annona* (Carandini et al. 1985: I 179, II 182–88; Whitehouse 1981; 1983).

Thus the economic evidence, such as it is, cannot by itself be decisive in assigning a cause and/or a date to the physical decline of Italian villas. If we return to my cautionary example—in *The Cherry Orchard*, the villa had endured "as is" for a long generation beyond its viability, and, after some tinkering by Lopahin, its estate was about to be revived. Leaving villas in "as is" condition for a while may have been an example of creative versatility on the part of their owners, and ultimately the abandonment of villas may have been due to causes other than those that prompted their slight change of use in the late first and in the first half of the 2nd century. The large-scale importation of produce for both the *annona* and the commercial market, which after all had been going on since the second century B.C., may well have discouraged Italian *agriculteurs* from building or adding onto their villas, but the process would not have been sudden. Owners of villas would have looked for resources outside estates to ensure their viability.

The annonarian measures, as well as the huge commercial food market in Rome, indirectly provided them with some resources: the *annona* gave owners of Italian agricultural estates the buildings and the marketing systems with which to offset the problems of storage, transport, and access to markets that they were experiencing. The buildings were the urban *horrea*, the commercial or official granary and general storage buildings in which agricultural produce could be stored close to metropolitan markets. The annonarian system had equestrian officials at both the *praefectus* and *procurator* levels, but even more interesting is that, by the late second century, Rome had a *procurator ad solaminia et horrea* (Pflaum 1960–61: III 1030; *solaminia* is food relief): the administrative innovation was presumably due to the physical and legal animation of the urban storage network. The marketing systems were the combination of commercial organizations and official purchasing agencies for the *annona* and for commercial brokers of large amounts of produce. When Cato was writing his manual, the construction of government *horrea* both to store food for distribution and to provision against lean years had not yet occurred: the first government *horrea* were built by Gaius Gracchus in 123 B.C. (the *horrea Sempronia*: Plut., *C. Gracch.* 5.6; Boren 1958; Pavis d'Escurac 1976: 6; Rickman 1980: 22, 47). By Varro and Columella's time, large *hor-*

rea—for example, the early manifestations of the *horrea Lolliana* and *Agrippiana*, and the *porticus Aemilia*—were an integral part of the urban landscape of Rome, though the two great *macella* (the *macellum Liviae* and *macellum Magnum*) were yet to be built in developed form (Rickman 1971: 87–104; Rickman 1980: 140–41; Colini 1980; *Misurare la terra* 1985: 180–89; De Ruyt 1983: 163–84). Petronius' Trimalchio owned urban *horrea* as an extension of his landholdings. Urban *horrea* of originally Republican or early Imperial date were many times rebuilt or added onto in Rome and Ostia in the second century, and the resulting total storage capacity grew significantly, both in government or government-leased buildings, and in private ones (Rickman 1971: 1–12, 121; Rickman 1980: 121–55, 198–201). It is important, however, to avoid being dazzled by the size and impressive architecture of the well-known *horrea* in Rome on the Tiber side under the Aventine. These, and the large Ostian granaries, were built for the grain, wine, and oil shipments coming from outside Italy, but in the urban landscape of Rome, they constituted, despite their size, only a fraction, about 15 percent, of the total number of *horrea* in Rome. Granted, many of the named or located *horrea*, which are known from the lists of the 4th-century *Curiosum* and *Notitia* descriptions of the city, must have been small, like those of Ostia (Rickman 1971: 38–43, 54–64, 76–86, 323–25). Even so, there were some 300 of them! Many, judging by their names and other evidence, were built in the second century, and many were in residential districts and around the major gates of the city on its east, northeast, and southeastern perimeter, in locations more appropriate to receive produce from Etruria, Latium, and Campania, where the villas were, than from Egypt, Africa, and Sardinia. In fact, the dozen or so large *horrea* of the Tiber side represent only the seaborne and riverine storage capacity of the city, not all of it in foodstuffs either, whereas the *horrea* of the regions must have represented the major part of the urban storage facilities. There were some that had specialized functions such as storing oil, wine, and other comestibles (Panciera 1980:*passim* and 239 n. 33; Rickman 1971: 9). Their total capacity cannot be accurately estimated. However, if we accept the estimates of historical sources, something of the increase in their gross capacity can be surmised from the following: in A.D. 51, Claudius had less than 15 days' food supply in the city, whereas when Septimius Severus died in A.D. 211, he left the city with seven years' worth of stocked food (on Claudius: Tac., *Ann.* 12.43; Suet., *Claud.* 18.2; Oros. 7.6.17; on Septimius Severus: *SHA* 7.7, 18.3, 23.2; Casson 1980: 24–25; Garnsey 1988: 223–25). The storage facilities to stock such a quantity as was left by Septimius Severus must have been built in the period under discussion here, that is, in the second century. They may represent a diversion

of investment by villa owners away from the countryside, in order to solve the storage and market-access problems they were experiencing.

The operation of these facilities was fairly standardized as were also their plans: *horrea* were set up as private or public corporations and were a source of lease money because the individual *tabernae* could be separately rented, for loose storage of grain as silos, or as units containing goods put up in *amphorae* and *dolia*, for baled manufactured goods (Rickman 1980: 134–43, 236–38). In a large city, of course, *horrea* represent a significant addition to the supple and quick provisioning of the populace with food, and their incidence within the city plans of both Ostia and Rome constituted, surely, one of the most prominent aspects of the urban landscape and activity. What is remarkable at Ostia is that very large *horrea* were not incompatible with small ones and did not absorb them: the variety of their sizes seems a clue to understanding the variety and versatility of their uses in the urban context. They were valuable properties and could replace prestigious, even historic, residences: one was built, in the 2nd century, on the north side of the Palatine Hill, on the site of an earlier aristocratic house (Carandini 1988: 359–87). These *horrea* thus constitute, for Rome and other cities, a secure method of ensuring that agricultural goods produced on rural estates could find storage near the principal centers of consumption in Italy, the bigger towns and cities. Owners of villas probably found that urban *horrea*, or ones they leased or to which they subscribed cooperatively, solved many of their marketing and distribution problems. In addition, the steady pace of governmental procurement for the civil and military *annona* probably led to the growth of cooperative ventures by Italian *agriculteurs* centered on cities; government officials are in general unwilling to enter into negotiations with small producers, and they much prefer to deal with brokers who can deliver produce on a large scale quickly and efficiently, besides being able to plan and anticipate annonarian requirements over several years (Rickman 1980: 219–30; Garnsey 1983: 121–30). Capitalizing such cooperative ventures and investing in the structures and leases of urban *horrea* required money, and it is to them that I suggest that the cash of the *alimenta* loans might well have gone. The large number of urban *horrea* in the *entrepôt* of Rome may well represent the diversion of money away from the countryside by villa owners anxious to solve problems of storage, transport, and market access; the result was the use of villas in "as is" condition.

For this reason I have termed Italian *villae rusticae* in the second century "alimentarian" and "annonarian." Owners of estates were no longer interested in spending money on the estates themselves, either the residential or utilitarian parts: they were interested purely in agricultural production. In this the govern ment may have been interested as well. But the net work of storage facilities and marketing possibilities in the market towns of Italy, which had for a long time been adequate, came to be inadequate by the beginning of the 2nd century, and something had to be done. In consequence, the city of Rome, and other *entrepôts*, came to have a network of both public and private agricultural warehouses, which solved the problems of storage and proximity to markets, and made large stocks of agricultural goods available as commodity for purchase and requisition by brokers and government agents. Ultimately, the urban *horrea* may have been counter-productive to the Italian owners of *villae rusticae*, because they were usable for any kind of goods from any source, but there are, of course, many other reasons for the dwindling of the Italian agricultural economy in Antonine times. The difficulties faced by Italian villa owners have been variously interpreted as a *repliement* of the slave mode of production, as an gradual exhaustion of productive imagination and material resources, or as a collapse in the face of competition from abroad (Carandini 1979: 128–31, 184–219; Carandini 1981; Dyson 1985). Still, their difficulties must always be seen in the context of their cultural attitudes—Pliny's, for example, happily living in an unchanging environment of villas built well before his time—and also of the infrastructure of viabilities, of what the *agriculteur* is going to do with his produce and how—storage, transport, markets. The target of production in the *villae rusticae* was always the cities, and the country-city interchange is at all times crucial in the Roman Empire. Of all that we hear of Italian cities and their decay in the late second century, conspicuously absent is the most successful of all the new phenomena, the *horrea*, which ensured commercial and annonarian operations. They seem not to have been affected by either the decay of cities or the dwindling of Italian agriculture. Paradoxically, the urban *horrea* are the second-century success story of Italian cities, even though rural agriculture in Italy, by which and for which they had in part been created, was in decline.

REFERENCES CITED

Abrams, P. and Wrigley, E. A. (eds.)
1978   *Towns in Societies: Essays in Economic History and Historical Sociology.* Cambridge.

Alarcão, J. and Mayet, F.
1989   "Les villa romaines de São Cucufate (Portugal)." CRAI **vol. no.?**:232–49.

Ascani, K. (ed.)
1976   *Studia Romana in honorem Petri Krarup septuagenarii.* Odense.

Barker, G. and Hodges, R. (eds.)
1981   *Archaeology and Italian Society: Prehistoric, Roman and Medieval Studies.* Papers in Italian Archaeology II, BAR 102. Oxford.

Bek, L.
1986   "Antithesis, a Roman Attitude and its Changes as Reflected in the Concept of Architecture from Vitruvius to Pliny the Younger." Pp. 154–66 in Ascani 1976.

van Berchem, D.
1939   *Les distributions de blé et d'argent à la plèbe romaine sous l'empire.* Geneva.

Boren, H. C.
1958   "The Urban Side of the Gracchan Crisis." AHR 63: 890–902.

Brunt, P. A.
1971   *Italian Manpower, 225 B.C.–A.D. 14.* Oxford.

Carandini, A.
1979   *L'anatommia della scimmia. La formazione economica della società prima del capitale.* Turin.
1980a   "Il vigneto e la villa del fondo di Settefinestre nel Cosano: un caso di produzione agricola per il mercato trasmarino." Pp. 1–10 in D'Arms and Kopff 1980.
1980b   "Roma imperialistica: un caso di sviluppo precapitalistico." Pp. 11–19 in D'Arms and Kopff 1980.
1981   "Sviluppo e crisi del manifatture rurali e urbane." Pp. 249–61 in Giardina and Schiavone 1981: II.
1982   "Sottotipi di schiavitù nelle società schiavistiche greca e romana." *Opus* 1:132–99.
1985   *I schiavi in Italia. Gli strumenti pensanti dei Romani fra tarda Repubblica e medio Impero.* Rome–Bari.

Carandini, A., et al. (eds.)
1985   *Settefinestre. Una villa schiavistica nell'Etruria romana*: I. *La villa nel suo insieme*; II. *La villa nelle sue parti*; III. *La villa e suoi reperti.* Modena.

Carlsen, J.
1984   "Considerations on Cosa and Ager Cosanus." *AnalRom* 13:49–59.

Casson, L.
1980   "The Role of the State in Rome's Grain Trade." Pp. 21–29 in D'Arms and Kopff 1980.

Colini, A. M.
1980   "Il porto fluviale del Foro Boario." Pp. 43–51 in D'Arms and Kopff 1980.

Cotton, M. A.
1979   *The Late Republican Villa at Posto, Francolise.* London.

Cotton, M. A. and Métraux, G. P. R.
1985   *The San Rocco Villa at Francolise.* London.

Corbier, M.
1981   "Proprieté e gestione della terra: grande proprieté fondiaria ed economia contadina." Pp. 427–44 in Giardina and Schiavone 1981: I.

D'Arms, J. H.
1974   "Puteoli in the Second Century of the Roman Empire: a Social and Economic Study." *JRS* 64:104–24.
1976   "Notes on Municipal Notables of Imperial Ostia." *AJP* 97:387–411.
1981   *Commerce and Social Standing in Ancient Rome.* Cambridge, MA.

D'Arms, J. H. and Kopff, E. C. (eds.)
1980   *The Seaborne Commerce of Ancient Rome: Studies in Archaeology and History.* MAAR 36. Rome.

De Robertis, F. M.
1971   *Storia delle corporazioni e del regime associativo nel mondo romano,* 2 vols. Bari.

de Ruggiero, E.
1961   *Dizionario epigrafico di antichità romane,* vol. I, reprint. Rome.

De Ruyt, C.
1983   *Macellum. Marché alimentaire des romains.* Publications d'histoire de l'art et d'archéologie de l'université catholique de Louvain 35. Louvain.

Duncan-Jones, R.
1964   "The Purpose and Organization of the Alimenta." *BSR* 32:123–46.
1982   "The Economy of the Roman Empire." *Quantitative studies* (2nd ed.). Cambridge.
1990   *Structure and Scale in the Roman Economy.* Cambridge.

Dyson, S. L.
1978   "Settlement Patterns in the Ager Cosanus." *JFA* 5:251–68.
1981   "Settlement Reconstruction in the Ager Cosanus and the Albegna Valley: Wesleyan University Research, 1974–1979." Pp. 269–74 in Barker and Hodges 1981.
1985   "The Villas of Buccino and the Consumer Model of Roman Rural Development." Pp. 69–84 in Malone and Stoddart 1985: IV.

Etienne, R.
1974   "Recherches sur l'ergastule." Pp. 249–66 in *Actes du Colloque 1972 sur l'esclavage.* Annales littéraires de l'Université de Besançon 163. Paris.

Finley, M. I.
1980   *Ancient Slavery and Modern Ideology.* New York.

Forlati Tamaro, B., Forlati, F., and Barbieri, F.
1956   *Il Duomo di Vicenza.* Vicenza.

Fouet, G.
1969   *La villa gallo-romaine de Montmaurin. Gallia* Suppl. 20. Paris.
1972   "Le sanctuaire des eaux de La Hillère à Montmaurin." *Gallia* 30:83–124.

Frazer, A. (ed.)
1998   *The Roman Villa*—Villa Urbana. Philadelphia.

Gabba, E.
1972   "Urbanizzazione e rinnovamenti urbanistici nell'Italia centro-meridionale del I sec.a.C." *Studi classici ed orientale* 21:73–111.
1977   "Considerazioni sulla decadenza della piccola proprietà contadina nell Italia centro-meridionale del II sec.a.C." *Ktema* 2:269–84.
1980   "Riflessioni antiche e moderne sulle attività commerciali a Roma nei secoli II e I a.C." Pp. 91–102 in D'Arms and Kopff 1980.

Garnsey, P.
1968   "Trajan's Alimenta: Some Problems." *Historia* 17:367–81.
1983   "Grain for Rome." Pp. 118–30 in Garnsey et al. 1983.
1988   *Famine and Food Supply in the Graeco-Roman World. Responses to Risk and Crisis.* Cambridge.

Garnsey, P., Hopkins, K., and Whittaker, C. R. (eds.)
1983   *Trade in the Ancient Economy.* London.

Garnsey, P. and Saller, R. P.
1987   *The Roman Empire: Economy, Society and Culture.* London.

Giardina, A. and Schiavone, A.
1981   *Società romana e produzione schiavistica:* vol. I,

L'Italia: insediamenti e forme economiche, vol. II, *Merci, mercati e scambi nel Mediterraneo,* vol. III, *Modelli etici, diritto e trasformazione sociali.* Rome–Bari.

Greene, K.
1986   *The Archaeology of the Roman Economy.* London.

Gualtieri, M., Salvatore, M., and Small, A. (eds.)
1983   *Lo scavo di S. Giovanni di Ruoti ed il periodo tardoantico in Basilicata.* Pubblicazioni del Centro accademico canadese 1. Bari.

Hesnard, A.
1980   "Un dépôt augustéen d'amphores à La Longarina, Ostie." Pp. 141–56 in D'Arms and Kopff 1980.

Hopkins, K.
1978   "Economic Growth and Towns in Classical Antiquity." Pp. 35–77 in Abrams and Wrigley 1978.
1983   "Introduction." Pp. i–xxvii in Garnsey et al. 1983.

Houston, G. W.
1980   "The Administration of Italian Seaports during the First Three Centuries of the Roman Empire." Pp. 157–71 in D'Arms and Kopff 1980.

Jasny, N.
1944   *The Wheats of Classical Antiquity.* Johns Hopkins University Studies 62. Baltimore.

Kahane, A., Murray-Threipland, L., and Ward-Perkins, J. B.
1968   "The Ager Veientanus North and East of Veii." *BSR* 36:1–218.

Kiechle, F.
1969   *Sklavenarbeit und technischer Fortschritt im römischen Reich.* Wiesbaden.

Labrousse, M.
1966   "Montmaurin." *Gallia* 24:420–21.

Lyttelton, M.
1980   "The Mura di San Stefano near Anguillara: a Roman villa?" Pp. 53–71 in Painter 1980.

MacDougall, E. B. (ed.)
1987   *Ancient Roman Villa Gardens.* DOP 10. Washington.

Malone, C. and Stoddart S. (eds.)
1985   *Papers in Italian Archaeology* IV: *the Cambridge*

conference, 4 vols. BAR 243–246. Oxford.

Martin, R.
1967   "Pline le jeune et les problèmes économiques de son temps." *REA* 69:62–97.
1971   *Recherches sur les agronomes latins et leurs conceptions économiques et sociales.* Paris.
1976   "Palladius." In *Traité d'agriculture,* vol. I. Paris.

McMullen, R.
1970   "Market-Days in the Roman Empire." *Phoenix* 24:333–41.

Meiggs, R.
1973   *Roman Ostia,* 2nd ed. Oxford.

Métraux, G. P. R.
1984   "Patronage and Style in the Mosaics of the Villa San Rocco, Francolise." *BullAIEMA* 10:139–49.

Misurare la terra
1983   — *centuriazione e coloni nel mondo romano: il caso modenese.* Modena.
1985   — *centuriazione e coloni nel mondo romano. Città, agricoltura, commercio: materiali da Roma e dal suburbio.* Modena.

Mrozek, S.
1987   *Les distributions d'argent et de nourriture dans les villes italiennes en haut-empire romain.* Collection Latomus. Brussels.

Pachtère, F. Georges de
1920   *La Table hypothécaire de Veleia. Etude sur la propriété foncière dans l'Apennin de Plaisance.* Bibliothèque de l'Ecole des hautes études, sciences historiques et philologiques 228. Paris.

Painter, K. (ed.)
1980   *Roman Villas in Italy. Recent Excavations and Research.* British Museum Occasional Paper 24. London.

Panciera, S.
1980   "Olearii." Pp. 235–50 in D'Arms and Kopff 1980.

Pavis d'Escurac, H.
1976   *La Préfecture de l'Annone: service administratif impérial d'Auguste à Constantin.* BEFAR 226. Rome.

Percival, J.
1976   *The Roman Villa: An Historical Introduction.* London.

Pesando, F.
1987 *Oikos e ktesis. La casa greca in età classica.* Perugia.

Pflaum, H. G.
1960–61 *Les carrières procuratoriennes équestres sous le haut-empire romain,* 4 vols. Institut français d'archéologie de Beyrouth, Bibliothèque archéologique et historique 57. Paris.
1982 *Les carrières procuratoriennes équestres sous le haut-empire romain,* supplément. Institut français d'archéologie du Proche-Orient, Bibliothèque archéologique et historique 112. Paris.

Potter, T. W.
1979 *The Changing Landscape of South Etruria.* London.
1987 *Roman Italy.* London.

Purcell, N.
1985 "Wine and Wealth in Ancient Italy." *JRS* 75:1–19.

Quilici, L.
1976 "Castel Giubileo (Roma). Saggi di scavo attorno a Fidenae." *NSc,* ser. 8, 30:263–326.

Rathbone, D. W.
1981 "The Development of Agriculture in the 'Ager Cosanus' During the Roman Republic: Problems of Evidence and Interpretation." *JRS* 71:10–23.

Rickman, G.
1971 *Roman Granaries and Store Buildings.* Cambridge.
1980a *The Corn Supply of Ancient Rome.* Oxford.
1980b "The Grain Trade under the Roman Empire." Pp. 261–75 in D'Arms and Kopff 1980.

Rougé, J.
1966 *Recherches sur l'organisation du commerce maritime en Méditerranée.* Paris.

Schlippschuch, O.
1974 *Die Händler im römischen Kaiserreich in Gallien, Germanien und in den Donauprovinzen Raetien, Noricum und Pannonien.* Amsterdam.

Small, A.
1983 "Gli edifici del periodo tardo-antico a San Giovanni." Pp. 21–37 in Gualtieri et al. 1983.
1985 "Introduction." Pp. xix–xxxiv in Cotton and Métraux 1985.

Tchernia, A.
1980 "Quelques remarques sur le commerce du vin et des amphores." Pp. 305–12 in D'Arms and Kopff 1980.
1983 "Italian Wine in Gaul at the End of the Republic." Pp. 87–104 in Garnsey et al. 1983.
1986 *Le vin de l'Italie romaine. Essai d'histoire économique d'après les amphores.* BEFAR 261. Rome.

Veyne, P.
1957 "La Table des Ligures Baebiani et l'institution alimentaire de Trajan." *MEFR* 69:81–135.
1958 "La Table des Ligures Baebiani et l'institution alimentaire de Trajan." *MEFR* 70:177–241.

White, K. D.
1970 *Roman Farming.* Ithaca.

Whitehouse, D. B.
1981 "The Schola Praeconum and the Food Supply of Rome in the Fifth Century A.D." Pp. 191–95 in Barker and Hodges 1981.
1983 "Ruoti, Pottery and Pigs." Pp. 107–9 in Gualtieri et al. 1983.

Widrig, W. M.
1987 "Land Use at the Via Gabina Villas." Pp. 223–60 in MacDougall 1987.

Wilson, R. J. A.
1985 "Changes in the Patterns of Urban Settlement in Roman, Byzantine and Arab Sicily." Pp. 313–34 in Malone and Stoddart 1985: IV.

Wiseman, T. P.
1987 *Roman Studies. Literary and Historical.* Liverpool.

2

HELLENISTISCHE VORLÄUFER DER RÖMISCHEN VILLA

Hans Lauter

Noch vor vierzig oder dreißig Jahren wäre es ein hoffnungsloses Unterfangen gewesen, die Frage nach hellenistischen—oder in weiterem Sinne griechischen—Vorläufern der römischen 'villa' überhaupt zu stellen. Inzwischen sind zwar bemerkenswerte Monumente bekannt geworden, die zu diesem Thema beitragen; insgesamt wird man das einschlägige Material aber immer noch als ziemlich mager und inkohärent bezeichnen dürfen. Publiziert ist es außerdem nur schlecht oder gar nicht. Es seien die folgenden Vorbemerkungen erlaubt.

Das Phänomen der römischen Villa ist ein sehr komplexes System, wenn man seine besonderen sozialen und ökonomischen Gegebenheiten in die Betrachtung miteinbezieht. Als solches ist es ein Produkt der spezifisch italischen Gesellschaftsstruktur zwischen späterer Republik und Kaiserzeit und daher *in toto* nicht mit 'Vorläufern' in der anders strukturierten, graeko-makedonischen Welt zu parallelisieren. Es wird also darauf hinauslaufen müssen, daß man sich hier mit vergleichbaren Teilaspekten zwischen griechischen 'Vorläufern' und römischer 'villa' beschäftigt. Deren gibt es freilich einige, und sie liegen insbesondere auf zwei Sektoren. Die 'villa' ist abgesehen von ihrer Funktion als agrarische Produktionsstätte (auch) ein ländliches, d.h. außerstädtisches Wohnhaus mit ausgeprägtem Nahverhältnis zu Natur und Landschaft,[1] deren Amoenitäten bewußt

genutzt werden. In diesem sind Griechen und Makedonen den Römern lange vorangegangen; schon seit dem 4. Jh. v. Chr. ist die Disposition, auf dem Lande—gegebenenfalls luxuriös—zu wohnen, archäologisch einwandfrei bezeugt; es sei hier nur der Name Mieza vorausgreifend genannt. Ich werde auf die Mentalität, die sich damit ausdrückt, zurückkommen. Ferner hat diese 'naturverbundene', ländliche Lebensweise bestimmte architektonische und künstlerische Erscheinungen zur Folge. So spielen z.B. Terrassierungen eine große Rolle; ein starkes Augenmerk gilt der 'Wasserarchitektur' usf.; dies ist unmittelbar mit der engeren Zweckbestimmung der Villen verknüpft. Nicht gar sehr spät dringen auch Motive aus der eigentlichen 'Herrschaftsarchitektur' in den Villenbau ein,—man denke nur an das Flügelrisalitmotiv, das die Gartenfront so vieler Landsitze in Italien, Gallien und Germanien auszeichnet. Der Grund für solche Übernahmen dürfte ein doppelter sein. Zum einen fügen sich entsprechende Motive vorzüglich in die gewollte landschafterische Gestaltung des Gebäudes, dessen Einbindung in das Ambiente dadurch verstärkt wird. Zum anderen demonstrieren sie aufgrund der semantischen Konnotationen, die sie unterschwellig immer noch transportieren, das Sozialprestige des *dominus*. Darauf soll hier nicht weiter eingegangen werden, weil das den Rahmen des engeren Themas sprengen würde.

---

1. In etwa dem römischen Wortgebrauch folgend, meinen wir unter dem Begriff '*villa*' hier nur den außerstädtischen Landsitz. Durch 'naturhafte' Verschönerung (z.B. durch Gärten) bereicherte Stadthäuser gab es, wie später im Römischen, zwar auch seit griechischer Zeit: Erinnert sei an den 'Kepos' des Epikur in dessen Haus im innerstädtischen Quartier von Melite zu Athen, vgl. Diog. Laert. 9 passim (zum Garten des Aristoteles in Chalkis vgl. Diog. Laert. 5.14); erinnert sei auch an die kunstvoll ausgestalteten Gartenperistyle des frühhellenistischen Pella in Makedonien (H. Lauter-Bufe [1975], in B. Andreae und H. Kyrieleis [Hrsgb.], Neue *Forschungen in Pompeji* [Recklinghausen] 169 Abb. 166; Heermann 1980: passim). Für die steigende Wertschätzung der 'Natur' im Wohnbau sind solche Beispiele zweifellos bedeutsam und zeichnen den Hintergrund

ab, auf dem die nachherigen Erwägungen gesehen werden sollten. Die Römer haben freilich landschaftlich gestaltete Stadthäuser stets als *domus* und nicht als '*villa*' bezeichnet (so z.B. die Domus aurea des Nero in Rom). Obwohl der Übergang zwischen den Gattungen in baukünstlerischer Hinsicht zumindest fließend, wenn nicht inexistent ist, soll es hier beim lateinischen Wortverständnis bleiben. Der Leser muß sich gleichwohl dessen bewußt sein, daß mit dieser definitorischen Zergliederung innerlich Zusammengehöriges auseinandergerissen wird. Nur unter Einbeziehung des sozio-ökonomischen Bedingungsfeldes der römischen '*villa*' erscheint solces einigermaßen gerechtfertigt; in unserem Zusammenhang wird dieses allerdings keine gravierende Rolle spielen können.

Überdies ist es ja leicht, die 'hoheitlichen' Motive in der römischen Villenarchitektur anhand der bekannten hellenistischen Großbauten zu verifizieren.

Im Hinblick auf die griechischen Vorläufer der römischen 'villa' kann es im folgenden nur um zwei Hauptpunkte gehen: Einesteils allgemein um das bewußte Wohnen (von Städtern!) in ländlicher Umgebung; andernteils um architektonische Besonderheiten der Villenbaukunst, die sich offenbar unabhängig von bestimmten historischen Grundbedingungen immer wieder einstellen. 'Villa' im modernen Sinn ist ja ein umfassenderer Begriff als das geschichtlich doch beschränkte Phänomen des römischen Villensystems mit seinen speziellen sozioökonomischen Bedingungen. Wir gehen hier von der übergreifenden Definition der 'villa' aus,[2] indem nur damit auch die Brücke zu den hellenistischen bzw. griechischen Vorläufern zu schlagen ist. Die Vergleichsmomente konzentrieren sich daher, um dies zu wiederholen, auf baukünstlerische Motive und auf das innere Verhältnis des (höheren) privaten Wohnbaus zur umgebenden Landschaft.

Wenn wir minoisch-mykenische 'Villen' einmal beiseite lassen—über deren nähere Qualität wir ausserdem fast nichts wissen—beginnt die europäische Villenarchitektur im engeren Sinne während der Spätklassik und erreicht noch gegen Ende des 4. Jh. v. Chr. erste Höhepunkte in Makedonien, die in gewisser Hinsicht niemals mehr übertroffen wurden.

I

Bei der Entstehung der—noch schlecht bekannten—hellenistischen Villenkultur, also bei der Ausbildung luxuriöser Landwohnsitze, spielen offenbar mehrere Faktoren eine Rolle, die hier nur kurz angeschnitten werden sollen.

Den Hintergrund bildet vielleicht die Gewohnheit griechischer Grundbesitzer, seit je isolierte Einzelgehöfte auf dem Land zu bewohnen. Das älteste, freilich noch mythische Zeugnis ist das Landhaus des Laertes in *Od.* 24.206ff., wo mit den Worten '*domata kala*' sogar schon ein gewisser baulicher Luxus angedeutet erscheint. Die Tatsache isolierter Einzelgehöfte ist von den Altertumswissenschaftlern bis in jüngste Zeit übersehen oder gar abgeleugnet worden; sie werden jedoch so etwas wie das Experimentierfeld für die sich entwickelnde Villenkultur der Griechen gewesen sein. Bei rezenten Forschungen

wurde vor allem in Attika, der Chora von Athen, eine große Fülle solcher Einzelhöfe nachgewiesen, unter denen sich nicht wenige anspruchsvolle und reiche Anlangen befinden (z.B. Lauter 1980: 283; weiteres reiches Material bald bei Lohmann 1990: passim); darauf ist gleich kurz zurückzukommen. Die von uns entdeckten, baulich anspruchsvollen, isolierten Einzelhöfe gehören im wesentlichen zwar erst dem 4. Jh. v. Chr. an, doch würde ich vermuten, daß sich schon die Passagen des Thukydides 2.13 ('Felder und Häuser des Perikles') und 2.65 ('die Güter der Reichen auf dem Land mit ihren Gebäuden und ihrem luxuriösen Inventar') auf vergleichbare, vielleicht villenähnliche Landsitze des 5. Jh. v. Chr. beziehen.

Ich meine, wir müssen uns ungefähr folgendes Bild machen. Die wohlhabenden Athener der klassischen Jahrhunderte, Mitglieder der Oberschicht, besaßen außer ihren Häusern in der Hauptstadt ein oder mehrere Güter auf dem Land, die sich oft völlig isoliert auch außerhalb der Dörfer erhoben. Der Vornehme wird normalerweise in seinem Stadthaus in der *asty* gewohnt haben, um seine politischen Pflichten und Ambitionen bequemer verfolgen zu können. Auf den Landgütern saßen Verwalter (*epitropoi*), Freie oder Sklaven, die den alltäglichen Betrieb besorgten. Es ist aber nur ganz natürlich, daß die Besitzer wenigstens gelegentlich Aufenthalt auf ihren Landgütern nahmen, schon um die Arbeit zu kontrollieren. Sollten sie zu einer Zeit, in der ein Aristophanes die Lieblichkeiten des Landlebens lyrisch zu preisen weiß, dann nicht aber solche Aufenthalte auch zu 'Ferien' o.ä. auszunützen verstanden haben? In unserem Zusammenhang: Die Mitglieder der Oberschicht werden in dem einen oder anderen ihrer Höfe Appartements eingerichtet haben, die ihren verfeinerten Lebensgewohnheiten und ihrem Vergnügen Rechnung tragen konnten. Der Übergang von ländlichen Farmen zu ländlichen Villen verflösse. Und daß dies tatsächlich der Fall war, scheint Thuk. 2.65 und das Testimonium der Denkmäler zu belegen.

Die obigen Erwägungen bleiben als solche immer noch theoretisch und spekulativ. Wir haben aber unverfängliche Beweise, daß die Einzelgehöfte von ihren Besitzern nicht nur als Produktionsbetriebe betrachtet, sondern auch emotionell gewürdigt wurden. Gerade bei den aufwendiger ausgestatteten Landhäusern finden sich recht häufig Familiengräber, was ja doch auf eine besondere Beziehung der Eigentümer zu ihrem Gut hinweist (wie sie auch immer begründet sein mag). Diese Beobachtung

---

2. In einer zeitgemäßen Definition der '*villa*' werden die Erfahrungen hinzuzunehmen sein, die mit dem Gegenstand seit der frühen Neuzeit gemacht wurden. Genauer gesagt: Villen seit der Renaissance und Villen des Barock sind in die Begriffsbildung zu integrieren. Selbst arabische 'Wüstenschlösser' wären zu berücksichtigen, um nur ein weiteres, dem Autor

besser bekanntes Material zu erwähnen. Es geht jedenfalls nicht an, den Villenbegriff auf seine speziell römische Erscheinungsform und die damit verbundenen (ausschließlich römisch) sozialen und wirtschaftlichen Grundlagen zu beschränken. Das anstehende Problem ist nach Überzeugung des Verfassers ein viel allgemeineres.

macht aus den klassischen 'Bauernhöfen'—oder doch aus einem Teil von ihnen—mehr als bloße agrarische Betriebseinheiten. Sie wachsen in eine andere Kategorie hinein.

Zu den unverzichtbaren Kennzeichen solcher herausgehobener Bauten gehören einige architektonische Elemente, die vereinzelt zwar nichts beweisen—da sie hie und da auch einmal in bescheideneren Anlagen auftreten können—die aber zusammen den Eindruck eines reichen, villenähnlichen Landgutes konstituieren: ein runder oder quadratischer Turm, das kostbar geschmückte Familiengrab und nicht zuletzt Räume (*androne*) von besonderer Größe und Ausstattung, die sich für Symposien u. dgl. eignen, womit eine über das nur Bäuerliche hinausgehende Lebensführung evident wird (Beispiele Lohmann 1990: passim). Fest eingerichtete Badezimmer mit Zementfußböden und Tonwannen erhöhen den Wohnkomfort. Inwieweit das rein landschaftliche Element, etwa in Form von Ziergärten o.ä., bereits Beachtung fand, ist verständlicherweise schwer zu beurteilen. Bemerkenswert ist immerhin z.B. der Nachweis einer Veranda über der Westterrasse des eher schlichten Hauses auf Kiapha Thiti, das man kaum als villenartig bezeichnen würde.

Zusammenfassend möchte ich sagen, daß die herrschaftlichen Landsitze der klassischen Zeit in Griechenland den Villengedanken insofern vorbereitet haben, als in ihnen ein auch luxuriöses Wohnen draußen auf dem Lande, fern von allen engen Habitaten erprobt werden konnte und offenbar eben auch stattfand. Echte Villen im Sinne von 'Lusthäusern' scheinen freilich bisher—etwa in Attika—nicht nachweisbar; und das überrascht bei der (wenigstens dem Geiste nach) gleichheitlichen Gesellschaftsstruktur der demokratischen Polis wenig. Allzu luxuriöse Lebensführung, wie sie sich im Bau großer Villen ausdrückt, ist eine Extravaganz, die selbst ein schwerreicher Polit eigentlich nicht wagen konnte. Doch mögen Charaktere wie Alkibiades auch hier schon Ausnahmen aufgestellt haben, die wir nur nicht kennen.

Wenn die Existenz herrschaftlicher Landsitze die Fähigkeit und die Bereitschaft der klassischen Welt bezeugt, die Freuden eines naturnahen Lebens und Wohnens wertzuschätzen, so ist zweitens auf die bereits erwähnte Erscheinung (Anm. 1) hinzuweisen, daß im Verlauf des 4. Jh. v. Chr. Gärten in die (Stadt-) Häuser integriert, also jeweils ein Stück gestalteter Natur in den Wohnbereich einbezogen wurden. Auch in diesem Phänomen, das nur scheinbar so selbstverständlich ist, drückt sich eine gewisse Disposition der Epoche aus, die die Villenkultur ermöglicht, ihr die Bahn geebnet hat.

II

Die Ausbildung echter Villen erfolgte auf diesem kulturellen Gesamthintergrund freilich aber nicht im eigentlichen Griechenland, sondern in Makedonien, wenn wir ausreichend unterrichtet sind. Ein entscheidender Grund dafür wird die noch monarchisch-adelige, halbfeudale Gesellschaftsstruktur des Staates gewesen sein; die Herrschenden gönnten sich hier eine (zeitgerechte) Lebensführung, wie sie in der Polis vielleicht nur schwer möglich war. Sie ließen sich veritable Landvillen oder Luxussitze in der Natur errichten, in denen sie der Muße und dem Vergnügen lebten.

Teile solcher Villen (im allgemeinen, nicht im beschränkteren römischen Sinn) sind nun seit einiger Zeit bekannt geworden. Das wichtigste und zugleich älteste Beispiel ist der Bau von Mieza beim heutigen Naoussa. Die nur ganz unvollständig erforschte Anlage von Kopanos stellt wahrscheinlich ebenfalls eine Villa dar und in gewisser Weise ist hier auch der Palast von Vergina-Palatiza zu erwähnen.

Diese spätklassisch-frühhellenistischen Villen Makedoniens weisen typische Züge der Naturanbindung und der Landschaftsgestaltung auf, die es verbieten, sie bloß als sozusagen außerstädtische Paläste einzustufen. Sie zeigen Formen und Eigentümlichkeiten, die die höhere Villenarchitektur auch anderer Epochen immer wieder kennzeichnen. Davon sei an dieser Stelle kurz die Rede.

Die Ruine einer Villa nahe der modernen Stadt Naoussa in Makedonien ist offenbar nur ganz unvollständig ergraben worden. Sie wurde versuchsweise mit jener Villa bei Mieza identifiziert, wo Aristoteles nach der Überlieferung den jungen Alexander erzogen haben soll. Deshalb ist sie als 'Schule des Aristoteles' in die Forschung eingegangen (Heermann 1986: 329–331). In der Tat ist das Gebäude in die 40er oder 30er Jahre des 4. Jh. v. Chr. zu datieren, wie dekorierte Dachziegel belegen; der eingebürgerte Kenn-Name mag also toleriert werden, auch wenn der Name in unserem Kontext eine höchst nebensächliche Rolle spielt. Entscheidend ist allein die Datierung und die Gestalt dieser höchst bedeutenden Anlage, von der freilich im Grunde nur eine in den Felshang geschlagene, L-förmige Stoa annähernd bekannt ist (Abb. 2.1–3).

Die Publikation (s.o.) ist so bescheiden—um es mild auszudrücken—daß ein Leser ohne Autopsie wohl nicht in der Lage ist, sich von dem Ensemble eine selbständige Vorstellung zu bilden.[3] Zum einen wird nur mäßig klar, daß auf dem stark überwachsenen Plateau über der freigelegten, in die Felswand ein-

---

3. Der Autor war in der glücklichen Lage, das Monument auf zwei Reisen 1967 und 1975 besichtigen zu können.

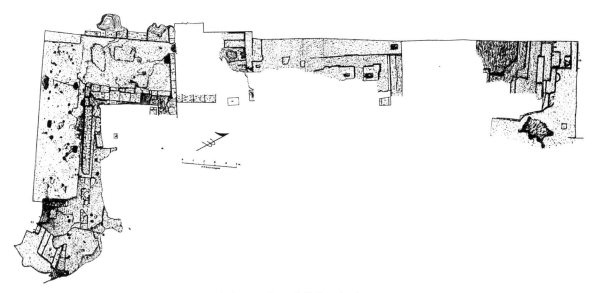

Abbildung 2.1. Villa von Mieza-Naoussa, Makedonien. Grundrißplan der Stoa.

geschnittenen Stoa weitere Gebäudeteile aufgeragt haben müssen; deren Spuren (Felseinbettungen) sind vor Ort besonders gut im Süden über der Halle bewahrt. Hier mögen sogar die Hauptanlagen der Villa mit den eigentlichen Wohnquartieren gelegen haben. Zum andern ist die eindrucksvolle Naturumgebung kaum angesprochen.

Wie schon gesagt, befindet sich die L-förmige Wandelhalle am oberen Ende eines Hanges und blickt von dieser hohen Lage weit nach Osten und Norden über die 'sandige' Hemathia hinaus, deren Horizonte sich in einer grünlich-blauen Ferne verlieren. Am Fuße des Hügelhanges, nur ein paar Meter tiefer als die Stoa, entspringt eine überaus kräftige Quelle, die den Talboden ringsum zu einer exuberanten, dschungelartigen Wildnis verwandelt. Nur mit Mühe ist heute durch Geschlinge und Geäst zum sprudelnden Quellteich durchzudringen.

Es muß dieses natürliche Phänomen—nicht ganz gewöhnlich in den trockenen subtropischen Ländern—gewesen sein, das die Errichtung unserer Villa an genau diesem Platze veranlaßt hat. Eine Verbindung zwischen dem Wandelgang und dem Quellteich war leicht herzustellen, wenn auch die Grabungen über ihr Wie keine Erkenntnisse gebracht haben (u.a. weil sie sich gar nicht auf diesen kritischen Bereich erstreckten).

Die Wahl dieses *locus amoenus*, das Gewicht, das der Aussicht, dem 'Bellevue,' zukommt lassen etwas von der fast schon romantischen Naturhingegebenheit ahnen, die den Bauherrn der Villa von Mieza leitete. Ein bauliches Detail kann diese Einschätzung verstärken. An die Rückwand der aus dem Felsen gehauenen Stoa schließt sich auf der südlichen Schmalseite eine Art Grotte an, die vielleicht als

natürliche Höhlung im Gestein schon vor Errichtung des Gebäudes bestanden hatte. Ihre Türe (in der rückwärtigen Felswand der Portikus) wird nun durch einen künstlich eingesetzten Sturz (Abb. 2.2, 2.3) überdeckt, der eine Art Bogen zeigt. Nur ist dieser Bogen nicht von abstrakt geometrischer Form, sondern unregelmäßig und eher kleeblattförmig gebildet. Diese bewußte und bisher einzigartige Irregularität spielt ganz evident auf 'natürliche' Erscheinungen, wie unberührte Höhleneingänge, an und sollte zweifellos den in die Landschaft eingebundenen Charakter des Bauwerks erhöhen, seine 'Naturbezogenheit' demonstrativ weiter verdeutlichen.

Diese sprechende Einzelheit und die Gesamtdisposition der 'Villa von Mieza' zeigen also Tendenzen, die für die höhere Villenarchitektur generell typisch sind: Landschafterei, Naturliebhaberei z.B.; charakteristische Details wie die Einbindung von 'Wasserkünsten' (hier eine natürliche Quelle) oder von Grottenarchitektur sind hervorzuheben. Die meist schlecht oder nicht veröffentlichten früheren römischen Luxusvillen (etwa in Tivoli oder an der Küste zwischen Rom und Neapel, die ich vor Augen habe) finden damit in der Villa von Mieza ältere ästhetische Parallelen.

Die Villa von Kopanos (Heermann 1986: 332–335) ist noch weit schlechter als die von Mieza-Naoussa bekannt (Abb. 2.4). Es ist noch nicht einmal völlig ausgemacht, daß die herrschaftliche Anlage wirklich eine freistehende Villa darstellt und nicht etwa einen 'Palast' innerhalb eines Habitats; doch spricht der Augenschein für das erstere (Autopsie des Verf. 1975). Ausgegraben wurde herzlich wenig, nämlich nur der Teil einer Substruktion, die an einen sanften

Abbildung 2.2. Villa von Mieza-Naoussa. Türreste in der Rückwand der Stoa.

Abbildung 2.3. Villa bei Naoussa, Makedonien. Türreste wie oben, Foto.

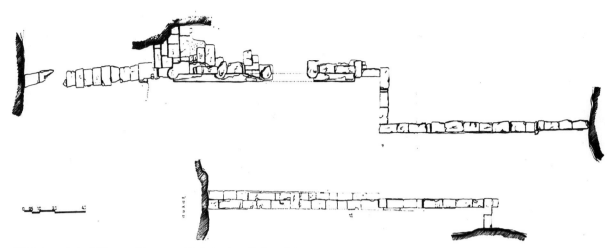

Abbildung 2.4. Villa von Kopanos, Makedonien. Substruktionen.

Hang gelehnt ist bzw. aus ihm hervortritt. Diese Substruktion bildete vielleicht eine Art Kryptoportikus. Doch soll darauf und auf ihren Säulenschmuck hier nicht näher eingegangen werden. Nur zwei Punkte seien herausgehoben: Zum einen der 'landschaftliche' Aspekt, der sich wiederum in dem Belvedere über die östlich ausgebreitete Ebene der Hemathia manifestiert; wichtiger aber ist die Tatsache, daß die ausgegrabenen Reste der Substruktion eindeutig das Vorhandensein eines Risalits bezeugen. Damit fassen wir (irgendwann um 300 v. Chr.) ein architektonisches Motiv, das in der späteren antiken Villenarchitektur so eminent fruchtbar werden sollte. Hinzuweisen ist wahrscheinlich noch auf das pure Faktum der kunstvollen Terrassierung am Gebäude von Kopanos—auch ein Motiv, das z.B. in der höheren römischen Villenarchitektur die breiteste Anwendung finden wird.

In diesem Zusammenhang muß nun doch noch der Palast von Vergina-Palatitza erwähnt werden, auch wenn er wohl eigentlich nicht als 'Villa' bezeichnet werden kann. Über seine Funktion haben wir an anderer Stelle das Nötige angedeutet (Lauter 1987: 346; Heermann 1986: 239–324). Was diesen Palast, der wohl unter Kassandros errichtet wurde, mit den *villae suburbanae* von Naoussa und Kopanos verbindet, sind zwei Züge. Einerseits ist die Tatsache nicht zu übersehen, daß es sich um einen terrassierten Bau handelt, bei dem das Terrassenmotiv ästhetisch bewußt—also nicht nur rein praktisch—genutzt ist. Und zwar wird es andernteils dazu genutzt, eine Aussicht, ein Belvedere, zu schaffen, das den Genuß des landschaftlichen Anteils ermöglicht; die lange Nordportikus über eben dieser Terrasse ist dafür untrügliches Zeugnis, und wer jemals von hier, von dieser heute stark zerstörten Substruktion, auf die Hemathia hinausgesehen hat, wird wissen, was ich hiermit aussprechen möchte.

III

Weiteres archäologisches Material zu unserem Thema existiert praktisch nicht. Ob es in den Luxusvororten der großen hellenistischen Metropolen wie Antiochia und Alexandria veritable Villen gegeben hat, ist ungewiß und jedenfalls nicht erwiesen—auch wenn ich mir schwer vorstellen kann, daß sie in Daphne oder Kanopos gefehlt haben werden. Über ihren möglichen Entwicklungsstand im Rahmen der Architekturgeschichte ist aber nicht das Mindeste zu vermuten.

So bleiben wir also tatsächlich auf die zwei oder drei schlecht erforschten, makedonischen Exempla aus dem späteren 4. Jh. v. Chr. zurückgeworfen, wenn sich die Frage nach griechischen Vorläufern der höheren römischen Villenarchitektur stellt, um es noch einmal auf diesen engeren Begriff (unter Ausschluß der spezifischen sozio-ökonomischen Implikationen des römischen Villenwesens) zu bringen. Fassen wir auf dieser dürftigen Grundlage zusammen.

1. Das Leben auf dem Lande (und wohl auch der Genuß eines solchen ländlichen Lebens) war dem griechischen Kulturkreis ein vertrautes Erbe. In klassischer Zeit hatte sich das Gefühl für die Natur und für die 'Landschafterei'—wie ich es oben einmal genannt habe—verstärkt, wie aus vielen Anzeichen hervorgeht, die sich ja nicht nur auf den schmalen Bereich der Villen beschränken (Lauter 1972: 49).

2. Nichtsdestoweniger stellen die makedonischen Villen des Frühhellenismus—wenn wir sie denn richtig interpretiert haben—ein Phänomen dar, das als solches gewissermaßen plötzlich und unvermittelt auftritt. Der herrschaftliche Lustsitz ist das Produkt einer monarchisch-aristokratischen Gesellschaftsstruktur, wie sie eben in den griechischen Poleis

vorher nicht vorhanden war. Erstaunlicherweise besteht darüber in der Wissenschaft auch eine Art von stillschweigender Übereinstimmung, indem die Anlagen von Mieza, Kopanos und Vergina (ziemlich ungeprüft) meist als unmittelbar königliche Bauten aufgefaßt werden. Die eine oder andere 'Villa' könnte aber sehr wohl auch einem sonstigen fürstlichen Herren zueignen; zukünftige Überlegungen sollten das in Rechnung stellen.

3. Die frühhellenistischen Villen in Makedonien weisen architektonische Züge auf, die späterhin in der römischen Villenkunst z.T. verbatim wiederkehren. Von dem Belvedere-Aspekt war ausreichend die Rede, von Terrassierungen, Risaliten, Wasserspielen, Grotten usf. Man kennt dies ja aber auch von Villen der Renaissance und des Barock. Ob die makedonischen Villen insofern direkte Vorbilder römischer Luxusvillen der späten Republik und der Kaiserzeit waren, oder ob die genannten gleichen Motive strukturelle, sozusagen überzeitliche Symptome aller Villenarchitektur repräsentieren, lasse ich daher ein wenig dahingestellt. Wer freilich das chronologische Nahverhältnis zwischen den makedonischen und den frühen italischen Villen in Anschlag bringt, und wer sich des starken architektonischen Einflusses der makedonischen Monarchien auf die mittel- und spätklassische Aristokratie Italiens erinnert, möchte wohl einen engeren Zusammenhang der beiden Erscheinungen für wahrscheinlich halten.

REFERENCES CITED

Heermann, V. (1986) *Studien zur Makedonischen Palastarchitektur* (Berlin)

Lauter, H. (1972) "Kunst und Landschaft," *Antike Kunst* (15).
id. (1980) "Zu Heimstätten und Gutshäusern im Klassischen Attika," in *Festschrift Bernhard Neutsch* (Innsbruck).

id. (1987) "La régia hellenistique," in E. Lévy (Hrsgb.), *Système palatial, en orient, en Grèce et à Rome* (Strasbourg).

Lohmann, H. (1993) *Forschungen zu Siedlungs- und Wirtschaftsstruktur des klassischen Attika* (Köln, Böhlau).

3

THE HOUSE OF THE SICILIAN GREEKS

Elizabeth Fentress

Although our knowledge of Sicilian cities continually expands, it is only recently that any attention has been paid to the countryside. The results of the project of survey and excavation carried out by the Soprintendenza ai Beni Culturali ed Ambientale di Trapani in the hinterland of Marsala and Mazara, though still partial, are thus particularly useful for the historical reconstruction of the economy of Lilybaeum and its hinterland.[1] Further, the plan of the partially excavated villa is extremely suggestive, pointing to a possible source for Vitruvius' discussion of Greek houses.

The Excavation

The scale of the villa as observed from the surface scatter suggested that it would be worthwhile to retrieve the maximum possible ground plan in the time available, as sites of this type are almost unknown (Figs. 3.1–3). This choice was also dictated by the workforce, which was large but not particularly skilled: by choosing to dig no deeper than the tops of the walls and the first undisturbed deposits, we avoided any damage to the stratigraphy in areas that could not be properly supervised. The site is bisected by a road, and although to the south of this the ground is open, to the north the site is covered with a vineyard, which it would have been difficult and expensive to remove. It was thus decided to strip the disturbed plowsoil in the southern sector mechanically to within 20–30 cm of the undisturbed deposit over an area of 50 x 25 m, and to hand-excavate within that area (area A). In the event, it was not possible to excavate the whole of area A, and certain sectors were not touched, particularly the central part of the peristyle. North of the road, in area B, a small trench of 4 x 6 m was opened in a clearing in the vineyard, in order to confirm the continuity of the villa in this sector. It revealed a wall aligned with the excavated structure, but limited time, and the difficulty of removing the earth from this deep trench, caused us to interrupt its excavation at the destruction layers of the villa.

Although much of the material awaits study, and the excavation itself cannot be considered complete, an outline history of the site's development is fairly clear. What follows is a summary account of this development.

PHASE 1A

Although in no case was a foundation deposit excavated, there seems to be little doubt from the residual material—2nd century B.C. black glaze and a few sherds of Greco-Italic amphorae—that occupation began during the 2nd century B.C., or, just possibly, at the end of the third. This view is corroborated by the mosaic of room b. This is a *semis* of dark blue

1. Excavations at the site of Timpone Rasta (sherd hillock) Contrada Mirabile, were undertaken initially by D.ssa Di Stefano in order to confirm the identification of the site as a large Roman Villa: C. A. Di Stefano, "La documentazione archeologica del III e IV secolo d.C. nella provincia di Trapani," *Kokalos* 26–27 (1982–1983):359. The site was originally identified by Dr. G. Alagna. To this end three small (5 m x 5 m) trenches were excavated to the first undisturbed deposits, and the results were sufficiently encouraging to warrant an excavation on a larger scale. This was undertaken in September–October of 1988.

This paper represents an updating of the preliminary publication of the site by Elizabeth Fentress, Derek Kennet, and Ignazio Valenti titled "A Sicilian Villa and Its Landscape (Contrada Mirabile, Mazara del Vallo, 1988)," *Opus* V (1986):75–90. The project was supported by D.ssa Rosalia Camerata-Scovazzo, director of the archaeological section of the Soprintendenza di Trapani, and the administrative direction was carried out by Ignazio Valenti. Elizabeth Fentress was responsible for the field direction of both the survey and the excavation, but the survey team was led by Derek Kennet. Dssa. Marisa Famà was unfailingly generous with support and hospitality.

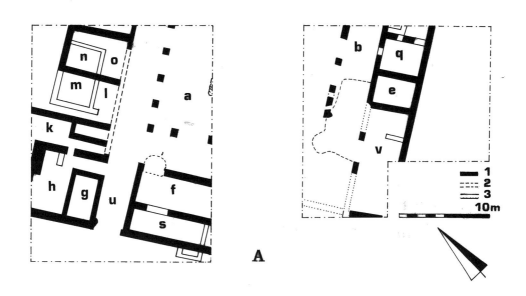

Figure 3.1. Villa of Contrada Mirabile near Lilybaeum, Sicily. Plan of the two areas excavated (a and b). 1: excavated wall, 1st phase. 2: robbed wall. 3: excavated wall, 2nd phase. 4: wall in section of modern road.

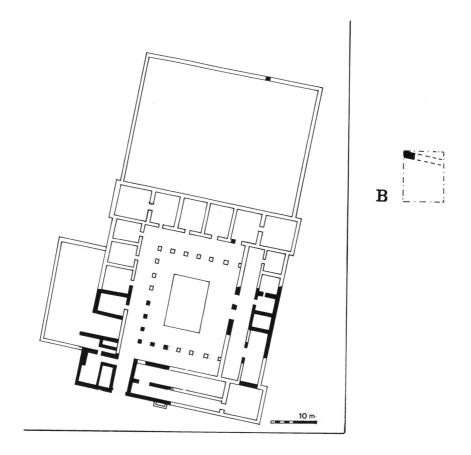

Figure 3.2. Villa of Contrada Mirabile. Reconstruction of the plan of the central portion.

Figure 3.3. Villa of Contrada Mirabile. Aerial view.

crosslets with white centers on a ground of white limestone chips, which could date anywhere from the beginning of the second century to the beginning of the first, and by two rhomboidal fragments of limestone *scutulatum* from the destruction layers of the same room, which again probably date to the second half of the second century.[2] Of course, without further excavation we cannot be sure that the villa was the first structure on the site: it is just possible that a small farm was replaced by the villa as late as the 1st century B.C. However, the consistent presence of residual black glaze pottery over the whole area of the excavation rather than in one small sector suggests that the original settlement was on a large scale, and it seems probable that it corresponds to the excavated structure.

Construction techniques were similar throughout

the villa: foundations and socles were built of roughly coursed pebbles in an earth mortar with the admixture of some yellow clay. These were leveled above pavement height with a course of carefully laid flat stones and tile, which served as a horizontal bedding for a course of rectangular tufa blocks measuring some 50 x 50 x 75 cm. The blocks had largely been removed in 1985 during the preparations for the vineyard, and a large pile of them lay on the edge of the excavation. The principal destruction layer of the west wing was composed of a thick layer of yellow clay, covering the fallen tile, which suggests that the upper part of the walls was constructed of *pisé de terre*.[3] Only in the collapse of the external east wall of the villa were sufficient stones present to suggest a construction entirely of stone.

The villa itself consisted of four wings surrounding

2. I am grateful to Mariette de Vos for drawing my attention to the four other examples of marble *scutulatum* known from Sicily: (1) the Casa di Leda at Solunto (M. de Vos , 1950, "Pitture e mosaico a Solunto," *BABesch* 50 (1975):195–205, p. 196); (2) from the Casa del Mosaico a Rombi in Agrigento: D. von Bomselager, *Antike Mosaike in Sizilien* (Rome 1983) pl. 32; (3) from Casa B in Piazza della Vittoria, Palermo: id., pl. 20; and (4) at Lilybaeum, C. A. Di Stefano, *Lilibeo, testimonianze archeologiche dal IV sec. a.C. al V sec. d.C.* (catalogue of the exhibition

at Marsala, 1984) 143. I am grateful to Rossella Colombi for identifying several fragments of black glaze: Morel forms 2974, 4111, 2737 a 1, and 2566 c1, all of which date to the 2nd century B.C., although a fragment of petites estampilles dates to the early 3rd.

3. Although this might have been decomposed mud brick, there was no trace of individual bricks. For this type of stratigraphy see A. Carandini, *Storie dalla terra* (Bari 1981) fig. 48.

a very large peristyle. If we may assume that the wall visible on the north side of the modern road represents the north wall of the peristyle, this measured 28 x 26.5 m. The scatter of building materials and the wall found in area B show that the building as a whole measured not less than 70 m x 42 m, so it is likely that other courtyards lay to the north and to the west of the excavated area. We may, however, be reasonably certain of the southern and eastern limits.

Although much of the plan was recovered, only one of the rooms, room b, was excavated to pavement level, and many of the details of the excavated plan remain obscure. The main entrance lay at the southwest corner of the building, and the position of the door was marked by a post footing. The west wing consisted originally of seven rooms, although the robbing of the east wall of this wing leaves us in some doubt as to the position of the doorways. At the southwest corner, in rooms g and h fragments of *signinum* flooring lay above the collapse of the walls, and the base of what may be interpreted as a staircase doubles the west wall of room h. The suggestion of a second story over these two rooms is supported by their relatively thick walls. This second story would have suggested a tower next to the main entrance, and similar structures may have been found at the other corners: these have been reconstructed on the plan.

Of the north wing we have only the one wall visible in the modern road section, which appears to give the northern limit of the peristyle, room a. This peristyle was almost square, with a row of roughly squared column bases running around it, at least on the south and west sides. The tile collapse between these columns and the walls of the peristyle confirm that the *ambulacrum* was covered. In its last phase the peristyle was paved with a very hard beaten earth surface, with much pottery and small stones. This was stepped slightly up along the line of the columns, ensuring that the floor of the covered walkway remained dry. A line of regular small blocks of fine-grained lime-stone, which emerge from the section near the center of the courtyard, may mark the edge of an open pool, or possibly an *impluvium*.

On the east side, room b, opening onto the peristyle through a wide double door, occupies the place of the portico. From it, a door leads to room q, which is further linked to a room to the north, r. To the south, the floor of room b was cut away by later activities, destroying its links with room v, which appears to be a large hall opening onto the enclosed space provided by room b, but the exact relationship between the two is not entirely certain. This whole wing was more elaborately decorated than the rest of the villa. Room b was originally paved with the mosaic of blue crosslets mentioned above, and the lintels of the narrow door that originally linked it to room q show traces of red plaster. The numerous tesserae in the destruction layers of room b were absent in the rest of the excavated sector, and may suggest that the *pars urbana* was limited to this wing of the building, while the other wings had more rustic functions. A fluted stuccoed column used in a later wall, and pieces of a fine stucco cornice—again from the east wing—imply that the decoration was of a fairly high quality.

Of the south wing little is known except for two long rooms to the right of the entrance hall, linked by a wide door. There is no trace of pavement or other architectural elaboration, and the size of the door may imply that the rooms were used for stabling or storage.

PHASE IB

At an unspecified period in the life of the building a series of small walls was added in the west wing, subdividing the rooms into smaller units. What is probably a watering trough was added to the front, to the right of the entrance, and various subdivisions were made within the building. At this or a later period a number of doorways were blocked, a column fragment was placed in the blocked doorway between rooms f and s; all imply that the building was not being well maintained. Possibly contemporary with this was the digging of a large pit between two of the columns of the western range of the peristyle. Without further excavation, however, we cannot understand either the chronology of these changes or their purpose.

DESTRUCTION

The complete destruction of the original building is signaled by a series of layers visible in the section of a robber trench and in the courtyard. The lowest of these is a thick layer of tiles, signaling the collapse of the roofs. This is covered by a layer of yellow earth interleaved with lenses of ash and of red burnt earth, which may suggest that the building was destroyed by fire. A *terminus ante quem* for the destruction is provided by two rubbish dumps covering the destruction layer. One of these, context 68, was found in the western range of the peristyle. Along with much charcoal and bone, the abundant pottery shows a very consistent date range between A.D. 80 and A.D. 130.[4] A tip of similar date was found in area B, covering the collapse of the wall.

---

4. The African Red Slip ware includes Hayes 3C and Hayes 8A; 8B is entirely absent from the deposit.

PHASE II

At some time after the destruction of the villa a new building was constructed in the east wing, reusing some of the existing structure. Only one of the rooms of this building was excavated, room c, and much of the rest of the plan remains un-clear. The construction of this room involved the cutting away of the floor of room b to a depth of almost a meter into the soft tufa bedrock. Walls constructed *a telaio* with stone packing between large blocks were then constructed against the sides of this cut. The floors seem to have consisted only of the level tufa at the bottom of the cutting. The construction is irregular, and we cannot specify the function of this building, although the rubbish tips over the rest of the site suggest that its primary function was domestic. Outside the east wall of the original villa a series of walls may represent a pen for animals, and may tentatively be linked to this structure. The rubbish tips previously mentioned may be contemporary with its occupation, as well as two further tips in area B, which date respectively to the first half of the 3rd century A.D. and the beginning of the fourth. Other structures may have existed in the unexcavated portion of the site, particularly to the north, although after the 2nd-century rubbish tips there was no occupation of any sort in the west wing. There African Red Slip C and D wares were entirely absent, even in the plowsoil, suggesting that a large, circular silo, cut into the destruction layers to the west of the rubbish tip, was contemporary with the beginning of this phase, around the middle of the 2nd century A.D.

PHASE III

In the second half of the 5th century room c was abandoned. Tips of rubbish interleave with the yellow material of the collapse of *pisé* walls. Pottery in these tips shows a consistent date range of 450–500.[5] However, the existence of these tips shows that occupation continued somewhere on the site. A small circular pit, carefully lined with stones in a yellow earth mortar, was dug into the destruction layers of room d. This may be interpreted as a silo, as there is no burning to suggest that it might have been an oven. The last rubbish deposit, which covers the possible

animal pen to the east, dates to the end of the 6th century or the beginning of the 7th.[6] It butted the old east wall of the villa, which must have remained standing. Our ignorance of the coarsewares in the period between the 7th and the 10th centuries does not allow us to rule out occupation during these periods; however, the absence of glazed pottery does suggest that the site was abandoned by the 11th century at the latest.

The Context of the Villa: the Survey

The opportunity provided by the Contrada Mirabile project for a systematic investigation of the surrounding countryside was too important to be ignored, and a small team led by Derek Kennet followed up preliminary work done by Dr. Giovanni Alagna. The national grid was used to select sampling areas of 2 x 2 km in three distinct zones: the valley of the Mazaro River, the ridge of raised beach on which the excavated site is located, and the *sciarre*, a rocky scrubland punctuated by quarries, which slopes down toward the coast and provides a marked division between the coastal plain and the interior (Fig. 3.4). This background sample was then filled out with the sherding of the sites known from Alagna's extensive survey, and a certain amount of purposive samples aimed at confirming the observed evidence for centuriation. The total area investigated was very small, but the almost continuous plowed vineyards allowed a very high level of site recovery, with abundant datable material.[7]

The modern landscape is notable for the impressive extent of its vineyards and the total absence of any modern occupation. The only structures visible are large courtyard farmhouses, or *bagli*, partially ruined and deserted. Although some of these are architecturally noteworthy, with wings constructed for the use of their urban owners, they are now given over to the storage of tools and temporary occupation during the wine harvest. In addition to these, and spaced at intervals of around 2 km, are found one-roomed stone buildings, one or two stories high, which were originally intended for field guards and for shelter during the harvest, but are now largely in

---

5. Hayes 76, 81, etc.
6. Hayes 104b, 91c.
7. Field walking was carried out at intervals of 10–20 m by a team of four or five. After a 0.5 km sample of the thick alluvium beds in the valley bottoms proved sterile these were not walked. The same policy was applied to the *sciarre*, although these would be reexamined in a later season. Off-site material was recorded cartographically in the form of colored dots indi-

cating the chronology of the material, but there was little of it, and no difficulty in distinguishing site concentrations, which usually provided abundant building material. Deep plowing seems in general to have brought up material from all phases of a site's occupation, but when observed in section some sites gave reason for doubt that the earlier periods were adequately represented.

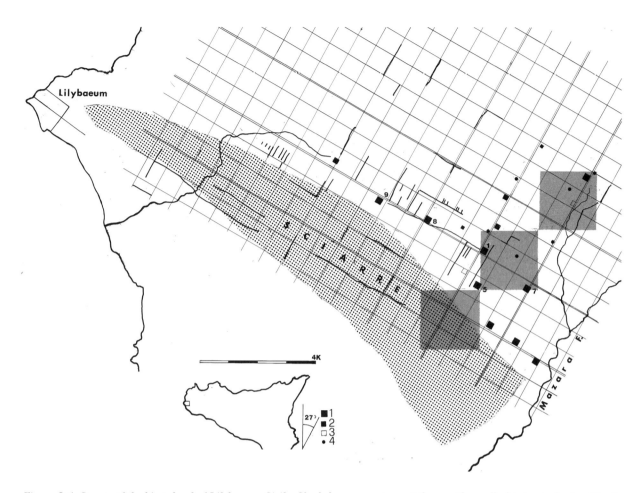

Figure 3.4. Survey of the hinterland of Lilybaeum, Sicily. Shaded squares represent the samples walked intensively. 1: villa. 2: large farm. 3: site with poor visibility. 4: small sherd scatter.

ruins. In the "badlands" between the coastal plain and the river terrace a single, isolated *baglio* seems to have been devoted to stock raising.

The results of the survey were extremely surprising in their uniformity. With the exception of two worked flints, no prehistoric material was found at all—in spite of the presence on the survey of two field walkers well acquainted with Sicilian prehistoric sites. The only prehistoric site was a series of rock-cut tombs on the edge of the *sciare*. This consisted of four tholos tombs, cut back from a sharp vertical face. The type is well known in the valley of the Mazaro, and probably dates to the Early Bronze Age.

The absence of prehistoric settlement here is in such sharp contrast to other areas of Sicily that we must suggest that previous to the 4th century B.C., if not later, the whole area had not been cleared for settlement. Four sites provided material datable to the 4th century B.C., including a sherd of local black

figure ware.[8] In all cases these were the sites of villas with substantial occupation in the Roman period, which has obscured the nature of the original occupation.

The vast majority of the farm sites presented material—black glaze and Greco-Italic amphorae—from the late 3rd and early 2nd centuries. This includes all the large villas, as well as the excavated site. Figure 3.4 shows these sites, as well as two doubtful cases, where visibility was extremely poor, and no black glaze was recovered. The sites were divided into three classes: small farm/sherd scatters, large farms, and villas. For the republican period there were seven in the first category, ranging in size between 0.1 and 0.25 ha, eight in the second category, between 0.25 and 0.96 ha, and nine in the third, between 0.64 and 4.00 ha. The criteria on which we distinguished these included both size and finds; crucial to the identification of a villa was some trace of architectural elabora-

8. I am grateful to D.ssa Maria-Luisa Famà for this identification.

tion, such as a column or mosaic fragment. These figures probably underestimate the number of small sites, although within the sample area the proportions are not very different: four villas, one large farm, and four tile scatters. Of course, we cannot assume that sites that appear now as villas had not started as small farms in the beginning of the 2nd century. However, only on one of these sites does black glaze pottery show a smaller distribution than the rest of the material, suggesting origins as a small farm.

The alignment of these sites along a series of parallel axes is immediately striking, and leads us to propose that the area surveyed was centuriated prior to the construction of the farms. The heavy black lines indicate the best fit of a 20 x 20 *actus* grid with the sites recovered, and the coincidence of this grid with modern roads and field boundaries.[9] Double lines indicate the axes for which we have the clearest evidence, as well as those with the largest sites, and the distance between these may indicate that the principal roads were laid out at intervals of 60 *actus*. Although the regularity of this pattern is extremely suggestive, it should be noted that we have *no* direct evidence for a Roman road, either on the air photographs or on the ground, and thus the proposed centuriation must still be treated as a hypothesis. Further, the proposed pattern has a different orientation from that of the urban grid of Lilybaeum, and no trace of this orientation can be found on the coastal plain. On the other hand, there seems little doubt that the five large villas that line up with Contrada Mirabile on an east-west axis were linked by a road that ran along the ridge and intersected one north-south road at the site, and another at Casal Vecchio, the villa site 7 immediately to the east. If we can accept this pattern, the dating of the sites along it to the late 3rd and early 2nd century leads us to suggest that it was laid out toward the end of the 3rd century.

Rather than developing over time, the pattern described above appears to remain static. A maximum of two sites were founded in the Julio-Claudian period, and, as we have seen, these were sites where tall grass impeded visibility, and the absence of black glaze wares may be more apparent than real. Almost all of the smallest sites disappeared before this period, but from the 1st century A.D. onward the drop-off is much less obvious. All sites produced large

quantities of African Red Slip (well over 1000 sherds were recovered) as well as late amphorae. Only in the middle of the 5th century do some sites appear to have been abandoned. On the four largest sites, 5, 7, 8, and 9, sherds of Hayes 104c, 105, and 109 indicate occupation into the 7th century. Evidence for medieval occupation was found on the same sites. On site 5 this consisted of a few sherds, including a fragment of a water filter, and the occupation may have been limited to the use of the ruins of the villa as a seasonal shelter, or as a quarry for building material. On sites 7, 8, and 9, however, large quantities of pottery may be dated to the 11th century:[10] the latest pottery found at these sites seems to indicate that they were finally abandoned at the end of the 12th century or the beginning of the 13th. The fact that the only medieval sites found were perched on large Roman villas that were inhabited until the 7th century makes a strong case for continuity of occupation, although our lack of knowledge of the pottery from the intervening three centuries does not allow us absolute certainty.

The Villa in Its Landscape

THE ARCHITECTURE OF THE VILLA

The two different lines of evidence, from survey and from excavation, intersect at the villa of Contrada Mirabile. The object of this final section will be to link the two to other evidence for settlement in Sicily. The villa itself is the obvious point of departure. There are no excavated parallels for it from Sicily. This is, of course, a function of the lack of excava-tion of rural buildings. Fifth century B.C. courtyard buildings with wings around three sides were exca-vated near Camarina,[11] but these were far smaller structures, measuring no more than 20 x 25 m over-all. A larger farmhouse with a covered portico was found near Gela, dating to the last quarter of the 4th century B.C.[12] The best parallel for the building tech-nique is a 3rd century, L-shaped farmhouse found near Akrai.[13] Here we find walls in exactly the same technique as those of Contrada Mirabile:

9. The positions of roads and field boundaries is derived both from older maps and from a series of air photographs dating to the early 1980s. Because of the vineyards crop marks are not visible, nor are there any notable soil marks. A 16 x 16 *actus* grid was tried as well, but no good fit emerged.
10. The most common form is a carinated basin found at Ajdabiya and published by J. A. Riley, "Islamic Wares from Ajdabiya," *Libyan Studies* (1982):85–104 fig. 2.1; A. Ragona, "La ceramica della Sicilia arabo-normanna," in *Rassegna dell'Istruzione Artistica* 1–2 (1984):11–26, from Piazza Armerina and Syracuse. Associated with this pottery on site 7 were some examples of a

type paralleled on Pisan churches that may be dated to the early 11th century: G. Berti and L. Tongiorgi, *I bacini ceramici Medievali delle Chiese di Pisa* (Rome 1981) fig. 86. One piece of spiral ware was recovered from site 8 and a fragment of *cobalto e man-ganese* from site 7.
11. P. Pelagatti, "L'attività della Soprintendenza alle Antichità della Sicilia Orientale, parte II," *Kokalos* 26–27 (1980–1981): 494–532.
12. D. Adamesteanu, "Contrada Priorato (Gela)," *NS* (1958): 364–373.

pebble so-cles in an earth mortar, capped with a line of tufa blocks, above which were presumably placed *pisé* or mud bricks. This extremely peculiar technique, which can only be explained in terms of the need to protect the earth walls from rising damp, was thus ap-parently Sicilian, either Greek or indigenous, in ori-gin, for it has nothing to do with either Roman tech-niques or with the *opus africanum* of Punic architecture.

In plan (Fig. 3.5), the building corresponds well to Vitruvius' well-known description of the contemporary Greek house. The beginning of this is worth quoting in full:

> The Greeks, not using atria, do not build as we do, but as you enter they make passages of scanty width with stables on one side and the porter's rooms on the other, and these immediately adjoin the inner entrance. The space between the two entrances is called in Greek "thyroron." You then enter the peristyle. This has colonnades on three sides. On the side which looks southward there are two piers at a fair distance apart, on which beams are laid. The space behind is recessed two-thirds of the distance between the piers. The recess by some is called *prostas* by some, *pastas* by others.
>
> As we pass in, there is the great hall in which the ladies sit with the spinning women. Right and left of the prostas are the bedchambers. . . . Round the colonnades are the ordinary dining rooms, the bedrooms and the servant's rooms. This part of the building is called the women's quarters, *gynaeconitis*.[14]

The text appears to fit our case very well. The entrance, to the south, is indeed a passage, as it must be to penetrate into the structure. On the left hand side, rooms h and g may plausibly be interpreted as the porter's lodge. The probable stair in room h would give the porter access to the tower: the same room controlled access to the rooms giving off the northwestern side of the building, which might have been devoted to productive and agricultural uses. To the right of the entrance passage two long rooms might have served as stables and barns (f, s); the presence of horses in the building is suggested by the later watering trough to the right of the entrance. Doors would probably be placed at either end of the passage, protecting the view of the courtyard from those whose business was with the porter or the activities of the northwest wing.

On the peristyle itself the northwestern wing might have served as slaves' quarters, and although we have no information at all about the northeastern wing, its southwestern exposure might have made it suitable for dining and for other bedrooms. On the southeastern side, room b, paved with a mosaic and giving onto the courtyard through a wide, double opening, is to be interpreted as the pastas, with bedrooms (q, e) and a hall (v) leading off it. The limits of the excavation make it impossible to know if the bedrooms lay at either end of the *pastas*, as Vitruvius' description seems to suggest, or whether they simply opened on to it like q. Room v, whose plan was much destroyed by later building, seems from its proportions to correspond to the *oecus magnus* where women spun and weaved. The apparent absence of any source of direct daylight in this room, impossible in a room used for weaving, may suggest that all of the rooms opening onto the pastas were lit by windows along the southeast wall. This whole wing seems to form an enclosed unit that might be interpreted as the *gynaeconitis*, the term applying to the wing rather than to the whole of the block containing the peristyle. However, Pesando argues convincingly that the term *gynaeconitis* should be applied to the whole of the main peristyle, to which male guests would not have been admitted, but which formed the center of the *oikos*.[15]

The reconstructed plan combines the excavated evidence with Vitruvius' account: the length of the peristyle is suggested by the fragment of wall seen on the north side of the modern road; it cannot be the back wall of the structure as the northeastern wing of the peristyle would then have fallen within the limits of the excavation. This solution is more satisfying from the point of view of the entrance to the pastas as well, which is thus roughly centered in the middle of the southeastern side of the peristyle. The pre-

---

13. P. Pelagatti, "La fattoria tardo-ellenistica di Aguglia," *NS* (1970):449–499. A single wall in a similar technique was found by R. Wilson, "Un insediamento agricolo romano a Castagna (Comune di Cattolic Eraclea, AG," *Sicilia Archeolgica* 57–58 (1985):14. This was apparently the earliest wall on the site, and dates from the end of the 2nd century B.C.
14. Vitr. VI, 7 (tr. Loeb). Recently K. Reber, "Aedificia graecorum," AA 1988, 653–666,has doubted the very existence of a house such as that described by Vitruvius. Two comprehensive recent studies of Greek houses are the work of F. Pesando, *Oikos e Ktesis: La Casa dei Greci in eta classica* (Perugia 1987); and *La Casa dei Greci* (Milan 1989).

See also D. Fusaro, "Nota di architettura domestica greca nel periodo tardo-geometrico e arcaico," *DdA* 4 (1982):5–30.
15. 1987, cited in n. 14, 187f.

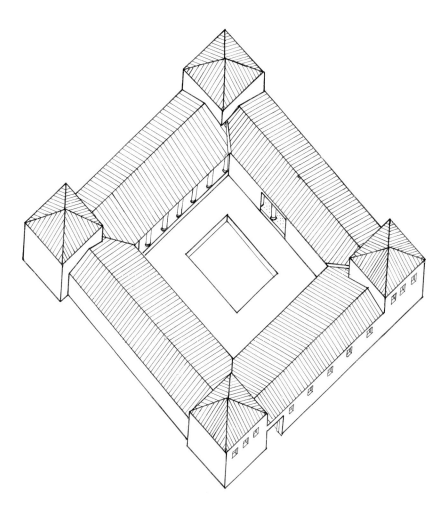

Figure 3.5. Villa of Contrada Mirabile. Axiometric reconstruction of the central portion.

sence of a further peristyle to the northeast is suggest-ed by the wall in area B, but we do not have sufficient evidence to do more than suggest that this was the *andronitis*.

The corner towers, although not mentioned by Vitruvius, are consistent with both our sources and with excavated parallels. Thus Seneca describes the villa of Scipio Africanus as turreted—"turres quoque in propugnaculum villae utrimque subrectas"—while in another letter he refers to the villas of Marius and

Cato as "Non villas . . . sed castra."[16] I know of no excavated example in Italy of a villa with corner towers, but their representation in Pompeian wall painting is frequent, and there is no doubt that they existed.[17] Although none are yet known from Sicily, square turreted villas are common in Greece, in Crimea, and in Macedonia.[18] Indeed, Grimal has suggested that the three essential structural elements of a Greek country estate were the tower, courtyard, and house.[19] Four towers are suggested here, for the sake of sym-

16. Sen. *ep.* 51, 11; 86, 4. I am grateful to A. Carandini for drawing these passages to my attention.
17. Several of these are reproduced in Carandini op.cit., 194, 195.
18. A much larger building on a similar plan is found on the Black Sea at Panskoje: A. Sceglov, "Un établissement rural en Crimée: Panskoje I (Fouilles de 1969–1985)," *DHA* 13 (1987):239–273, fig. 22 (4th century B.C.). A smaller site from the Crimea with a single tower is illustrated by M. Nowicka, *Les maisons à tour dans le Monde Grec* (1973) 114. For the palace at

Vergina, see D. Pandermalis, "Beobachtungen zur Fassadenarchitektur und Ansichtveranda im hellenistischen Makedonien," *Hellenismus in Mittelitalien* (Göttingen 1976) 387–395. Towers were important in smaller Greek farms as well: J. Pečírka, "Homestead Farms in Classical and Hellenistic Hellas," in M. I. Finley ed., *Problèmes de la terre en Grèce ancienne* (Paris 1973) 120–132, 126f.; J. H. Young, "Studies in South Attica: Country Estates at Sounion," *Hesperia* 25 (1956):122–146.
19. P. Grimal, "Les maisons à tour hellénistiques et romaines," *MEFR* 56 (1939):28–59.

metry, but there are a number of examples of large houses with only a single tower, and the position over the main entrance was clearly the most important.[20]

Thus both in construction technique and in plan it is clear that the villa at Contrada Mirabile is a Hellenistic type of building, whose origins may lie in the Greek colonization of the island, or may represent a Mediterranean *koiné*. Although houses on Delos and elsewhere have open peristyles, the precise form of the peristyle with a pastas seems to be rarer than Vitruvius' description would suggest.[21] The plan found here has its closest parallels in Sicily itself, rather than in mainland Greece. At Morgantina, the House of the Official has two peristyles, one of which opens onto a *pastas* very similar to that at Contrada Mirabile. Here the bedrooms, *thalamos* and *amphithalamos*, lie at either end of the *pastas*, and there are two symmetrical halls beyond it. The three-sided peristyle is a later feature, constructed after the destruction of 211.[22] A similar plan is found in other houses at Morgantina, such as that of the Arched Cistern.[23] Here, again, the peristyle is a secondary addition to the *pastas* court. Both of these houses date from around the middle of the 3rd century, and we seem to be seeing a specific local development combining the *pastas* and the peristyle. It is thus possible that Vitruvius' knowledge of the Greek house was derived from information about Sicilian Greek houses rather than direct evidence from Greece itself.

There may indeed be some connection with North African types of the same period. No Punic house so far excavated at Carthage can be compared to the Sicilian town houses.[24] However, the absence of any excavated examples of 3rd- or 2nd-century villas from the countryside leaves open the possibility that they had similar plans. We know that intensive plantation agriculture developed early at Agrigento, and Toynbee has suggested that this development might be linked to the subsequent intensification of Punic agriculture after the First Punic War.[25] Although we know as yet very little of rural building in North Africa, a survey on the island of Jerba suggests that large villas of the same period were found there.[26] Certainly African villas of the Roman period are regularly large peristyle buildings, and the villas frequently shown on late Roman mosaics from Africa have been interpreted as courtyard farmhouses. Corner towers can be found on a number of these.[27] There is little evidence, either in Sicily or in North Africa, for the development of buildings with an atrium plan,[28] and it is clear that our villa forms part of a separate and distinct scheme from that of the standard Roman model. This seems to offer some confirmation for J. Ward Perkins' observation that North African reception of Hellenistic models was more closely related to that of Sicily and Magna Graecia than to Rome,[29] without its being clear in which direction the model is traveling.

THE LANDSCAPE OF PRODUCTION

Even in the limited area studied, the villa of Contrada Mirabile is not unique: at least eight other sites are on a similar scale, and six more are almost as big. As we have seen, there is good evidence that the farms near Contrada Mirabile were laid out on a centurial grid, on land that had only recently been cleared when they were built. Four sites present one or two sherds of the 4th century, but the vast majority belong to the beginning of the 2nd. This has all the hallmarks of a political geography—a settlement pattern conditioned by a deliberate political decision rather than by organic growth.[30] We do not have to look far for the historical context of such a decision.

20. For example, Cersonesus, Heraclea, cited in Peǎrka op. cit., 126, fig. 6; Andrea Carandini, "La villa romana," in E. Gabba and A. Schiavone, eds., *Storia di Roma* 4: *Caratteri e Morphologie.*101–200, p. 158–159.

21. For Delos J. Chamared, *Le Quartier du Théatre, EAD* 8 (Paris 1963). A good discussion of the plans of houses with a *pastas* at Olynthus and elsewhere is found in J. E. Jones, A. J. Graham, and L. H. Sackett, "An Attic Country House below the Cave of Pan at Vari," *Annual of the British School at Athens* 68 (1973):355–452, p. 431–435.

22. R. Stillwell, "Excavations at Morgantina (Serra Orlando)," *AJA* 67 (1963):163–197, fig. 10.

23. These houses have been studied by Barbara Tskargis, "The Domestic Architecture of Morgantina in the Hellenistic and Roman Periods," Ann Arbor, unpublished disseration (1985).

24. The largest Punic houses from Carthage are those excavated by F. Rakob: F. Rakob, ed., *Die Deutschen Ausgrabungen in Karthago* (Mainz 1991) 238–241. These are far smaller than the Morgantina houses, although they have a small open court approached through an entrance corridor.

25. Diod. XXII, 18; A. Toynbee, *Hannibal's Legacy* (London 1965) 162f.

26. Unpublished data, American Academy–Institut National du Patrimoine–University of Pennsylvania survey.

27. N. Duval, "L'iconographie des Villas Africaines et la Vie Rurale dans l'Afrique Romaine de l'Antiquité tardive," *Histoire et Archéologie de l'Afrique du Nord* III (Colloque internationale, 1986) 163–176. He inexplicably draws corner towers onto the main buildings rather than onto the outer wall, where they seem to be indicated, and where they are found on our one known parallel, Nador (L. Anselmino et al., *Il castellum di Nador: Storia di una fattoria romana tra Tipasa e Caesarea, I–VI sec. D.C.* (Rome 1989).

28. R. J. A. Wilson, "Towns of Sicily during the Roman Empire," *ANRW* II, 11, 1, 19, 90–206, p. 161, notes the two atrium houses known from Lilybaeum and another from Agrigento (p. 178). A villa dating from the 1st century A.D. on a more or less Roman plan was found near Camarina: M. Aoyagi, "Ripresa degli scavi nella villa Romana di Realmonte," *Kokalos* 26–27 (1980–1981:668–674.

29. J. B. Ward Perkins, "From Republic to Empire: Reflections on the Early Provincial Architecture of the Roman West," *JRS* LX (1970):1–19, p. 14–19.

30. For this distinction, I. Attolini et al., "Political Geography and Productive Geography in the Ager Cosanus/Albegna Valley," in G. Barker, ed., *Roman Landscapes* (1991) 142–152.

Toynbee has drawn attention to the passages in Strabo referring to the governorship of Valerius Laevinus (210–207 B.C.), who after the Second Punic War restored the agriculture of the island:

Omnes in urbis, in agros suos reductos arare, serere, desertam recoli terram, tandem frugiferam ipsis cultoribus polulique romano pace ac bello fidissimum annonae subsidium.[31]

The clearing, surveying, and allocation of this area of *ager publicus* near the city of Lilybaeum, seat of one of the island's quaestors, would be just what we might expect of a policy designed to restore Sicily's devastated agriculture.[32] As we have seen, at least in the case of Contrada Mirabile, the type and the construction of the villa suggest that its owner was probably Sicilian, possibly from one of the hellenized parts of the island. Two cases of the use of Sicilians to resettle land elsewhere in the island are cited by Cicero: in 197 the Senate instructed the governor of Sicily to bolster the population of Agrigento with settlers from elsewhere, and a similar resettlement took place under P. Rupilia at Heraclea.[33] The territory of Lilybaeum, expanded after the First Punic War to include that of Selinus,[34] would have been an obvious subject for resettlement.

Resettlement with Hellenized Sicilians would suggest a basis for Diodorus' statement that many of the rich proprietors in the next century were Sicilians: he notes that at the time of the slave wars "in fact, the Sicilians who had acquired much wealth were now rivalling the Italians in arrogance, greed and villany."[35] But whoever they were, there can be no doubt that this is not the landscape of the *latifundium*, nor yet that of a myriad of small-holders. In an ideal situation, between a major town and the port at Mazaro, Contrada Mirabile (and probably much of coastal Sicily) was occupied by the *fundus* rather than the *saltus*. A. Giardina has opposed "paralia," or zones devoted to intensive agriculture, to "mesogeia," inland zones given over to a sylvo-pastoral economy.[36] This is certainly the best image for Sicily; indeed, the survey conducted by J. Johns in the territory of Monreale has revealed far fewer Roman sites.[37]

We do not yet have enough data to calculate more than very roughly the distance between sites, or the size of the properties, but naturally this is not going to stop us from guessing. For the group of sites around Contrada Mirabile there appear to be three *centuria* for each major farm or villa, giving around 1.5 km², or 600 iugera, each. The smaller sites presumably had smaller allotments, or perhaps the owners rapidly sold up their holdings to the nearby villas. This property size may be compared with that suggested for the Valle d'Oro near Cosa, where the average holding appears to have been around 500 iugera, or 125 ha.[38] There it has been demonstrated that the economy of the villas was based on the production of wine for export, and this cultivation may explain the smaller holdings. Traditionally, it has been assumed that wheat was Sicily's principal crop, but the fact remains that the holdings around Contrada Mirabile seem almost too small to justify the size of the villas if only wheat was produced. At Contrada Mirabile the find of a pruning knife (*falx arboraria*) suggests that at least some tree crops were grown, but there is still no basis for suggesting that anything other than wheat was produced for the market. In contemporary Jerba the villas were almost certainly producing wine, as the discovery on their estates of amphora kilns producing copies of Italian wine amphorae demonstrates,[39] but none of these were found in the immediate neighborhood of Contrada Mirabile. Possibly the villas of the area ran flocks on the ager publicus (the sciare?), but without further excavation and field survey the question cannot be answered.

Using the calculation of Saserna that one person can cultivate eight *jugera* we can estimate a minimum labor force of 19 or 20 for each villa.[40] This could not have been provided by free peasants on the small farms in the vicinity, as these simply are too few in

31. Strabo III.5. The passage is discussed by M. Mazza, "Economia e società nella Sicilia Romana," *Kokalos* 26–27 (1980–1981):694–732 and Toynbee, op.cit., 210–228. The economy of Republican Sicily has been the subject of much recent debate: A. Fraschetti, "Per una prosopografia dello sfruttamento: Romani e Italici in Sicilia, 212–44 a.C.," in A. Giardina and A. Schiavone, eds., *Societm romana e produzione schiavistica* (henceforward *SRPS*) (Bari 1981) 51–66; F. Coarelli, "La cultura figurativa in Sicilia dalla conquista romana a Bisanzio," in *Storia della Sicilia* II (Naples 1979) 371–392; id., "La Sicilia tra la fine della guerra annibalica e Cicerone," *SRPS*, 2–19; G. Clemente, "Considerazioni sulla Sicilia nel'impero romano (III sec. a. C.—V sec. d.C.)," *Kokalos* 26–27 (1980–1981):192–249; G. Manganaro, "La Sicilia da Sesto Pompeio a Diocleziano," *ANRW* II, 11, 1 (1988):3–89; E. Gabba, "La Sicilia romana," in M. Crawford, ed., *L'impero romano e le strutture economiche e sociali delle provincie* (Como 1986) 71–85. On Laevinus, R. Marino "Levino e la 'formula provinciale' in Sicilia," *Sodalitas: Scritti in onore di A. Guarino* (Naples 1984) 1083–1094.
32. The reordering of the street grid of Lilybaeum in the early part of the 2nd century was probably related to the reorganization of her territory: C. A. Di Stefano, op.cit. in n. 4.
33. Verrine Orations 2:122–124.
34. It remained so in the Roman period, as dedications from Mazara show: *CIL* X:7205, 7211.
35. Diod. XXXIV–XXXV 2:26–28, tr. Loeb. However, Manganaro points out that no Sicilian Senators have Greek names: "i senatori di Sicilia," in *Epigrafia e ordino senatorio Tituli* 5, II (1982):369–375, p. 370.
36. A. Giardina, "Allevamento ed economia della selva," *SRPS*, 87–113, p. 89; Strabo VI, 1, 2–3.
37. P. Perkins and J. Johns, pers. comm. The best survey of Roman rural settlement in Sicily is found in Roger Wilson's *Sicily under the Roman Empire* (1990) 189–225.
38. M. G. Celuzza and E. Regoli, "Ville e centuriazione," in A. Carandini, ed., *Settefinestre, una villa schiavistica in Etruria romana* (Modena 1985) 53.
39. Jerba survey, unpublished.
40. Giardina, op.cit. in n. 27.

relation to the number of villas. There thus seems little doubt that some of the rooms at Contrada Mirabile served as housing for slaves, but again this would have to be confirmed by further excavation.

THE HINTERLAND OF LILYBAEUM DURING THE EMPIRE

The development of this fairly articulate settlement pattern over time can only be described in terms of a gradual stagnation. Figure 3.7 shows the decrease in the number of sites over time, with the stippled bars representing new sites. There is no sign of any destruction caused by the slave wars, but these seem to have had their epicenter elsewhere on the island. Most, but not all, of the small sites in our area seem

to have been abandoned by the Julio-Claudian period, and by the 2nd century A.D. the farms in the area were uniformly large—possibly expanding physically, as their properties increased. If we were to judge by surface evidence alone, we would have to conclude that although all new building stopped in the 1st century A.D., most of the villas were continuously occupied until the Vandal conquest. There is no evidence of a general fall-off in economic activity; huge amounts of African Red Slip Wares and African amphorae demonstrate a continuity of trade with North Africa, even after the Vandal conquest.[41]

It is here that the excavation of the villa provides us with a new way of interpreting this material. As we have seen, the villa collapsed, possibly because of a fire, at a time when rough rebuilding—the blocking of a door with fragments of a fluted column—and the digging of pits inside the peristyle itself had se-

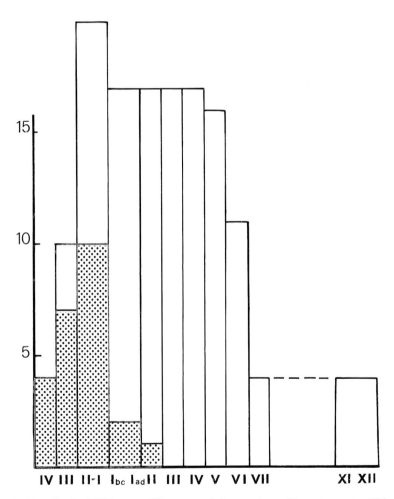

Figure 3.6. Farms in the hinterland of Lilybaeum. Histogram of site numbers, 4th century B.C.–12th century A.D. Stippling represents new foundations.

---

41. For the relative upswing in finds of ARS in Sicily after the middle of the fifth century, see E. Fentress and Ph. Perkins,

"Counting ARS," in A. Mastino, ed., *Africa Romana* 5 (Sassari 1988) 205–214.

verely degraded the original *pars urbana*. This event can be dated somewhere between 80 and 130 A.D. However, the site did not cease to be occupied. A new building on a far more modest scale was constructed against the east wall of the peristyle, and the wide distribution of domestic refuse suggests that it was not the only one. This structure was occupied until the middle of the 5th century, and, although we have no later constructions in the excavated area, refuse tips suggest that occupation continued elsewhere on the site until the end of the 6th or the beginning of the 7th century. It was also noted at site 7 that a medieval village occupied the site of an early Roman villa. This leads us to suggest that most, if not all, of the villas became agglomerations, or villages, by the end of the early empire. The sites may have continued to be estate centers, they may even have been the residences of the *vilicus*, but they were no longer villas in any accepted sense of the word. In this context it is noteworthy that the four sites that survived into the 7th century were by far the largest. Site 5 covered 1.20 ha, site 9 at least 2 ha, and sites 7 and 8 almost 4 ha. It might be suggested that these hamlets continued to grow as the others were abandoned, and the settlement of the area became increasingly agglomerated. In this form they survived into the medieval period, the sort of sites described in Arab texts as "rahal."[42]

There is no certain a priori link between the abandonment of the villas as even temporary residences of their owners in the early empire and the dissolution of their apparently productive economy. Wheat cultivation, with slaves or free labor overseen by a *vilicus* or *conductor*, could, and probably did, continue. The modern landscape, exploited to the last square meter by the wine production of Marsala, is marked by the *bagli* of the 16th and 17th centuries, whose *partes urbanae* have long since fallen out of use, and which tend to be subdivided by inheritance into dozens of separate properties. However, we suspect that this was not the case in the later empire. Survey in Tunisia has shown just how complex the settlement pattern of the upper Mejerda was in the 3rd and 4th centuries: new sites were being founded continuously, and while there were almost no villas with any trace of luxurious appointments, the highly complex settlement pattern, with major farms, small sites and villages, leaves us in no doubt as to its vitality.[43] As we have seen, this is not the case at Contrada Mirabile.

L. Cracco Ruggini describes this period in Sicily as "una fase di prolungata marginalità politica, di stagnazione sociale e produttivà, di depressione culturale . . . dopo l'incapsulamento nell'orbita di Roma l'isola, per dirla con Marziale, '*vivebat*,' ma '*non valebat*.'"[44] The reasons for this stagnation are obviously complex, but several points stand out. First, the size and solidity of the villas of the 2nd–1st century B.C. goes a long way towards explaining this inertia: even as systems of estate management changed, the landscape was, in a certain sense, weighed down by its villas, as the agricultural structures which replaced slave production still used the same buildings. This is one reason why it is difficult to grasp archaeologically the economic structures of the late Empire. We perceive the rarefaction of the villas, but not the way in which they were adapted to new economic conditions.

Nevertheless, the lack of new building can be equated with a lack of investment in agriculture. A spiral had apparently begun, wherein lower profits gave the absentee owners less incentive to invest, especially in the slave manpower by which the economic system had previously functioned. Like the buildings which housed them, the slaves were not replaced. Further, the disappearance of local municipal elites had left a vacuum in which no local initiative was likely to emerge. The landlords, never resident, became entirely absentee. In contrast, in the strong African economy, fueled by the demand for corn and oil, local elites remained a major element among landowners, and most of the labor was provided by *coloni*, tenant farmers with a direct interest in the results of their labor. Even on the vast senatorial estates were *conductores* replaced local landowners as overseers, the *coloni* continued to invest. In Africa, then, the economy was sufficiently buoyant to allow for a continual renewal of settlement structures. Why was the Sicilian (or Tyrrhenian) economy unable to change over to a similar form of production? The answers to this question are complex, but one common factor stands out. In the areas dominated by slave villas the small peasants, and the farms they lived on, had disappeared by the end of the Julio-Claudian period. There was no indigenous peasantry available to take up farming leases when slaves became expensive and unprofitable. The very success of the slave villas was thus, in time, their downfall.

42. H. Bresc, *Un Monde Méditerranéen: Economie et Société en Sicile, 1300–1450* (Rome 1985) 8–9.
43. R. B. Hitchner, "The Kasserine Archaeological Survey,"

AntAf 24 (1988):1–41.
44. "La Sicilia fra Roma e Bisanzio," *Storia della Sicilia* III, 3–96, p. 3.

4

THE VILLA AS CULTURAL SYMBOL[1]

Andrew Wallace-Hadrill

The Roman villa was a power-house: at once a su-preme symbol of the individual's power, resources and ability to control the environment and its popu-lation, and a place where that power was actively gen-erated through the harnessing of slave and other de-pendent labour to profitable production.[2] The trans-formation of the Italian landscape in the 2nd century B.C. by the emergence of the villa and the specific forms of control of labour and of agricultural pro-duction it embodies is the immediate consequence of conquest.[3] Though it is hard to sustain the asser-tion that the Romans engaged in warfare in order to supply their villas, it remains true that the villa is closely linked to certain features of conquest, the massively unequal distribution of booty to individuals that put new levels of workable capital in the hands of the office-holding class, and the influx of slave-la-bor of war-captives linked to the absence from their land of the free Italian peasantry, engaged in this in-cessant warfare.[4]

But if to us the villa is a symbol of a brutal but un-questionable Roman power, to contemporaries its symbolism was more complex and ambivalent, simul-taneously straddling the cultural polarities of town and country and of Greek and Roman.[5] In crude terms, the villa draws its power as cultural symbol by expressing the dominance of the one over the other: in the midst of the country, it expresses the domi-nance of the city, the control of men from the urban center with their urban tastes and ways;[6] and in the midst of rural Italy, it expresses the superiority and sophistication of the imported Greek culture of the aristocracy who in conquest reduce the Greek east to

their personal booty. The boorish Italian peasantry are to be dazzled by this display of imported and ur-banized values. And yet, if this is how the villa works, it is in another sense how it fails to work. The rela-tionship of the Roman elite to the countryside was a central focus of Roman discussion and agonising. Cato's treatise on agriculture is the earliest surviving work in Latin prose;[7] while Varro's three books on the same subject constitute the only one of his nu-merous productions that survives in full.[8] The paral-lel survival of these texts and abundant archaeologi-cal remains highlights the problematic nature of the cultural issues at stake.

Cato's attitude to what we think of as "the villa," that is the cluster of buildings at the heart of the es-tate, emerges more from silence than from explicit comment. The treatise is concerned with agricultural systems, how to extract the best profit from a hold-ing, the different modalities of wine and olive pro-duction, the management of a slave labor force, and so on: but though it finds room to explain how to construct mangers which will prevent the cattle wast-ing fodder, it offers no specific advice on the con-struction of residential buildings, except to urge cau-tion in the expenditure of money.

> In his youth a head of household should concen-trate on planting. He should think long before starting building work, but get on with planting without further thought. When you reach the age of 36, then finally, once the estate is planted, you should put up buildings . . . A head of household should have a well-built working

1. The argument of this paper remains the same as that ori-ginally presented at Philadelphia; but it has benefited not only from discussion on that occasion, but also from subsequent dis-cussions in Princeton, St Andrews and Copenhagen.
2. H. Mielsch, *Die römische Villa. Architektur und Lebensform* (Munich 1987) 45–49.
3. M. Rostovtzeff, *The Social and Economic History of the Roman Empire* (Oxford 1957) 17; A. J. Toynbee, *Hannibal's Legacy* (Oxford 1965) 296ff.; K. Hopkins, *Conquerors and Slaves* (Cambridge 1978) 48ff.

4. W. V. Harris, *War and Imperialism in Republican Rome, 327–70 B.C.* (Oxford 1979) 48ff.
5. J. H. D'Arms, *Romans on the Bay of Naples* (Cambridge Mass. 1970) in general for villa culture.
6. Cf. J. S. Ackerman, *The Villa: Form and Ideology of Country Houses* (Princeton 1990) 10ff.
7. A. E. Astin, *Cato the Censor* (Oxford 1978) 189ff.
8. E. D. Rawson, *Intellectual Life in the Late Roman Republic* (London 1985) 137ff.

farmstead (*villa rustica*), cellars for oil and wine, plenty of vats . . . (details follow). You need good cowbyres, good sheep pens, and latticed feed racks with bars one foot apart (if you do this, the cattle will not scatter their feed). As for residential buildings (*villa urbana*), build them to suit your resources. If you build a good residence on a good estate, and site it in a good position, the result of living comfortably in the country is that you will come more willingly and more often. That way, the estate will improve, less will go wrong, and your profits will rise: the forehead leads the backhead, as they say (Agr. iii.1ff.).

We hear from elsewhere of Cato's attacks on the *villa expolitae* of his contemporaries, villas elaborate with citrus wood and ivory and Punic pavements, and his boasts that no stucco was to be found on the walls of his own farm buildings (the moulded stucco of the "incrustation" style being the fashionable decoration of the day).[9] In this context, we may note, he concedes a logic to investment in a more luxurious resi-

dence: the landowner who visits his estate more willingly and frequently will help to maximise his returns. But that concession embeds the rationale of villa building in a context of profitable production, rather than wasteful consumption. The treatise, then, is not just concerned with offering practical advice and ancient rustic lore. It seeks to insert the practices of contemporary agriculture within a value-system, associating the use of slaves to maximise returns with a Roman morality as traditional as the medicinal use of cabbage, and excluding the construction of buildings he would categorise as "luxurious." Consequently Cato's treatise is repeatedly cited in analyses of the archaeological remains of villas, but only with reference to their agricultural production (questions like the number of hectares of vineyard assumed by the storage capacity). So persuasive is Cato in suggesting that these are the practicalities of the villa, while building is merely for show, that we forget that in excavating wine-presses and storage vats we are also uncovering moral values. These too are "for show," as their conspicuous survival confirms (Fig. 4.1).

Figure 4.1. Pompeii, Villa dei Misteri, view of wine-pressing room (48).

---

9. J. D'Arms (supra n. 5) 10, citing Cato in H. Malcovati, *Oratorum Romanorum Fragmenta* (Turin, 2nd ed. 1955) fr. 174 and 185; Plutarch *Cato major* 4.4.

Catonian morality is treated by later writers as definitive: here as elsewhere the voice of Cato achieves the apotheosis it seeks as "the voice of ancestral tradition." Varro and Columella (i.6) both dutifully observe the convention that agricultural production, and not residential building, is the proper theme of an agricultural treatise. It is Varro who is most explicit about the values at stake:

> Those great men our ancestors had good cause to prefer rustic Romans to city-dwellers. They thought that countrymen who lived in the villa were more idle than those who spent their time at work in the fields, and that those who sat around in the town were more idle than those who tilled the land. They divided their time by spending every eighth day on business in town, and the remaining seven tilling the land. So long as they preserved this institution, their acres were more productive and their bodies more physically fit, and they had no need for the urban gymnasia of the Greeks. These days one gymnasium each is hardly enough, and people think do not have a real villa unless it tinkles with Greek names which they attach to particular spaces, *procoeton, palaestra, apodyterion, peristylon, ornithon, peripteron, oporothece.* That is why fathers of families have now sneaked inside the walls, abandoning sickle and plough, and now prefer to wave their arms about in theatre and circus than among corn and vines . . . (*RR* ii.1).

The moral antitheses are deftly aligned: Roman *maiores* versus Greeks, country versus town, industry versus idleness, morality versus corruption. The villa-owner's slave-worked fields are surreptitiously associated with a form of personal *ascesis*: hard work in the fields is a form of physical exercise that is morally superior to the "Greek" exercise of the gymnasium, let alone the theatre (where, according to its critics, Roman manliness, *standi virilitas*, was sapped).[10] Exactly the same antithesis is developed by Seneca in his reflections on the villa of Scipio Africanus at Liternum (*ep* 86.5): the bath, being so much smaller and darker that the baths of contemporary corruption, is represented as the bath of a man who has sweated in the fields rather than the gymnasium. Seneca slides over Scipio's own record of attendance in the gymnasium (Livy xxix. 19.2), and the link between the sort of sweating bath he describes, the by then unfashionable *laconicum*, and the gymnasium,[11] in order to generate a fantasy of the aged general working up a sweat with. a mattock. But this is precisely the trick

which both the agricultural treatises and the villa remains constantly play on us: the sweat and industry of slave-worked agricultural production stands by transference for the sweat, industry, moral probity and ancestral Romanness of the owner.

Varro follows the Catonian lead in neglecting to offer prescriptions for the villa buildings. Even so, by a series of ironical contrasts he keeps the luxury features of the villa before the reader's eyes, and establishes a moral counterpoint between the "rustic" spaces he invests with value, and the "urban" spaces that are ironically divested.

> Certainly a farm derives more profit from its buildings if you construct them on the model of the diligence of the ancients rather than the luxury of the moderns . . . In those days a villa was praised if it had a good country kitchen, ample stables, and wine and oil storage to suit the size of the estate . . . Nowadays they concentrate their efforts on having an urban villa as large and polished as possible, and they compete with the villas of Metellus and Lucullus built to public ruin. Hence their preoccupation is with the aspect of summer triclinia towards the cool east, and of winter ones towards the sunny west, while the ancients cared about the side the wine and oil cellars had their windows, since wine production requires cooler air on the vats, oil production warmer air. (*RR* i.6–7)

Aspect is indeed, as we see from Vitruvius, a preoccupation of 1st century B.C. construction: Varro manages to construct rustic aspect and urban aspect as parallel and alternative systems. Such parallelisms are developed with considerable ingenuity. The luxurious picture-galleries, *pinacothecae*, of Lucullus are held up for opprobrium, in contrast to the alternative and natural luxury of the "fruit-gallery," *oporotheca* (i.2.10); one can feast as richly in one as in the other (i.59.2). The Greek pseudo-formation *oporotheca*, found only here, shadows and mocks the fashionable Greek label of *pinacotheca.*[12]

Varro's sense of humour affects our reading of his moralization. Here is an author with *villae urbanae* of his own, writing a dialogue in which none of the participants are exemplars of ancient Roman rusticity. It is an issue on which they tease each other. The third book is dedicated to Pinnius, who has a villa "spectacular for its plaster-work and inlay and noble pavements of *lithostroton*," which Pinnius further adorned with his own writings, and Varro now complements with further produce, a discussion *de villa perfecta*

---

10. So Valerius Maximus ii.4.2 on the destruction of the stone theatre of 154 B.C.
11. I. Nielsen, *Thermae et Balnea: The Architecture and Cultural*

History of Roman Public Baths (Aarhus 1990), vol. 1, 159.
12. I owe to Nicolas Purcell the observation that a satirical vein runs through the *Res Rusticae.*

(iii.1.10). The participants sit down for their discussion in the Villa Publica on the Campus Martius. The setting is used to form one pole of two separate contrasts. First Appius compares it favourably, being constructed by *maiores nostri* and frugal, to Axius' polished villa at Reate, with its citrus wood and gold, rich pigments of minium and armenium, its mosaic and marble inlay (*emblema* and *lithostroton*). But Axius hits back by contrasting the paintings and statues (works of Lysippus and Antiphilus) of the Villa Publica with the works of the hoer and shepherd to be found in his own. Hay in the loft, wine in the cellar, grain in the granary are the real ancestral marks of a villa (iii.2.3–6). The banter continues, as the speakers produce further examples of villas that are or are not decorated, do or do not have agricultural produce. The moral contrasts fold in on themselves as it emerges that the ass which is the proudest rustic boast of Axius' villa cost a staggering 40,000 sesterces (2.7), and that the best way to make profit from a villa may be "villatica pastio," the breeding of bees or birds or fish, which directly serve the luxury of the city (2.16). In the end, rustic and urban, fruitful production and luxury consumption, feed off each other.

The problem, then, is to relate the moral antitheses in terms of which such discussions structure the whole idea of the villa and the practices to which the archaeological remains so abundantly testify. The trap into which we fall is to swallow the antithesis while stripping out its moral evaluation. The rustic elements are assumed to be genuinely "Roman" and in some sense a static heritage of tradition; while the luxurious urban elements are seen as the product of "Hellenization." It is assumed that the villa owners themselves did not share the moral qualms of a Varro, and that they saw the luxury appurtenances of their properties as a form of desirable modernisation in line with the fashion for the Greek. But there is a double objection to this reductionism. The first is that there are no true Greek precedents for the Roman luxury villa. It is not the borrowing of an existing Greek type of construction, but a startling Roman innovation.[13] The second is that since Varro and his friends *are* the villa-building class, we risk misunderstanding by blinding ourselves to the moral values which they attribute to their structures.

Vitruvius again proves a revealing witness. We might expect that, even if agricultural writers stick to farming and pass over building, for an architect the villa would be one of the most interesting buildings to discuss. What else were the sort of well-off and educated *patres familiae* whom he addresses putting their money into at this period? We may then register with considerable surprise (the more so if we insist on identifying Vitruvius with Caesar's assistant Mamurra, byword for luxury) that Vitruvius is an orthodox Catonian. His account of the villa (vi.6), which immediately follows that of the town house, is a purist discussion of "rustic practicalities," of barns and vats and stables, and of the very down-to-earth considerations that govern their disposition. There is nothing here to which Varro could take exception: in stressing again the importance of aspect, it is certainly not the orientation of winter triclinia he concerns himself with:

> Similarly cowbyres will be not impractical if situated outside the kitchen in the open facing the east: for when in winter in clear weather the cows are brought across to them in the morning, their condition improves from taking fodder in the sunshine. (RR vi.6.5)

So resoundingly practical and rustic is the advice that we may forget that these cows are the luxurious counterpart of their owners, getting sleeker (*nitidiores*) by breakfasting of a winter's morn in the sunshine.

Vitruvius has not forgotten the *villa urbana*: it is a question of strict categories. The urbanity of the luxurious features of the villa is their defining characteristic; they can only therefore be discussed as part of the town house. At the end of his authentically "rustic" winter cowbyres, the architect notes another side to the villa:

> If anything needs to be made of a more delicate sort in villas, they should be constructed according to the rules of symmetry given above for urban buildings, but in such a way that no obstruction is caused to rustic practicalities. (Vitr.vi.6.5)

The *villa urbana* is thus presented not as an organic part of the estate, but as the transposition of an alternative and contrary set of considerations from town into country. The countryside is the place of production, *fructus*, and the dominant considerations must be the practical ones of maximising returns. The town is, except for the humble tradesmen also concerned with practicalities, a place of social display, of decorum, the dignity imparted by elegance. Its symmetries can indeed be transposed into the countryside, provided that production does not suffer thereby.

This principle may seem to leave the owner rather at a loss as to how to shape the rustic and urban parts of his villa. But indeed he will find all the necessary prescriptions in his Vitruvius, not only in the rules for the town house, but in the ensuing discussion of

---

13. On the problem of Greek precedents for the villa, see Mielsch 1989, 32–34 and Lauter in this volume. There are clear links with the architecture of hellenistic palaces, yet these are no villas: I. Nielsen, *Hellenistic Palaces: Tradition and Renewal* (Aarhus 1994) 164–180.

the Greek house, and then in the next book with its instructions on decoration, on pavements and wall-plaster, and on the use of expensive pigments like minium and armenium, which Vitruvius like Varro sees as luxuries (vii 5.7–8), but nevertheless details (vii.8–9). As for overall planning, he offers a single, but illuminating, hint:

These principles (*rationes*) will apply not only to buildings in the city, but also in the country, except that in the city atria are normally next to the entrance, whereas in the country pseudourban villas have peristyles immediately at the entrance, then atria with pavemented porticoes around them looking out to palaestras and walks. (Vitr.vi.5.3–4)

At a single, brilliant stoke, Vitruvius turns the villa into the mirror image of the town house. In town you move from atrium to peristyle, in country from peristyle to atrium. To "urbanise" the country is to stand the town on its head.

The actual diversity of plans of excavated villas shows that Vitruvius' principle of inversion was not universally respected.[14] But Vitruvius is not in the business of describing how the Romans do things, but of imposing *ratio* on *consuetudo*. His rationality is an attempt to create order, giving a more secure basis to the sometimes messy or contradictory tendencies in Roman usage.[15] There is perhaps only one villa that follows his principle of inversion precisely, the Villa dei Misteri at Pompeii. But this is an illuminating example to consider, both because it makes explicit the rationale of the town/country antithesis, and because it exposes modern incomprehension of that rationale (Fig. 4.2).

The villa is a model Vitruvian exercise in symmetry and aspect. Its entrance, which lies to the east on the road from Pompeii, is set on a strongly marked east/west axis which defines the symmetries of the building, passing from the entrance through the center of the peristyle, through the atrium with its impluvium, to the so-called tablinum and the semicircular room called the exedra. This axis corresponds to the characteristic sightline of the town house, but visibly inverts the usual sequence. It is perhaps no coincidence that modern publications frequently offer pictures of the sightline in reverse, from atrium back to peristyle and entrance (Fig. 4.3), and not the view presented to the ancient visitor (Fig. 4.4), a tendency much encouraged by the modern construction of an approach road and entrance at the western facade, i.e. the back, of the villa.

The east/west axis is crosscut by a north/south axis which is invisible to the visitor, but basic to the plan. Running along the wall between peristyle and atrium, it divides the building into two contrasting areas. It precisely bisects the east/west axis, as measured from the formal entrance point marked by the doors (these are preceded by a cluster of irregularly shaped buildings) to the edge of the portico which surrounds the atrium end on three sides. (The semicircular room which extends this line is in fact a later addition to the main plan). The plan is inscribed in a square which has as its centre the point on the central visual axis of crossing between atrium and peristyle (Fig. 4.5). But the architecture deliberately complicates this square. Whereas the edges of the eastern end conform to the square, the western end is extended by the cryptoporticus that runs round its three sides. The effect is that while the underlying symmetry of eastern and western ends is preserved, they also contrast sharply with each other, the western end being marked off by the cryptoportico (and by many other constructional features) as more pronounced in its symmetries and evidently more prestigious.

The two halves of the square, eastern and western, are contrasted in architecture and types of room. The eastern half is the *pars rustica*, with a string of service rooms, decorated simply if at all, along the eastern side, the kitchen area to the south, and to the north the handsomely constructed pressing room and storage vat area beyond. There are no finely decorated reception rooms opening onto the peristyle, though to the south the bath complex (including a small but beautifully constructed *laconicum*), approached through its own "tetrastyle" atrium, adjoins the kitchen, and to the north an impressive room with an apsidal end was under construction in the final phase of the villa, perhaps as a new bath suite.

The western half forms the *pars urbana*. Several phases of highly elaborate decoration are apparent. The atrium, though of the usual rectangular shape around a central impluvium, lacks the canonical tablinum and alae. The room (2) referred to as a "tablinum" appears to have been cut off visually from the atrium by a solid wall. The atrium acts as distribution center for access to four sets of rooms, each of them forming a neat square, symmetrically disposed around atrium and "tablinum." The arrangement of this central block replicates the symmetries of the villa as a whole; its east/west axis is cut by a north/south axis which divides the sets of rooms, though this time the north/south axis is visually demarcated by the two corridors that open to

---

14. See Carandini in the present volume.
15. Recent discussions of Vitruvius include: H. Geertman and J. J. de Jong (eds.), *Munus non ingratum: Proceedings of the International Symposium on Vitruvius' De Architrectura and*

the Hellenistic and Republican Architecture, Leiden 20–23 January 1987 (Leiden 1989); P. Gros et al., *Le Projet de Vitruve. Objet, destinataires et réception du de architectura* (Coll.Ec.Fr.Rome 1994).

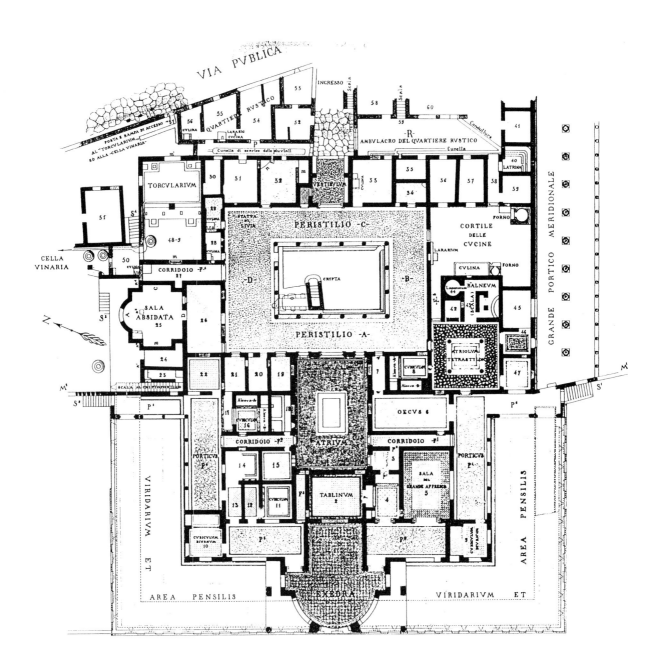

Figure 4.2. Villa dei Misteri, general plan.

Figure 4.3. Villa dei Misteri, view from atrium back toward entrance.

Figure 4.4. Villa dei Misteri, view from entrance across peristyle toward atrium.

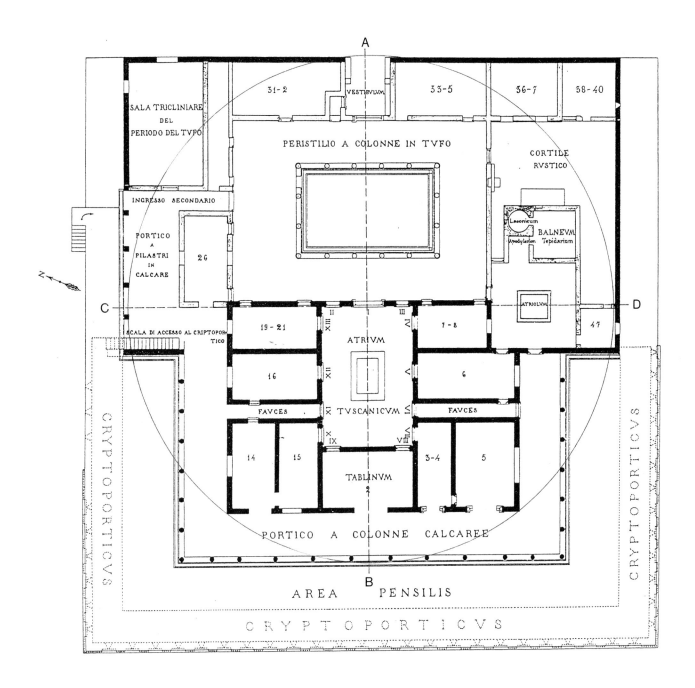

Figure 4.5. Villa dei Misteri, reconstruction of original layout according to Maiuri, with basic layout marked (A/B, C/D).

right and left of the west end of the atrium.

The excavator of the villa, Maiuri, with good reason posited an earlier phase in which the four suites of rooms had a somewhat simpler internal arrangement (Fig. 4.5). This makes clearer a pattern still detectable in the later arrangement: each set has a large reception room (triclinium) with a different orientation, and a cubiculum beside it with a double alcove for two beds. In the final phase, two of these "sets" survive, those with the sunniest and most visually spectacular orientations, to south and west, and these also contain the most spectacular decoration. Outside the four sets are linked by a double "walk": beside the rooms a handsomely paved colonnade, and beyond this the open walk of the garden the runs above the cryptoporticus.

The *pars urbana* thus conforms exactly to Vitruvius' prescription for a villa. Here is the "atrium with pavemented porticoes looking out to palaestras and walks (*ambulationes*)" (vi.5.3). But we also find elements of his prescriptions for the Greek house, which he so carefully contrasts with the Italic tradition. The villa neatly fits his discussion of the vocabulary of the *xysti* and *paradromides* of the Greek house (vi.7.5) in which he distinguishes covered and open-air walks. If the garden can be regarded as a sort of compact palaestra, it offers the alternative of covered and open-air walks which Cicero and his philosophising friends took in the *ambulationes* of their "gymnasia."[16] The orientation of the four suites with their different aspects fits his (and Varro's) discussions of aspect. And perhaps a further link can be detected in the corridors that lead to the suites. Vitruvius' "Greek" house features *hospitalia* guest suites with independent access, and their own cubicula and triclinia (vi.7.4). These are linked to the main peristyles by corridors, strictly called *mesauloe* but "wrongly" Latinized as *andrones*. There is a good chance that the corridors here, handsomely decorated in highly polished plasterwork, were meant to be thought of as "andrones" and the room suites as "hospitalia."

The important point in this analysis is not so much that the plan of the villa conforms in detail to Vitruvian prescriptions, but that it embodies the moral dichotomies which the literary sources offer so insistently. The *pars rustica* parades the "practicalities" and productivity that the "true" villa is all about. The *pars urbana* is a supplement, not obstructing the rustic practicalities, but adding "something more delicate," urbanity in a rustic setting. The urbanity is "Greek," a potential repertory of the sort of "Greek" names with which the luxury villa tinkles. The two parts stand counterposed in symmetrical antithesis.

Seen from the sightline of the visitor, this villa or-

ganizes its constituent antitheses, of rustic and urban, Roman and Greek, practical and luxurious, in careful sequence. The entrance presents the visitor with what they should expect of the Roman countryside: traditional Roman rusticity. As we step over the threshold from peristyle to atrium, we move from rustic to urban, from production to luxury. We also begin to cross a threshold from Roman to Greek, except that the atrium is itself reassuringly Roman, as the piles of arms depicted in the decoration underline. But as we pass down the *andromes* to the *hospitalia* with their views of *porticus* and *xysta* and gaze at exquisite decoration featuring crocodiles and the symbols of Egyptian Isis, or in the climactic west-facing suite scenes of Dionysus and Ariadne and the exotic mysteries of Bacchic initiation, we know that we have moved into another world.

The significance of this sequential arrangement becomes more marked if we return to the urban axial vista which, in accordance with Vitruvian rules, it inverts. In the town, to enter the atrium is to be confronted with an assertion of Roman identity, with the image, if not the practice, of patronal power; to pass through to the peristyle is to cross the threshold from urban to rural (gardens and fountains), from the practical to the luxurious, and from the Roman to the Greek (statuary, Rhodian peristyles and Corinthian *oeci*). In both city and country, then, despite or rather because of the inversion of atrium and peristyle, the Greek represents a level of privilege, less accessible but more desirable than the Roman. That can be translated into the inclusion and exclusion of visitors according to their status. In the town, the humble townsman may be received in the atrium, so close to visible reminders of the humble practicalities of the town (shops flank the entrance); to pass through to the Greek and rural is a privilege. In the country the opposite sequence of town and country is required: it is the rustic peristyle in which the countrymen can do their humble business, and the privilege consists in advancing to the *pars urbana*.

Failure to appreciate the importance of such sequential experience of the contrasts a house builds has led to the modern misrepresentation of the Villa dei Misteri. The modern visitor, as we have seen, is led directly into the western facade by a route impassable in antiquity, since the cryptoporticus on this side lifts the villa level high above the surrounding fields. From this illicit entrance, the visitor can advance directly to the much-advertised "room of the Mysteries," and relish, out of context, its exotic sexuality. Thereafter the peristyle, if the visitor advances so far, can only be anticlimactic.

This modern sequence of reactions appears to mir-

16. E.g. Cicero *de Rep.* i.18; *de Div.* i.8; cf. D'Arms (supra n. 5) 55ff.

ror that of the excavator himself. Maiuri evolved the thesis that the villa had, in the Augustan age, belonged to a family of refined taste and high social distinction, who were responsible for the fine decoration of the western part. But in the final phase it had fallen into quite different hands, doubtless a family of servile extraction, who were more intent on profit than good taste. The clinching proof of this thesis was the pressing-room. It was tasteless to degrade so fine a villa with such conspicuous rusticity, and the wine presses "must have been" a subsequent installation in what was originally the largest and finest reception room of the house.[17] Archaeological evidence for this supposed conversion and degradation of a dining room into a wine-pressing area is wholly lacking: the rough walls show no trace of earlier window openings or decoration to grace a fine reception room. On the contrary, it is perfectly shaped and decorated for its purpose as pressing room. Nor is there the slightest architectural sense in placing a grand reception room so close to the roadway, and on a northern aspect. No decorator's ingenuity could elevate this room above the "room of the Mysteries" with its views west and south through broad windows past the columns of the porticoes and out over the panorama of the Bay.

The deep implausibility of Maiuri's construction (which he so successfully wished on the modern visitor) flows from the refusal to accept the *morality* of the Roman villa, the value system which agricultural writers set out. The *torcularium*, fascinating to any reader of Cato and Varro, must be allowed to recover its positive moral connotations, a conspicuous centre of fruitful production and rustic virtue. It stands in moral (as well as aesthetic) antithesis to the "room of the Mysteries" at the diagonally opposite corner of the villa. Here Romanness, rusticity, productivity and virtue; there foreignness, an exotic oriental cult once driven by the senate from the land, the corruption of hellenistic luxuries. The architecture "moralises" no less than Varro. But the antithesis that separates also binds together, and the connection should not be missed: for here the fruits of the vine gush richly out to flow into the vats, while there the orgiastic mysteries of Bacchus, the god of the vine, are celebrated.

The Villa dei Misteri, despite its Vitruvian correctness, need not be turned into a literal blueprint for "the Roman villa." Plans are endlessly diverse, as indeed Vitruvius' refusal to elaborate might lead us to predict. The essential point is that the value system that shapes literary discussion of the villa equally in-

forms the architecture. The tensions between rustic and urban, Roman and Greek, the interplay between them, and the ambivalences to which they give rise, are central to the experience of the villa. We must abandon the cherished delusion of Italian archaeology that the "villa rustica" and the "villa urbana" are separate types.[18] One achievement of Carandini's handsome publication of the villa at Settefinestre was to show, with constant reference to agricultural writers, how the two hang together.[19] The power of the *dominus* is expressed by the complementary messages of the *pars rustica* and the *pars urbana*, in the rustic quarters by the control over manpower manifested in slave gangs and the control over the land manifested in the vintage and the oil pressing, and in the urban quarters by the control of wealth and the ability to impose on the countryside an alien cultural language. Neither part diminishes the other, since together they express an embracing dominance, of country and town, production and consumption, moral rectitude and transgression, the Roman and the non-Roman.

It may seem strange that the Roman ruling class chose to advertise its dominance in language so ambivalent and risky. But the ambivalence is itself the source of power. In Horace's fable (Satires ii.6.77ff.), the Roman does not know whether he wants to be a town mouse or a country mouse; when in one, he longs to be in the other. The hesitation was natural for men who had an equal ideological investment in both, and whose superior status was bound up in the ability to play off one against the other. As landowner and rural patron, the villa owner derived authority from his links with the city, from the wealth and political power he could generate there; he was the broker between country and town. But as politician in the city, he owed his clout also to the strength of his country backing, the wealth of his acres and the support of the countrymen who turned up to vote for him or his candidate on polling day.[20] The double face presented by both his villa and his town house reflects this duality. He must be able at once to impress the townsman by the ideological force of his rustic credentials, and the countryman by the sophistication of his urbanity.[21] The villa thus asserts urban values in the middle of the countryside, but on condition that the town house asserts rural values in the midst of the town. This sense of reciprocity is elegantly encapsulated in Vitruvius' vision of the villa as inversion of the town house.

By the same token, the ambivalence between

17. A. Maiuri, *La Villa dei Misteri* (1931), esp. 93 and 100.
18. A. Carandini (ed.), *Settefinestre. Una Villa schiavistica nell'Etruria Romana* (1985), vol. 1, 126: the non-agricultural villa is the product of selective excavation.
19. Carandini 107–137, an invaluable analysis.

20. Cf. A. Wallace-Hadrill, *Patronage in Ancient Society* (London 1989) 72.
21. Cf. J. W. Rich and A. Wallace-Hadrill (eds.), *City and Country in the Ancient World* (London 1991) 244–249.

Greek and Roman is a source and symbol of power.[22] The development of the villa is due to the example of the conquering aristocracy of the late republic, men from Scipio Africanus to Lucullus who subjected the eastern Mediterranean to Roman power. Their authority rested on a dual dominance: the ability to subject the Greek kingdoms to Roman military might, and their ability to dazzle their fellow-country-men with the booty of the east. Their villas and houses incorporate this moral ambivalence: they must at once be the authoritative expression of Roman power, and yet be able to rise above and transgress the rules by importing the exotic and alien. The same men are the guardians of ancestral tradition, and the innovators who redefine it.

22. The ambivalences of Roman hellenization have been explored recently by E. Gruen, *Culture and National Identity in* *Republican Rome* (Ithaca, NY 1992) and K. Galinsky, *Augustan Culture* (Princeton 1996).

5

THE ESQUILINE HORTI: NEW RESEARCH*

Chrystina Häuber

The subject of this paper is the Esquiline hill in Rome. I shall refer especially to the *horti* of Maecenas, that famous patron of poets and friend of the emperor Augustus.

Horti was another term for "luxury" *villae*, used by the Romans exclusively for *villae* in Rome that were inside the Servian city-wall, where the vegetable gardens (*horti*) had been. As a group, these Republican *horti*, and the *domus* (houses) of the Roman urban aristocracy, first attracted the interest of antiquarians in Rome during the Renaissance. Research was mostly based on literary sources, until building activities between 1870 and the beginning of the 20th century revealed parts of the architecture in question. The finds were poorly documented, however, and in recent years the Italian authorities in Rome have been concentrating on the enormous task of recovering and incorporating these finds into our previous knowledge about the urban topography and history of Rome. By their invitation, many archaeologists from the foreign academies in Rome have enjoyed the opportunity to collaborate.

In 1981 Eugenio La Rocca, then director of the department of antiquities at the Musei Capitolini, invited me to study the provenances of the statues excavated by the Commissione archeologica communale di Roma during the above-mentioned period. My own idea was to study only the statues in the *horti* of Maecenas on the Esquiline hill. Some of the results of this study were presented at the Villa Symposium.

In order to identify this specific group of statues, all of the reported "new" finds (roughly 1000 statues) had to be checked, since some of the provenances hitherto applied to extant statues in Roman museums had proved incorrect. On the basis of unpublish-ed archival material in Rome, including notes written by the excavators, photographs and maps, the provenances of the statues were established. Such was the approximate state of research at the Villa Symposium; at that point it was clear that the statuary decoration of Maecenas' *horti* was extremely rich. Since the Symposium, the focus of my research has shifted from the contents of the *horti* of Maecenas to their setting, and finally to *horti* Romani in general.

As with the study of any given monument or building in ancient Rome, research on the *horti* of Maecenas requires many different methods of approach. A full project demands a synopsis of literary sources, previous literature, and unpublished excavation notes, a survey of the remains, and, if possible, "re-excavation" in order to understand the reports of earlier archaeologists. This paper describes one aspect of this process, focusing on the topography of the *horti* of Maecenas and its precise location in the current land survey.

The literary sources

By 1930 A. Kappelmacher had already thoroughly collected the literary sources concerning Maecenas,[1] but N. Purcell was the first to focus a discussion on the only extant description of his *horti* in the *Elegiae in Maecenatem* (1.33–36).[2] Other literary sources also contribute significantly to our knowledge of the history, location, and buildings of the *horti*.

Horace (*Sat.* 1.8.7–15) mentions that the new *horti* of Maecenas were located where the cemetery of the

---

* In this paper I shall refer to my article about the topography of the *horti* on the Esquiline, which is supplemented by four maps: C. Häuber (1990) "Zur Topographie der Horti Maecenatis und der Horti Lamiani auf dem Esquilin in Rom," *KölnJb* (23) 11–107 [= *Topography*]. Parenthetical references

(A–L 1–13) indicate the position on those maps of the ancient and modern buildings which are mentioned here.
1. RE XIV 207–229, s.v. "Maecenas" 6 and "Maecenas und die zeitgenossische Literatur..
2. "Horti of Rome," typescript, no date.

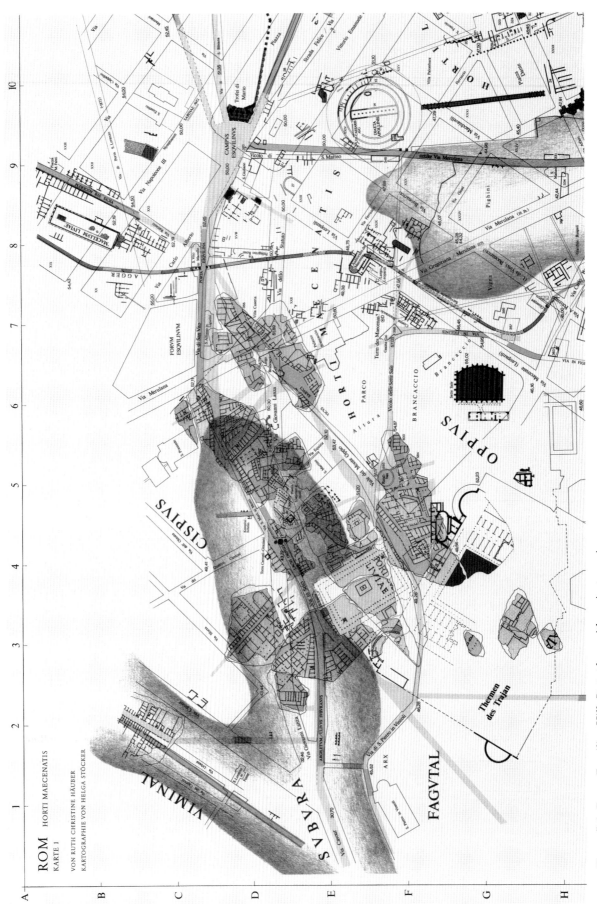

Figure 5.1. Rome, Esquiline Hill. State plane with ancient remains.

poor used to be. In his own day, he tells us, it was possible to walk along the *agger*, the so-called Servian (city) wall, with its rampart and ditch. Only the 2nd-century author Porphyrio suggests that Maecenas was the first to have *horti* on the Esquiline (*Schol. Hor.*). Horace (*Carm.* 3.29.5–11) describes a view from the palace of Maecenas towards the Alban hills. Noting its imposing structure, he compares it to a "skyscraper." In *Epod.* 9.3–4, Horace mentions the *alta . . . domus* of Maecenas; the *domus* is also mentioned by Suetonius (*Aug.* 72.2). Nero connected the buildings on the Palatine hill with the *horti Maecenatis* by means of his *domus transitoria* (*Tac., Ann.* 15.39–40). There Suetonius (*Nero* 38.2) mentions the *turris Maecenatiana*, from which Nero watched the great fire in A.D. 64. Orosius (*Adv.Pag.* 8.6) describes this same tower as *altissima*.

When Maecenas died (8 B.C.), it was presumably Augustus, his universal heir (Cass. Dio 55.7.5), to whom the *horti* were bequeathed. Suetonius (*Tib.* 15) informs us that Tiberius occupied the *horti Maecenatis* in A.D. 2. By the mid-2nd century, M. Cornelius Fronto[3] claimed that he (*Ep.* 1.8) was their owner. We may then conclude that his universal heir Aufidius Victorinus[4] received the *horti* from him. Pseudo-Acro wrote in the 5th century[5] that the *horti Maecenatis* used to be at the site where the baths of Trajan stood in his day.

In A.D. 40, Philo Alexandrinus (*De leg. ad Gaium* 351) writes that the *horti Maecenatis* and the *horti Lamiani* were situated next to each other and that both were near to the city. *CIL* VI 8668 mentions the *horti Lamiani* and the *horti Maiani* together.[6] R. Lanciani suggested on his *Forma urbis Romae*[7]—and this idea was never challenged—that the ancient road, called by the modern name Via Merulana (G 9) (Fig. 5.1),, was the original boundary between the *horti Maecenatis* and the *horti Lamiani*, and that the *horti Maiani* were situated east of the *horti Lamiani*. According to Lanciani's proposal, therefore, the *horti Lamiani* occupied, more or less, the area of the former Villa Palombara (F 10). This latter assumption was first drawn by A. Nibby on his map in 1826,[8] who based his idea on F. Nardini's hypothesis of 1666.[9] (Personally, I wonder whether the ancient Via Merulana may not have been built until late antiquity, which would mean that the area hitherto taken for the horti La-

mani formed instead part of the *horti Maecenatis*.[10] My suggestion has, however, the disadvantage of not offering an alternative site for the *horti Lamiani* and the *horti Maiani*.)

The Regionary catalogues of Constantine's reign[11] do not mention the *horti Maecenatis*, but Constantine did present a *possessio Micinas Augusti* to the Basilica S. Lorenzo.[12] In the 12th century, a Casa Frontoniana was mentioned by Magister Gregorius.[13] In the middle ages, the area of the *horti Maecenatis*/Villa Caserta (D 7) was called "Massa Juliana."[14] Because of this and because of the fact that the so-called Auditorium of Maecenas (E 8)[15] was so obviously covered by later buildings (compare maps 3 and 4),[16] I suggest that it formed part of a building in the *horti Maecenatis* that was venerated as a *monumentum*.[17]

History of scholarship

After the so-called Auditorium of Maecenas was found in 1874 and, in its vicinity, a waterpipe with an inscription of M. Cornelius Fronto,[18] the following combination of ideas was generally taken for granted: the "graves of the poor" (Hor., *Sat.* 1.8.10) were identified with the *puticuli*, although Horace does not use this technical term himself. We learn from Varro (*Ling.* 5.25), that the *puticuli* were situated beyond the city-gate on the Esquiline hill, and from Festus (*De sign. verb.* 240), that they were to be found near the *Porta Esquilina* (C 8). The archaeologists who excavated the Esquiline in the late 19th century (erroneously) located the *puticuli* in the area beyond the *agger* north of the *Porta Esquilina* (B–C 8–9),[19] an idea based, as Lanciani informs us, on L. Canina.[20]

According to literary sources (Strabo 5.3.7; Dion. Hal. 4.13) the *agger* ended at the *Porta Esquilina*. The 19th-century excavations proved instead that it extended at least up to the so-called Auditorium of Maecenas, which was built into its rampart.[21] F. Coarelli and G. Colonna offer a new idea concerning the *puticuli*.[22] They identify this technical term with the so-called "al pozzo" graves. These were found on the Esquiline hill exclusively between Via dello Statuto

3. RE IV 1312–1340, s.v. "Cornelius" 157.
4. RE II 2296–2297, s.v. "Aufidius" 41.
5. Schol. Hor., Sat. 1.8.14.
6. For the *Horti Maiani*, see *Topography* (supra n.*) n. 370.
7. R. Lanciani (1893–1901) *Forma urbis Romae* (Milano) fol. 23–24.
8. A. P. Frutaz (1962) *Le piante di Roma* (Roma) II, pl. 84.
9. *Topography* (supra n.*) 15.
10. *Topography* (supra n.*) 15, 30, 103.
11. A. Nordh (1949) *Libellus de regionibus urbis Romae* (Lund) 76–77, 80–81.
12. G. Lugli (1938) *I monumenti antichi di Roma e Suburbio* (Roma) III, 459.
13. T. P. Wiseman (1981) *PBSR* (49) 153 with n. 23.
14. R. Lanciani (1897) *The Ruins and Excavations of Ancient Rome* (London) 412.
15. *Topography* (supra n.*) 59–61.
16. *Topography* (supra n.*) 62 with n. 157.
17. See J. Bodel's contribution to this symposium, *passim*.
18. *CIL* XV 7438; *PIR* (1st edn.) II, 322–24, no. 1364.
19. Lanciani 1893–1901 (supra n. *) 7/fol. 23.
20. L. Canina (1874) *BullCom* (2) 48.
21. Canina 1874 (supra n. 20) pls. 12–15.
22. F. Coarelli and G. Colonna (1979) *Archeologia Laziale* (2, CNR 3) 202 with n. 19, 230, 232.

(D 8) and the so-called Auditorium of Maecenas (E 8), that is to say, inside the Servian wall, a fact which has not entered previous discussions of the *horti Maecenatis*.[23]

Summing up, we may conclude that Maecenas, after clearing the Republican cemetery, could just as well walk "on top of the graves of the poor" and, as well, "on the rampart of the *agger*" in the area south of the *Porta Esquilina*. It is hardly necessary to assume that parts of the *horti Maecenatis* extended as far north as the area outside the *Porta Esquilina* where Lanciani situated the *Macellum Liviae* (B 8) on his *Forma urbis Romae*.[24] Jordan-Hülsen[25] and Platner-Ashby[26] nevertheless suggested this idea. A. M. Colini[27] proposed the same topographical location for the *horti Maecenatis* as I do here, although with different arguments.

The area that was hitherto taken for that of the puticuli was destroyed by the building which Lanciani understood as the *Macellum Liviae*.[28] C. De Ruyt[29] challenges this identification and suggests that this building ought instead to be identified with the *Forum Esquilinum* together with a market-place.

Horace calls the *horti* of Maecenas "new" (*Sat.* 1.8.7). Grimal[30] suggested, therefore, that Maecenas enlarged pre-existing "old" *horti* with a "new" part outside the city wall that was gained by clearing the graveyard. It is commonly accepted that the *horti Maecenatis* partly belonged to Regio III (inside the city wall) and partly to Regio V (outside the city wall). L. Cianfriglia[31] offers a new solution. She claims that Horace simply alluded to the fact that the *horti Maecenatis* "as a whole" were built recently. Collecting the results of the excavations of the 19th century and drawing a map of all ancient buildings found at that stage, her suggestion seems to make sense.[32] The so-called Auditorium was part of a greater building complex which I identify as the *domus* of Maecenas.[33] Furthermore, it is obvious that Maecenas built his *domus* over the Servian wall. We may therefore ask ourselves whether, at his time, the *pomerium* still followed the line of the city wall. M. T. Boatwright has recently studied the question of whether or not Augustus enlarged the *pomerium*.[34]

To find the boundaries of the *horti Maecenatis* in the north and in the west, we may refer to recent studies by E. Rodriguez Almeida. He studied fragment nos. 593, 584 and 600 of the Severan marble plan and suggested its location on the *Mons Oppius* (F 5), assumptions that have meanwhile been proven by excavation.[35] The round building which is visible on fragment no. 593 was excavated exactly where Rodriguez Almeida located this fragment. Cianfriglia,[36] following Rodriguez Almeida, takes this round building for the "hot water basins" that Maecenas, according to Cassius Dio (55.7.6), was the first in the city of Rome to own. I myself suggest instead that these warm water basins alluded to the *Diaeta Apollinis*.[37]

Following Colini,[38] the boundaries of the *horti Maecenatis* to the north are the *Porticus Liviae* (F 4) and the *Vicus Sabuci* (F 6–C 8), and in the east the ancient *Via Merulana* (G 9). According to Cianfriglia,[39] the boundary in the south is defined by the north boundary of the *Domus transitoria/Domus aurea* (wherever that may be). The archaeologists who discussed the *horti Maecenatis* in the exhibition catalogues on the *horti Maecenatis*[40] and on the *horti Lamiani*[41] agree with these definitions of the boundaries.

Only Coarelli[42] and Grimal[43] maintain that the eastern boundary of the *horti Maecenatis* is unknown. Previous scholarship was almost entirely based on study of the literary sources. In order to have a better chance to find the boundaries of the *horti*, I began to collect evidence for a reconstruction of the original orography of the area, as well as of the ancient streets. I argue that there were roads that divided the numerous *horti* on the Esquiline (see Figs. 5.1, 5.3, and 5.4).

New research

As mentioned above, vast areas in Rome were uncovered during the period after 1870, when the city was rebuilt as the capital of Italy. The archaeologists

23. *Topography* (supra n.*) 64 with n. 172, fig. 43.
24. *Topography* (supra n.*) 101–102.
25. H. Jordan and Ch. Hülsen (1907) *Topographie der Stadt Rom im Altertum* (Berlin) I.3 346–348.
26. Platner-Ashby, s.v. "horti Maecenatis."
27. A. M. Colini (1979) *RendLinc* (34, Fasc. 5–6) 243.
28. R. Lanciani (1874) *BullCom* (2) 212–219 no. 37.
29. C. De Ruyt (1983) *Macellum. Marché alimentaire des Romains* (Louvain-La-Nueve) 171–172.
30. P. Grimal (1984) *Les jardins romains* (3rd ed.) 146–147.
31. L. Cianfriglia (1976–77) *Horti di Mecenate* (unpublished tesi di laurea, Roma) 74.
32. *Topography* (supra n.*) map 3.
33. *Topography* (supra n.*) fig. 67.
34. M. T. Boatwright (1986) *Historia* (35) 13–27.
35. E. Rodriguez Almeida (1975–76) *RendPontAcc* (48) 263–278; see *Topography* (supra n.*) 18, 40; F. Astolfi, L. Attilia,

and L. Cordischi (1989–90) *BullCom* (93.1), 59–68; ead. (1990) *BA* (2) 176–184.
36. Cianfriglia 1976–77 (supra n. 31) 81–83.
37. *Topography* (supra n.*) 95 with n. 309. It is of course odd that he does not call this building a "bath"; it might just as well have been something else.
38. Colini 1979 (supra n. 27) 243, 245.
39. Cianfriglia 1976–77 (supra n. 31) 70.
40. C. Häuber (1983) in *L'Archeologia in Roma capitale tra sterro e scavo* (Roma capitale 1870–1911) Auditorio di Mecenate Rome, Nov. 1983–Jan. 1984 (Venezia) 204.
41. M. Cima (1986) in M. Cima and E. La Rocca (eds.), *Le tranquille dimore degli dei. La residenza imperiale degli horti Lamiani* (Venezia) 47.
42. F. Coarelli (1980) *Roma* (Guide arch. Laterza, Roma-Bari) 219.
43. Grimal 1984 (supra n. 30) 148.

of the Commissione Archeologica of the city of Rome took many notes of ancient buildings visible in these building sites, but did not succeed in publishing these. These notes and sketches are still unpublished and are scattered throughout many archives in Rome (e.g., the Comune di Roma). Others are kept by the Soprintendenza and by the Vatican library, which has part of the collection of notes previously owned by Lanciani. The old buildings and streets (which were to be destroyed by the new residential quarters; Fig. 5.2) were documented by the most recent land survey of 1866. Every sketch made by the archaeologists on building sites was therefore keyed to this land survey, the original drawing of which I found in the Archivio dello Stato. In order to reconstruct what the archaeologists of this period had actually seen, we used the original drawing of this land survey for our maps[44] instead of the survey of 1882/83 which Lanciani used for his *Forma urbis Romae* (because this shows the new residential quarters). Thus we managed to integrate the original sketches of ancient buildings in our maps in a way that significantly differs from Lanciani's map. Consequently, we reconstruct the outline of the Servian wall on our maps differently than Lanciani did. Notice its route between the so-called Auditorium of Maecenas (F 8) and the modern Via Angelo Poliziano (H 7).

I suggest that the boundaries of the *horti Maecenatis* were formed by roads which were much older than the *horti* itself. In the west there was the *Via in figlinis* ("of the terracotta-kilns"; G 7).[45] This road is mentioned by Varro (*Ling.* 5.49–59), and the identification was suggested by Rodriguez Almeida.[46] If this hypothesis is correct, then the *Via in figlinis* on the *Mons Oppius* would have been lined by compital shrines which were still worshipped in the Roman Empire, as well as by one shrine of the Argei (*Argeorum sacraria*). Maecenas, who discussed with Augustus so many new laws related to religion, may also have proposed the restoration of this archaic cult, chatting with him in his *horti*. If the former Vicolo delle Sette Sale was in fact this sacred road, even Maecenas would not have been powerful enough to suppress it. On the contrary, considering the content of the *Elegiae in Maecenatem*[47] we may assume that he was at-

tracted by these shrines. (Consider the fact that the *horti Sallustiani* incorporated the old cult of Venus Erycina which became Venus Sallustiana.[48]) If so, then Maecenas lived in a real "sacro-idyllic" landscape which is described, according to Grimal,[49] surprisingly often by those Augustan poets who formed part of the famous "circle of friends" of their patron Maecenas. Classicists take these descriptions for mere fiction.

I think that the northern boundary of the gardens of Maecenas was formed by another road, the *Vicus Sabuci* (E 6–C 8),[50] which leads beyond the *Porta Esquilina* (C 8) towards the *Campus Esquilinus* (D 9) and the *Via Labicana-Praenestina* (E 12). Following Colini,[51] I assume that there was an ancient road underneath the modern road Via E. Filiberto (H 12), which formed the eastern boundary of the *horti Maecenatis* (according to Colini the ancient *Via Asinaria*). Drawing its outlines, the northeastern corner of the *horti Maecenatis* is marked by the so-called Casa Tonda (E 11), a tomb of Late Republican date (maps 1, 3), which I take for Maecenas's *tumulus*, beside which Horace was buried.[52] Rodriguez Almeida came to the same conclusion.[53]

I locate the *Diaeta Apollinis* (F 10), described in the inscription *CIL* VI 29774, unfortunately lost, east of the ancient *Via Merulana*.[54] My suggestion is partly based on the fact that the *Elegiae in Maecenatem*[55] mention that he worshipped Phoebus (Apollo) and Pallas (Athena) in his *horti*. I take the latter literally as well, because the Regionary catalogues mention for Regio V (the area in question) a temple of Minerva Medica.

To the south of the *Diaeta Apollinis* I assume there was a park (F–G 10).[56] South of the modern Piazza Dante, we reach buildings on top of a hillock (H 10–11).[57] It may well be that there was already a sanctuary on this promontory before Maecenas built his *horti*. In 1908[58] terracotta votives to a healing god were found here, unfortunately after Lanciani had published his *Forma urbis Romae* (which explains why this fact has been forgotten).

I think that the southwest corner of the gardens of Maecenas was also defined by older buildings. G. Pisani Sartorio[59] assumes that the sacred grove of the *Mons Oppius* formed part of one of the above mentioned compital shrines. The grove is mentioned in

44. *Topography* (supra n.*) 12 with n. 2, figs. 34.1–4, 2–5 [= Lanciani 1893–1901 (supra n. 7), fol. 23, 24, 30, 31].
45. *Topography* (supra n.*) 21–22.
46. Häuber 1983 (supra n. 40) 107–108 fig. 1.
47. *Elegiae in Maecenatem* 1.17–18.33ff.
48. I. Mariotti, ed. (1972) *Gaio Sallustio Crispo. Opere. Con un appendice di F. Castagnoli* (on the horti Sallustiani) 388; G. Cipriani (1982) *Horti Sallustiani* (Roma) 65.
49. Grimal 1984 (supra n. 30) 381.
50. *Topography* (supra n.*) n. 5.
51. A. M. Colini (1944) *MemPontAcc* (7) 77; *Topography* (supra n.*) 91, 101 maps 3, 4.

52. *Topography* (supra n.*) 65 with n. 185, 91 with n. 270.
53. E. Rodriguez Almeida (1987) in *L'Urbs. Espace urbain et histoire (Ier siècle av. J.-C.-IIIe siècle ap. J.-C.)* (CEFR 98, Rome) 417 with n. 13.
54. *Topography* (supra n.*) 82–98 maps 1–3.
55. Supra n. 47.
56. *Topography* (supra n.*) fig. 67.
57. *Topography* (supra n.*) 89–90.
58. (1908) *BullCom* (36) 92.
59. G. Pisani Sartorio (1988) *BStorArt* (31) 23–24; *Topography* (supra n.*) 14 with n. 5; 22 with n. 35; 57 fig. 73.
60. *Topography* (supra n.*) 54–56.

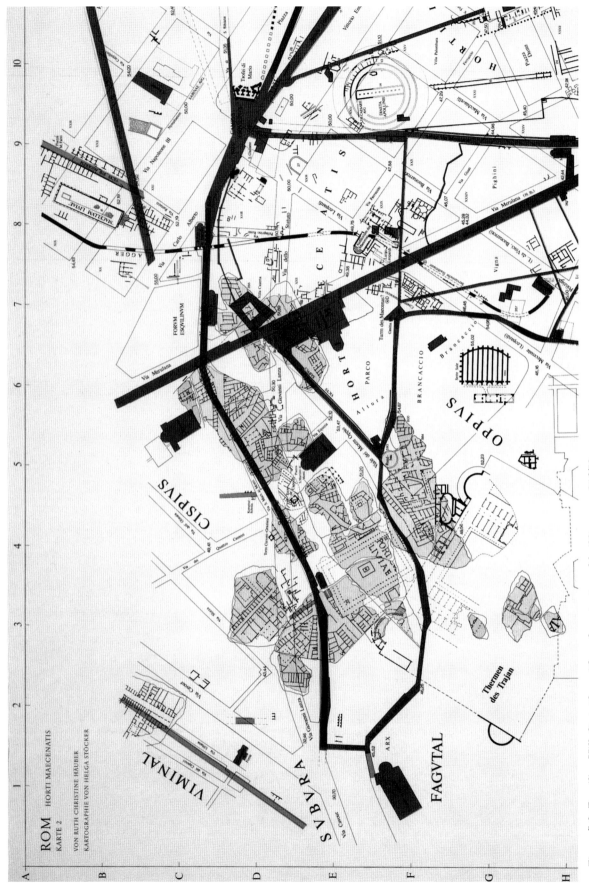

Figure 5.2. Esquiline Hill. State plan with modern streets and buildings as of 1870.

the inscription CIL VI 32455, found near the so-called *Aedicula di Minerva Medica*.[60] Next to this Lanciani located on the *Forma urbis Romae* a sanctuary of the Egyptian gods (I 7).[61] If my reconstruction of the Servian wall in this area proves to be correct we find ourselves inside the city-wall, that is to say in Regio III.

Lanciani suggested that this was the Egyptian sanctuary which gave its name to Regio III: *Isis et Serapis*. The archaeologists who excavated here found walls which were dated to regal or else to the Republican period and imperial-period sculptures.[62] Coarelli suggested locating the Republican temple "Isium Metellinum" here.[63] In my opinion, both Lanciani and Coarelli were cor-rect.[64]

Besides we learn from the inscription CIL VI 2234 that near the temple of Isis and Serapis in Regio III there was the *aedes* to Bellona (the goddess Mâ from Cappadocia brought to Rome by Sulla), built by some Rufilius. And from the inscription CIL VI 2462 that the Dea Syria (Atargatis/Astarte) was worshipped near this sanctuary too. The chronology of all these cults is so far unknown, as well as the precise boundaries of the *horti* of Maecenas and of the Domus Transitoris/Domus Aurea in this part of the Mons Oppius.

Some reflections may be useful for further discussion. Firstly the very name of Regio III is striking. Considering the importance of the Amphitheatrum Flavium/Colosseum, the fact that it did not give its name to the Regio can only be explained by assuming that the temple must be older than the amphitheatre. Secondly we should keep in mind that the emperor Nero was not only attracted by Egypt (Suet. *Nero* 47,2)—one of this tutors was the Egyptian priest Chaeremon (*FGrH* 618)—but also by the goddess Dea Syria, who was the only divinity he worshipped during most of his life (Suet., *Nero* 56). According to Pliny (*NH* 36.46), Nero built a temple to Fortuna, using *phengites*, a translucent stone that was discovered during his reign in Cappadocia, called "*aedes Fortuna Seiani*" (which means it replaced an earlier temple), which was originally founded by Servius Tullius. Nero incorporated it into his Domus Aura.

Therefore we may just as well ask ourselves whether or not the Egyptian sanctuary at some stage formed part of that section of the Imperial Horti, which had previously been the Horti Maecenatis, or of the Domus Transitoria/Domus Aurea of Nero, or of both.

Outside the Servian wall between the so-called Auditorium of Maecenas (G 7)[65] and the former Convento dei Cappuccini (I 8)[66] a couple of ancient houses were excavated, built against the city wall. One of these, entirely constructed in *opus reticulatum* (H 8),[67] was found while building Via Buonarroti/Poliziano. I suggest that these were the houses of Horace, Vergil and Propertius who, according to literary sources, had houses in or near the *horti Maecenatis*.[68]

In my opinion, the above mentioned *Diaeta Apollinis* should be compared to the famous Museion in Alexandria (Strab. 17.794)[69] which, thanks to Augustus, regained its former splendor in this period.[70] We learn that Augustus, when he felt ill, stayed in the *domus* of Maecenas.[71] It may be, therefore, that the medical doctor and freedman Antonius Musa cured Augustus's serious illness of the year 23 B.C. with his new cold-water therapy in the *Diaeta Apollinis*. This cure saved Augustus's life after the warm-water therapy of C. Aemilius had failed. Musa received knighthood as compensation and was highly esteemed;[72] Horace was also his patient (*Epist.* 1.15.2–3). Musa was the student of the famous Asklepiades of Prusa, who was a *diaitetikos* (dietician).[73]

As mentioned before, Maecenas was, according to Dionysios of Halikarnassos (55.7.6), the first in Rome to own "hot water basins." In addition, we learn in the *Elegiae in Maecenatem* (1.33) that he worshipped the "nymphs of the fountains" in his *horti*. The presumed existence of a book with the title *de tuenda valetudine ad Maecenatem* by Antonius Musa has been taken for a learned forgery.[74] But this detail, as well as the whole biography of Maecenas, have unfortunately not been studied recently; new work might change our view as much as that about the topography of his *horti*. It is well known that Maecenas suffered from serious illnesses in the last years of his life (e.g., Sen. *Ep.* 101, 110 ff.).[75]

61. *Topography*(supra n.*) 43–54.
62. *Topography*(supra n.*) 54–55.
63. F. Coarelli (1982) *EPRO* (92) 53–58.
64. In the meantime, M. de Vos has found new evidence in order to locate the temple of Isis and Serapis in this area (unpublished conference papers): M. de Vos, "L'Iseum di via Labicana a Roma," *Atti dell'incontro di studio sul tema I grandi santuari della Grecia e l'Occidente* (Università degli Studi di Trento, 12 Mar. 1991); id., *Sixth International Congress of Egyptology* (Turin, 1–8 Sept. 1991).
65. *Topography*(supra n.*) 59–61.
66. *Topography*(supra n.*) map 2.
67. (1886) *BullCom* (14) 91–92.
68. *Topography*(supra n.*) 100–101.
69. RE XVI 797–821 s.v. "Museion" (Müller-Graupau); L. Canfora (1990) *The Vanished Library. A Wonder of the Ancient World*

(2nd edn. Berkeley) *passim.*
70. RE XVI 816 s.v. "Museion" (Müller-Graupau).
71. Suet., *Aug.* 72.2.
72. Cass. Dio 53.30; Suet., *Aug.* 59.1: *Medico Antonio Musae, cuius opera ex ancipiti morbo convaluerat, statuam aere conlato iuxta signum Aesculapi statuerunt* and ibid. 81: *. . .quia calida fomenta non proderant, frigidis curari coactus auctore Antonio Musa.* See: J. André (1987) *Etre médecin à Rome* (Paris) 36, 61, 71, 106, 139, 143–144, 178; RE I 2633–2634 s.v. "Antonius" 79, "Antonius Musa" (M. Wellmann). But see J. D'Arms (1970) *Romans on the Bay of Naples* (Michgan) 79 with no. 32.
73. André (supra n. 72) s.v.; RE II 1632–1633 s.v. "Asklepiades" 39 (M. Wellmann).
74. According to Wellmann (supra n. 72).
75. Else Pliny, *NH* 7.172; Hor., *Carm.* 2.17.

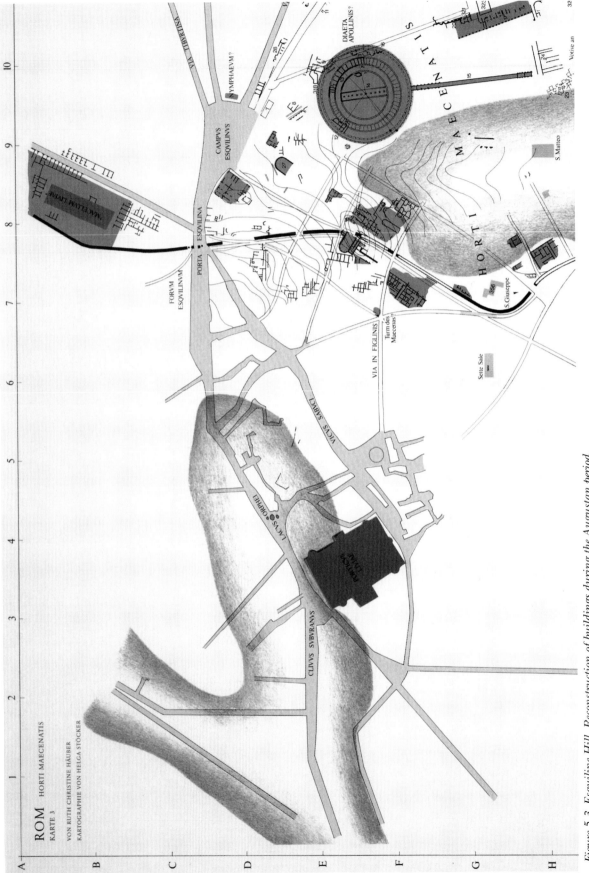

Figure 5.3. Esquiline Hill. Reconstruction of buildings during the Augustan period.

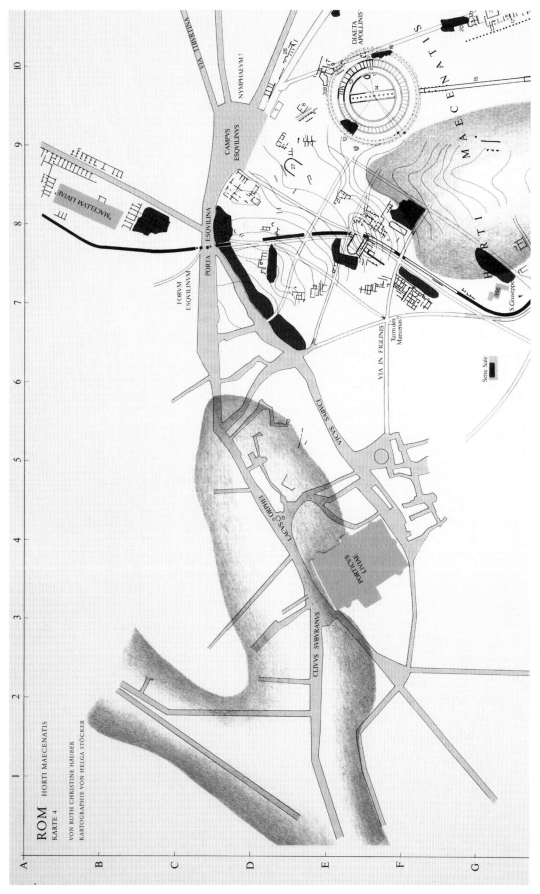

Figure 5.4. Esquiline Hill. Reconstruction of buildings to the end of the 3rd century A.D.

Maecenas also worshipped Apollo and the Muses in his *horti*.[76] May we interpret this remark in the *Elegiae in Maecenatem* as a hint at the fact that Maecenas built a structure called *Diaeta Apollinis* in his gardens modclled after the Muscion in Alexandria? If so Maecenas, who lived next door to the *Diaeta* in his *domus*, could compare himself to the Ptolemaic kings. They had built the Museion inside their palace-quarter, because it formed an important part of their lives. The fact that the poets of his circle lived in the *horti* of Maecenas as well (or else owned houses there) hints at a similar arrangement.[77]

Vitruvius (1.5) mentions towers only when he talks about city-walls. But we know that buildings in Roman villas (*horti*) were often designed in order to resemble entire cities (e.g., Suet., *Nero* 31.2 on the *Domus Aurea*). Therefore the famous *turris Maecenatiana* (tower of Maecenas) must have been part of a wall, very much like the garden wall of the Villa at Settefenestre or like those shown on the stucco reliefs from the Roman villa underneath the Villa Farnesina.[78] Else the tower was part of a building or was a free standing structure as Colini, who located the tower near S. Martino (E 5), suggested, following F. Nardini.[79]

I myself locate the tower of Maecenas on the highest spot in the area (F 7),[80] in the present Parco Brancaccio. Old maps such as the map of G. B. Falda (1676),[81] or that of G. B. Nolli (1748) show a building here.[82] If there had been a tower it surely would have had strategic value and could have been used for the transmission of information. Compare the (undescribed) tower of Tiberius at his Villa Iovis at Capri (Suet., *Tib.* 65).

We can only guess when the *horti Maecenatis* were built. In 38 B.C., Horace was introduced to Maecenas (Hor., *Sat.* 1.6.54). The publication of the first volume of his satires was dated in the year 35 B.C.[83] In 33 B.C. Octavian/Augustus and Agrippa began reorganizing the water supply of Rome. We might assume that the *horti Maecenatis* could only be built after a sufficient water supply was guaranteed. And there-

fore a wall built in *opus reticulatum*[84] which was found underneath the so-called Trofei di Mario/Nymphaeum Alexandri (D 10) may have been part of an earlier nymphaeum, built by Augustus. Since G. Pace[85] challenged the assumption that the Trofei di Mario nymphaeum was built for the *Aqua Julia*, Italian archaeologists have tried hard to learn more about the aqueducts entering the city on the Esquiline hill.

In fact, gardens do need water; we hear from Seneca (*Prov.* 1.3.10) that Maecenas especially enjoyed the murmuring of the fountains in his *horti*. Because of this, and also because Maecenas broke the old city-wall with his so-called Auditorium (a part of his *domus*) in a spectacular way, I suggest that he built his *horti* in the year 29 B.C. in order to commemorate the triple triumph of Octavian/Augustus, as a clear sign of *pax Augusta*. This presumed dedication may explain why the so-called Auditorium of Maecenas was covered by later buildings as a kind of *monumentum*.

As noted above, urban *horti* were "luxury" villas, the main buildings of which were called *domus*. It seems obvious that the *horti* of the Late Republic developed from the much older *domus*, originally built exclusively by the urban Roman aristocracy (and only later also by freedmen). As a result of the gradual conquest of an empire, the members of this class transferred parts of their riches to places outside Rome (from as early as the 3rd century B.C. onward). The old Latin term for farm, *villa*, was later used also for luxurious residences in the "country-side," which sometimes served no agricultural purposes at all.

I suggest, therefore, that later pleasure-villas across the Roman Empire, as well as the "middle-class" houses of Pompeii, may all (at least to some extent) be traced back to Republican *domus* and *horti* in Rome. *Domus*, *horti* and *villae* always seem to come in groups and should therefore be studied as a "group phenomenon," with emphasis on the group of the Republican urban Roman aristocracy since it was they who created the *domus*, *horti* and "luxury" *villae* as outward expressions of their life-style.

76. Supra n. 47.
77. Canfora (supra n. 69) *passim*, especially the chapter "In the cage of the muses," 37ff.
78. *Topography* (supra n.*) 36–38, esp. 38 with n. 77, fig. 23.
79. Colini 1979 (supra n. 27) 250.
80. *Topography* (supra n.*) 36, 38.
81. Frutaz 1962 (supra n. 8) III, pl. 359; *Topography* (supra n.*) fig. 37.
82. Frutaz 1962 (supra n. 8) II, pls. 408, 411; *Topography* (supra

n.*) fig. 12.
83. *Topography* (supra n.*) 65 with n. 180.
84. D. Cattalini (1985) in Soprintendenza Archeologica di Roma (ed.), *Lavori e studi di Archeologia pubblicati dalla Soprintendenza Archeologica di Roma*. (6,II ROMA Archeologia nel centro. La città murata) 504–505 with n. 8. Prop. 4.8.1–2 calls the Esquiline "rich in water." Underneath building no. 318 (E 10) there was a spring, see *Topography* (supra n.*) n. 214.
85. P. Pace (1983) *Gli acquedotti di Roma*, 150–152; Cima 1986

6

VILLA HADRIANA. RAUM, LICHT UND KONSTRUKTION

Adolf Hoffmann

In der Kaiserresidenz der Villa Hadriana gelangte die römische Villenkultur zu einem neuen Höhepunkt. Lebensvorstellungen und -formen, die zuvor eher der Privatsphäre vorbehalten waren, wurden in den offiziellen Bereich der kaiserlichen Repräsentation und Hofhaltung übertragen, und dies nicht innerhalb der Stadt selbst, wie es Nero mit der Domus Aurea versucht hatte, sondern weit außerhalb in freier Landschaft, d.h. in einer der Villa adäquaten Umgebung. Es steht nach jüngeren Überlegungen und Erkenntnissen kaum noch in Frage, daß die Villa Hadriana nicht nur ein privates, auf individuelle Bedürfnisse zugeschnittenes Refugium des Kaisers, sondern zeitweilig ebenso Verwaltungsmittelpunkt und Steuerungszentrale des Imperiums gewesen ist.[1]

Bei dem in mehreren Schritten gewachsenen Gesamtkomplex konnte Hadrian, dem selbst entscheidender Anteil an der Planung seiner Residenz-Villa zugeschrieben wird,[2] auf ein breit gefächertes architektonisches Repertoire zurückgreifen, wenn auch kein verbindliches Gesamtmodell existierte, wie es etwa aus der barocken Schloßbaukunst bekannt ist.[3] Mit der stadtrömischen Palastarchitektur waren in flavischer Zeit gültige Lösungen für die Aufgabe gefunden worden, öffentliche Repräsentation des Kaisers und privates Wohnen zu einer Einheit zu verbinden.[4] Für die gleichen Anforderungen hatten sie in ländlicher Umgebung allerdings keine Gültigkeit. Hier rückten die Ideale der Villenarchitektur in den Vordergrund, zumal das Kernstück der Villa Hadriana ohnehin eine republikanische *villa urbana* gewesen ist.[5]

Den Stellenwert der Villa Hadriana machen keine revolutionierenden und die weitere Entwicklung der Architektur unmittelbar beeinflussenden Neuschöpfungen aus. Aber eine höchst phantasievolle Experimentierfreude, die noch während des fortgeschrittenen Bauprozesses Planänderungen erlaubte, ließ sehr abwechslungsreiche, oft neu interpretierte Einzelräume und Raumkombinationen entstehen. Deren ordnende Organisation und Verknüpfung war nur mit 'städtebaulichen' Überlegungen zu bewältigen. Im Vordergrund stand dabei nicht die Gestaltung eines übergreifenden, groß dimensionierten Gesamtprospekts, sondern die Schaffung reizvoller und immer neue Überraschungsmomente liefernder Einzelkomplexe. Noch in der Gegenwart fasziniert die Villa Hadriana als ein Lehrstück der Architekturkomposition Bauhistoriker und Architekturtheoretiker bis hin zu R. Venturi, einem der Wegbereiter der sogenannten postmodernen Architektur.[6]

Variationsreichtum auch bei Materialien und Formen belebte das von der Ausstattung der Oberflächen bestimmte, den Vorlieben der Zeit entsprechende Erscheinungsbild der Villa Hadriana. Das meiste davon ging verloren, so daß sich an keiner Stelle die Architektur dem heutigen Besucher in der gleichen Gestalt darbietet wie dem, der sie bald nach ihrer Fertigstellung sehen konnte. Wohl aber sind umfangreiche Teile der Rohbaustrukturen erhalten geblieben oder anhand der Überreste zu rekonstruieren, die heute ehemals ganz verborgene Einblicke bieten.

---

1. s. u.a. die Bemerkungen von S. Salza Prina Ricotti (1973), in *Les cryptoportiques dans l'architecture romaine* (CEFR 14) 219, und H. Rahms (1989) in: *Frankfurter Allgemeine Zeitung* (Nr. 266 vom 15.11.1989, N 3).
2. Zu Hadrians Rolle bei der Planung der Villa s. zuletzt M. Ueblacker (1985), *Das Teatro Marittimo in der Villa Hadriana* (Sonderschriften des DAI Rom, Bd. 5) 53.
3. Vgl. F. Rakob (1973) "Der Bauplan einer kaiserlichen Villa," in: *Festschrift Klaus Lankheit*, 116.

4. Zu den flavischen Palästen auf dem Palatin s. F. Rakob (1967) in: Th. Kraus (Hrsg.), *Das römische Weltreich* (PropKg 2) 189 mit Bibliographie, und G. Wataghin Cantino (1966) *La Domus Augustana. Personalità e problemi dell'architettura flavia*, dazu jedoch kritisch F. Rakob (1968), *Gnomon* (40) 187.
5. G. Lugli (1927), *BullCom* (55) 139ff. Grundlagen und Entwicklungsablauf der Villa Hadriana hat zuletzt F. Rakob aufgezeigt, Rakob 1973 (supra n. 3) 116ff.
6. R. Venturi (1966) *Complexity and Contradiction in Architecture*.

Im Konstruktionswesen stand die Architektur der Villa Hadriana auf der Höhe der Zeit, hat vielleicht auch neue Impulse gegeben. An einigen charakteristischen Beispielen soll dies demonstriert werden. Die mit dem Thema formulierte Fragestellung zielt dabei auf die Abhängigkeiten von Raumgestalt, Raumwirkung und konstruktiver Lösung. Nicht die gesellschaftsbezogenen oder wirtschaftspolitischen Aspekte aus der Frühzeit der Villa sind also Gegenstand dieser Betrachtungen, sondern einige Fragen zu Architektur und Konstruktion. Mit den anfänglichen Zielen und Aufgaben der Villenkultur hatte die kaiserliche Residenz-Villa nur noch begrenzte Gemeinsamkeiten. Das Streben nach den Annehmlichkeiten ländlicher Umgebung im Kontrast zu städtischem Leben allerdings bestimmte nach wie vor ganz wesentlich die Entwurfsüberlegungen.

In der Villa Hadriana ist der Bezug von innen nach außen, d.h. die Öffnung der Gebäude auf umgebende Freiflächen unterschiedlichster Gestalt ein vorrangiges Anliegen gewesen. Möglichst viel Licht sollte eingefangen und zugleich sollten vielseitig wechselnde Ausblicke gewährt werden. Wenn dies auch als ein allgemeines Charakteristikum der Villenarchitektur gelten kann, lassen sich in der Villa Hadriana im Zusammenhang mit raumgestalterischen Zielen doch ganz spezifische Versuche nachweisen, neue Möglichkeiten zu erproben.

Zwei aus statisch-konstruktiven Überlegungen eigentlich unvereinbar erscheinenden Architekturprinzipien bzw. ihrer Kombination galt bei der Planung der Villa Hadriana ein besonderes Interesse: der Säulenarchitektur und dem Gewölbebau. Aus dem Gliederbau sind in der Regel ausschließlich Vertikallasten in die Fundamente abzuführen, Gewölbekonstruktionen ergeben zu einem großen Teil auch Horizontallasten bzw. Schubkräfte. Beide Prinzipien aus gestalterischen Überlegungen miteinander in Einklang zu bringen, hat die römischen Baumeister seit republikanischer Zeit herausgefordert. Die bisher frühest bekannten Beispiele der Überwölbung einer Säulenportikus in monumentalen Dimensionen finden sich im Fortuna-Heiligtum von Praeneste aus dem späten 2. Jh.v.Chr. gleich in mehrfacher Ausführung.[7] Kolonnaden von korinthischen oder ionischen Säulen trugen massive, an der Unterseite kassettierte Tonnengewölbe aus *opus caementicium*. Durch große Auflasten über den Säulen in Form

hoher Attiken, einem neuen, aus bautechnischen Überlegungen erwachsenen Element der italisch-römischen Architektur, ist das statische System dieser Bauten ins Gleichgewicht gebracht worden. Sowohl architektonischräumlich als auch konstruktiv waren mit diesem frühen Experiment der *caementicium*-Bauweise kühne und zukunftweisende Lösungen gefunden worden, doch stehen sie zunächst noch lange Zeit isoliert. Sehr viel massiver ist z.B. das überwölbte Arkadengeschoß des nicht sehr viel später errichteten Tabulariums in Rom proportioniert.[8] Anders als in Praeneste wurde hier die statisch besonders gefährdete Arkadenzone durch schwere und recht eng stehende Pfeiler gesichert. In der Kombination mit vorgelegten Halbsäulen ist in dieser Ausbildung ein allgemein gültiges und die weitere Entwicklung prägendes System gefunden, das römische Gewölbe- und Massenarchitektur mit den Elementen des als Würdezeichen dienenden griechisch-hellenistischen Gliederbaus verbindet.[9]

In der zeitgleichen kleinmaßstäblichen Privatarchitektur werden mit den korinthischen Oeci vergleichbare Raumvorstellungen als Scheinarchitekturen ausgeführt, die ein anderes, in der Monumentalarchitektur nicht erreichbares Entwurfsideal der Baumeister widerspiegeln: Luftige oder gar zierliche Säulenstellungen sollten mit gewölbten Decken zu einer Raumeinheit verbunden werden. Architektonische Wunschbilder der Baumeister liefen hier den technischen Möglichkeiten allem Anschein nach voraus. Nur in Stuck über leichten Stützkonstruktionen konnten sie ausgeführt werden.[10]

In augusteischer Zeit wird das Thema der Kombination von Kolonnade bzw. Arkade und Gewölbe erneut aufgegriffen. Die Beispiele betreffen unterschiedliche Bauaufgaben, für die ganz individuelle Lösungen gefunden wurden: In einem Nutzbau wie den Horrea Agrippiana am Nordfuß des Palatin, zwischen 20-10 v.Chr. entstanden,[11] finden sich ähnlich schwere Proportionen wie beim Tabularium. Nicht Säulen, sondern enggestellte Pfeiler mit vorgeblendeten Halbsäulen trugen auch hier in zwei Geschossen übereinander die Deckenkonstruktion. Spätestens ab dieser Zeit aber wurden die außerordentlichen und ganz neue Dimensionen des Konstruierens eröffnenden Qualitäten des Baustoffs Eisen erkannt: Anstelle hoher Auflasten wie in Praeneste stabilisierten im Obergeschoß der zweigeschos-

7. s. F. Fasolo und G. Gullini (1953) *Il Santuario della Fortuna Primigenia a Palestrina* [= 'FG']; H. Kähler (1958) "Das Fortuna-Heiligtum von Palestrina Praeneste," *AnnSarav* (7.3-4) 189ff. [= 'K']. Portiken kombiniert mit Gewölben finden sich im Fortuna-Heiligtum an folgenden Orten: Rampenportiken zur Terrasse IV: FG 97ff., K 200; Hemizyklien der Terrasse IV: FG 128ff., K 201; zweischiffige Portiken der Terrasse VI: FG 177; zweischiffige Ringportikus der Terrasse VII: FG 185ff., K 206. Vgl. hierzu zuletzt F. Rakob (1990), *RömMitt* (97) 62, 67f. mit Abb. 23.

8. R. Delbrueck (1906) *Hellenistische Bauten in Latium* I, 33ff.

9. In der Privatarchitektur findet sich die Verbindung von (Blend-) Arkaden und Halbsäulen bereits in den spätrepublikanischen Exedrafassaden der Villa von Anguillara Sabazia (R. Vighi [1941], *Palladio* [5] 145ff. Abb. 4-5, 10) und der Villa della Farnesina in Rom (G. Lugli [1938], *MEFRA* [55] 5ff. Abb. 2, 3).

10. A. Maiuri (1937), *Palladio* (1) 121ff. und zuletzt ein Beispiel bei A. Carandini (1985) *Settefinestre. Una villa schiavistica nell'Etruria romana* II. *La villa nelle sue parti* (Modena) 21ff.

11. H. Bauer und A. Pronti (1978), *ArchCl* (30) 107ff. und H. Bauer (1978), *ArchCl* (30) 132ff.

sigen Portiken zugbeanspruchte Eisenanker das Baugefüge.[12]

Die umfangreiche Verwendung von Eisenankern gab ebenso einem sehr viel fragileren Gebäude, der 14 v.Chr. errichteten Basilica Aemilia, die notwendige statische Festigkeit. Auch hier waren Gewölbe und Arkadenarchitektur in der zum Forum orientierten Vorhalle zu einer Einheit verbunden, bei der offen-sichtlich auf elegante Leichtigkeit großer Wert gelegt worden ist; ein Ziel, das nur mit dem Einsatz von Eisen erreicht werden konnte. Sowohl als Längsaussteifung der Arkadenarchitektur als auch zur Eliminierung der Schubkräfte aus den Gewölben sind nach Beobachtungen H. Bauers, dem ebenso die Analyse der Horrea Agrippiana zu verdanken ist, Eisenanker eingefügt worden.[13]

Ein dritter Bau augusteischer Zeit, die Portiken des Augustusforums, zeigt bei verwandter Entwurfsaufgabe jedoch, daß man den neuen technischen Möglichkeiten des Konstruierens mit Eisen vor allem bei großen Dimensionen wohl nicht immer vertraute. Dies mag umso mehr gegolten haben, wenn Pfeiler mit Halbsäulen, die–abgesehen von den Beispielen in Praeneste–bei allen zuvor genannten Bauten wohl als zuverlässiger Garant für eine standfeste Architektur angesehen worden sind, durch Säulen ersetzt werden sollten. Vergleichbar den Saalbauten der Privatarchitektur überspannten die Säulenportiken des Augustusforums nach Bauer an hölzernen Dachbindern aufgehängte, kreissegmentförmige Scheingewölbe.[14] Anscheinend barg die Kombination von Säulen und massivem Gewölbe mit großen Spannweiten (c.15 m) nach wie vor Probleme; die erstrebte Raumwirkung freilich wußte man auch auf anderen Wegen zu erzielen.[15]

Das architektonische Ideal der Kombination von Gewölbe und Säulen wird noch einmal mit dem trajanisch begonnenen Bau des Pantheon in Rom deutlich.[16] Die älteren bzw. die etwa gleichzeitigen Groß-kuppelbauten von Baiae hatten auf Säulen ganz verzichtet.[17] Entgegen der statisch-konstruktiv existierenden Verhältnisse täuschte der Architekt des Pantheon dagegen ein Erscheinungsbild vor, das dem Betrachter suggerierte, die gewaltige Kuppel des Rundbaus werde (zumindest in wesentlichen Abschnitten) von Säulen getragen. Tatsächlich konnte diese Aufgabe nur der dahinterliegende und optisch bewußt in den Hintergrund gedrängte Mauerzylinder mit seinen enormen Abmessungen übernehmen.

Um das Entwurfsideal vor allem mit großen Spannweiten zu erreichen, waren demnach Hilfskonstruktionen notwendig: Entweder waren die scheinbar gewölbetragenden Säulen statisch weitgehend irrelevant wie beim Pantheon oder die Säulen trugen wie bei den Portiken des Augustusforums nur ein Scheingewölbe, das von der eigentlichen Dachkonstruktion abgehängt war. Freilich muß dies keineswegs bedeuten, daß die eine oder die andere Konstruktion als geringerwertig betrachtet worden wäre. Grundsätzliche und gravierende Konsequenzen ergaben sich jedoch für die Lichtführung. Beim Pantheon konnte Licht nahezu ausschließlich vom Kuppelscheitel her einfallen;[18] eine Lichtquelle, die nur bei einem Bau mit einem bestimmten, eingeschränkten Aufgabenbereich zu tolerieren war. Gebäude für einen längeren Aufenthalt, allemal im Zusammenhang einer Villa, erforderten dagegen möglichst viel Seitenlicht und zugleich vor allem Ausblicksmöglichkeiten.

Die ausführlichere Schilderung dieser Voraussetzungen erleichtert es, architektonische Eigenarten und Besonderheiten der Villa Hadriana zu verstehen und einzuordnen. Die Auseinandersetzung mit Gewölben und Säulen nimmt bei diesem Bauvorhaben in ganz unterschiedlichen Zusammenhängen einen dominierenden Platz ein. Dabei interessieren in diesem Rahmen weniger die überwölbten Räume mit Säulenfronten, die–durch die Wölbung allerdings in

12. Vgl. hierzu A. Hoffmann (1991) "Konstruieren mit Eisen," in: A. Hoffmann, E.-L. Schwandner, W. Hoepfner, und G. Brands (Hrsg.), *Bautechnik der Antike* (Diskussionen zur Archäologischen Bauforschung 5) 99ff. Die Verwendung von Eisenankern zieht Rakob 1990 (supra n. 7) 68, schon für die überwölbten Portiken in Praeneste in Erwägung.
13. H. Bauer (1977), *MittDAV* (8) H. 2, 8ff., und ders. (1988), in *Kaiser Augustus und die verlorene Republik* (Berlin) 200ff.
14. Bauer 1988 (supra n. 13) 184ff.
15. Bei der Verfolgung des geschilderten Entwurfsgedankens unter konstruktiven Gesichtspunkten ist (entgegen J. Packer, der z.Zt. eine genauere, aber noch unpublizierte Untersuchung des Gebäudekomplexes durchführt) möglicherweise vor allem ein Bau aus trajanischer Zeit von Bedeutung: Die Basilica Ulpia des Trajansforum, s. C. M. Amici (1982) *Foro di Traiano: Basilica Ulpia e Biblioteche* (Spoleto) 32. In den Seitenschiffen der Basilica wurden nach bisheriger Kenntnis zum ersten Mal seit Praeneste schlanke Säulen wahrscheinlich mit Massivgewölben verbunden, ohne daß der Konstruktion–wie etwa bei den Thermen–durch die Einbindung in einen Sicherheit garantierenden Großblock aus Mauerwerk zusätzliche Stabilität gegeben wurde. Möglich war dies nur mit dem

16. W.-D. Heilmeyer (1975), *JdI* (90) 316ff. Vgl. jetzt aber K. S. Freyberger (1990) *Die stadtrömischen Kapitelle aus der Zeit von Domitian bis Severus Alexander*, 55 Anm. 217, der–die wohl noch nicht abgeschlossene Diskussion zur Datierung des Pantheon resümierend–für den 'konventionellen' Ansatz in frühhadrianische Zeit plädiert.
17. Der Kenntnisstand zum römischen Gewölbebau allgemein hat sich in den letzten Jahren gerade in bezug auf die Kuppelkonstruktionen entscheidend verbessert: F. Rakob (1988), *RömMitt* (95) 257ff. und Rakob 1990 (supra n. 7) 61ff. mit grundlegend zusammenfassenden Überlegungen zu Technik und Entwicklung des römischen Kuppelbaus; vgl. zuvor J. J. Rasch (1985), *Architectura* (15) 117ff. (bzw. ders. [1989], in R. Graefe [Hrsg.], *Zur Geschichte des Konstruierens*, (17ff.) mit ausführlicher Bibliographie zum Thema; s. jetzt auch J. J. Rasch (1991), *JdI* (106) 311ff.
18. Zur Belichtung des Pantheon s. W.-D. Heilmeyer (1990), in: W.-D. Heilmeyer und W. Hoepfner (Hrsg.), *Licht und Architektur*, 107ff.

Einfügen eiserner Zuganker, wie sie in ähnlicher Form bei den augusteischen Bauten erschlossen werden konnten. Vgl. o. Anm. 11ff.

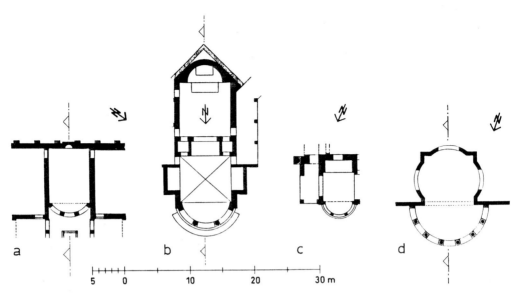

Abbildung 6.1. Säulenapsiden in der Villa Hadriana, Grundrisse; a. 'Piazza d'Oro', westlicher Hauptsaal der Querachse; b. 'Lateinische Bibliothek'; c. 'Canopus', westlich flankierender Pavillon; d. Trikonchos vor den 'Bibliotheken'. a. Rakob (Anm. 19), b. Kähler (Amn. 19), c. Aurigemma (Anm. 48), d. Rakob (Anm. 20)

ihren Raumqualitäten gesteigert–seit republikanischer Zeit eine allgemeingültige und weit verbreitete Bauform nicht nur der römischen Privat- und Villenarchitektur sind.[19] Auffällig in der Villa Hadriana ist jedoch die Variante mit konvex vorspringender Krümmung einiger Säulenstellungen: Die ausschwingenden Fronten der Hauptsäle in der Querachse der 'Piazza d'Oro' (Abb. 1a) sind zwar als eine Antwort auf die Kurvenformen des zentralen Peristyls zu verstehen; als isoliertes Element begegnen sie uns bereits an der 'Lateinischen Bibliothek' (Abb. 1b), einer der wahrscheinlich frühen Anlagen der in mehreren Schritten gewachsenen Kaiservilla.[20] Die Bauform zunächst in massiverer Ausbildung, d.h. mit Fensterwänden anstelle von Säulenkolonnaden, ist in der Villen- und Thermenarchitektur gleichermaßen verbreitet;[21] die Säulenapsis markiert dabei ohne Frage den krönenden Endpunkt einer Entwicklung zu immer größerer Auflösung der tragenden Wände, zu immer mehr Lichteinfall und unbegrenzter Ausblicksmöglichkeit.

Im Gegensatz zu den spielerischen, nahezu phantastischen Kurvenexperimenten der 'Piazza d'Oro' hatte die ausschwingende Kolonnade der 'Lateinischen Bibliothek' eher die ganz zielgerichtete Auf-

gabe, den wohl als repräsentativen Empfangsraum genutzten Saal in der Tradition der *oeci cyziceni* in den Garten ausgreifen zu lassen, diesen gleichsam in die Architektur hineinzuziehen und zugleich möglichst viel Licht in den Raum zu holen.[22] Die Verknüpfung von innen und außen konnte mit diesem architektonischen Kunstgriff entscheidend intensiviert werden.

Wie steht es jedoch mit der Ausbildung von oberem Raumabschluß und Dachkonstruktion dieser Säulenapsis? Bei relativ kleinen Dimensionen (Durchmesser knapp 6 m) bereitete die von F. Rakob zurecht angenommene Überwölbung der Segment- oder Halbkreisräume der 'Piazza d'Oro' trotz des feingliedrigen Unterbaus offenbar keine Schwierigkeiten (Abb. 2a), wenn wir auch zunächst noch nicht wissen, wie diese Konstruktionen im Detail gelöst gewesen sind. Trotz des etwas größeren Durchmessers (8 m) können wir relativ sicher sein, daß ebenso die Säulenapsis der 'Lateinischen Bibliothek' in der von Rakob vermuteten zweigeschossigen Form mit einem Massivgewölbe überdeckt war, wie es bereits H. Kähler für den eingeschossigen Zustand angenommen hatte (Abb. 2b). Selbst bei leichtem Säulenunterbau scheinen also diese Apsiden der Villa Hadriana mit

19. Als ein Beispiel dieser Gattung seien die Flügelräume an den Seitenatrien der 'Piazza d'Oro' genannt: F. Rakob (1967) *Die Piazza d'Oro in der Villa Hadriana bei Tivoli* (Diss.) Abb. 1, 6-7, 14-15. Konstruktiv sind die beiden Elemente Kolonnade und Gewölbe hier unabhängig voneinander eingesetzt.
20. Rakob 1967 (supra n. 19) 20, Abb. 1, 3, 11 (s.o. Anm. 4), und H. Kähler (1950) *Hadrian und seine Villa bei Tivoli*, 32, 111, Abb. 1.
21. F. Rakob (1987), *RM* (94) 1ff. hat Geschichte und Aufgabe der befensterten Apsis in der kaiserzeitlichen Architektur

aufgezeigt und sie für den Bereich der Villa in Anlehnung an Vitruv überzeugend als eine Spielart des *oecus cyzicenus* interpretiert. Vitruv (6.3.10; 6.7.3) schildert diesen Raumtyp und nennt dabei vor allem den Gartenbezug über große Fenster-Türen als sein besonderes Charakteristikum.
22. Rakob 1987 (supra n. 21) 23f. hat zusätzlich auf die Bedeutung der vorgelagerten (nachträglich angefügten) Freitreppe "als Zeichen direkter Vermittlung an der Grenze zwischen Innenraum und Gartenfläche" hingewiesen.

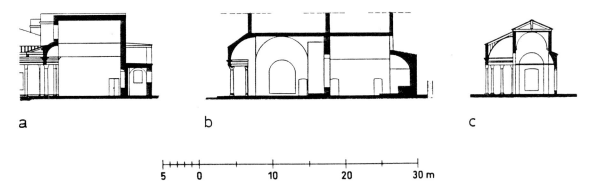

a   b   c

Abbildung 6.2. Säulenapsiden in der Villa Hadriana, Rekonstruktionsversuche, Schnitte; a. 'Piazza d'Oro', westlicher Hauptsaal der Querachse; b. 'Lateinische Bibliothek'; c. Trikonchos vor den 'Bibliotheken'. a. Rakob (Anm. 19), b. Kähler (Anm. 19), c. Verf.

Kugelkalotten aus *opus caementicium* überdeckt gewesen zu sein.

Einen bis dahin vollkommen unbekannten Vorläufer zu der Apsidenkolonnade der 'Lateinischen Bibliothek' hat Rakob vor kurzem vorgestellt:[23] Zwischen 'Lateinischer' und 'Griechischer Bibliothek' stand ehemals ein isolierter Saalbau (Abb. 1d), ein Trikonchos, der sich wahrscheinlich nach drei Seiten auf angrenzende Gartenzonen öffnete, lehnte sich gegen eine den Garten nach Norden, zum Tal hin abschließende Mauer. Aus dieser Mauer trat eine mit halbkreisförmiger Kolonnade ausschwingende Säulenapsis vor. Als ein architektonisches Signal der Villa wirkte diese Apsis nach außen, ermöglichte und intensivierte zugleich aber auch den Ausblick aus dem Saal in die umgebende Landschaft. Nach ihren Abmessungen im Verhältnis zum Saalbau zu urteilen, hatte sie sicher auch eigenräumliche Qualitäten als Aussichtsexedra (Durchmesser c. 10.5 m), wie z.B. ein ähnlicher Saal der Villa Iovis auf der Insel Capri, der freilich in seinem nach Rakob möglicherweise luftigen, allerdings von Pfeilern getragenen Obergeschoß nahezu doppelte Abmessungen erreichte (Durchmesser c. 20 m).[24] Die Fensterapsiden pompejanischer Stadtrandvillen reflektieren wahrscheinlich das Vorbild der Kaiservillen in bescheideneren Dimensionen und bezeugen die Wertschätzung dieses architektonischen Motivs schon ab der frühen Kaiserzeit ebenso in der bürgerlichen Baukunst.[25]

Zwei Säle hintereinander bestimmen, wie es Kähler herausgearbeitet hat,[26] als Basisidee auch den Entwurf der beiden 'Bibliotheken'; in mehrfacher Hinsicht lassen sich folglich mit dem Trikonchos-Aussichtsbau Parallelen zu den Nachfolgebauten aufzei-

gen, zu deren Gunsten der ältere wohl abgerissen worden ist. Vielleicht sind hierfür nicht zuletzt konstruktive Mängel ausschlaggebend gewesen. Eine detaillierte Rekonstruktion des ersten Saalbaus ist von Rakob noch nicht vorgelegt worden, doch rechnet er auf Grund der geringen Mauerdicken zurecht mit einer leichten Dach- und Deckenkonstruktion für den Trikonchos,[27] die analog auch für die Kolonnadenapsis anzunehmen ist. Entsprechend der anspruchsvollen Grundrißgestaltung kann man sicher davon ausgehen, daß Saal und Apsis, wie H. Bauer es ähnlich für die Exedren des Augustusforums vorgeschlagen hat,[28] in abgehängtem Leichtbau mit Gewölbeschalen aus Stuck versehen gewesen sind (Abb. 2c). Nur so jedenfalls würde die Raumform dem Planentwurf gerecht geworden sein.

Wohl in Anpassung an die wachsenden Aufgaben, die Hadrian seiner Villa übertrug, wurden Abmessungen und Differenzierung des Grundrisses bei den vermutlich nacheinander entstandenen 'Bibliotheken' erheblich gesteigert, die zugleich wohl auch eine größere konstruktive Stabilität anstrebten. Wie die Säle erhielt aller Wahrscheinlichkeit nach auch die Säulenapsis—wie bereits ausgeführt—eine massive Gewölbekonstruktion. Zwar wurde mit dem zweiten Bau die überaus großzügige Lösung der ersten Aussichtsexedra nicht wieder erreicht, doch konnte mit der deutlich größeren Weite und damit größeren Lichtdurchlässigkeit der Apsisinterkolumnien doch ein gewisser Ausgleich geschaffen werden.

Bessere Möglichkeiten des Ausblicks zu erzielen, mehr Licht und mit einer Orientierung nach Süden zugleich auch mehr Sonnenwärme einzufangen, erstrebten die Baumeister der Villa ebenso in der

---

23. Rakob 1987 (supra n. 21) 21.
24. Rakob 1987 (supra n. 21) 11, Abb. 12.
25. s. etwa den Cubiculum-Erker der Diomedesvilla aus neronisch-flavischer Zeit(?), A. Maiuri und R. Pane (1947) *La Casa di Loreio Tiburtino e la Villa di Diomede* (Monumenti Italiani Ser. II Fasc. I) 14, Grundriß Tav. IX; vgl. zur Aussichtsexedra der Villa dei Misteri: Rakob 1987 (supra n. 21) 13f.
26. Kähler 1950 (supra n. 20) 106ff.

27. Rakob 1987 (supra n. 21) 21 Anm. 45. Zwei grundsätzlich unterschiedliche Wölbformen sind über dem Trikonchos vorstellbar: Eine einheitliche (gegen die Säulenapsis allerdings beschnittene) Kuppel über den zum Kreis ergänzten Segmentapsiden oder über einem oberhalb der Apsiden frei stehenden Mauerquadrat ein Kreuzgratgewölbe, hier Abb. 2c.
28. Supra n. 13.

Thermenarchitektur. Der für Caldarien bevorzugte Rundraum mit Kuppel wurde einer allgemeinen Strömung der Zeit folgend durch immer höhere und immer größere Fenster aufgelöst. Während in den Großen Thermen der Villa Hadriana ein entsprechender Rundraum mit einer Fensterfront auskommt, die etwa ein Drittel der Außenfläche umfaßt, erreicht der Heliocamino genannte, überkuppelte Rundraum der Thermenanlage zwischen 'Teatro Marittimo' und 'Gartenstadion' bei nahezu gleichem Durchmesser von 12 m eine Auflösung von fast der Hälfte des Mauerzylinders (Abb. 3a, b).[29] Mit diesen Abmessungen übertrifft der kühne Bau selbst die Maße der Leichtkonstruktion des ersten Saalbaus zwischen den 'Bibliotheken'. Die etwas schwerere Ausbildung der Stützen als Pfeiler wurde auch am 'Heliocamino' durch größere lichte Weiten zwischen diesen ausgeglichen.[30] Bezeichnenderweise war der in seiner Wirkung sicher großartige und ebenso als großartige technische Leistung wohl auch empfundene Saal Bestandteil einer Thermenanlage, die wahrscheinlich nicht der Allgemeinheit zugänglich war. Nach Lage und Zuordnung ist sie wie die Audienzsäle der 'Bibliotheken' vermutlich nur einem reduzierten Kreis hochrangiger Gäste vorbehalten gewesen.

Daneben existierten in der Villa Hadriana andere Arten von Kuppelräumen mit Säulen.[31] Besondere Aufmerksamkeit bei der Verfolgung des Problems der Kombination von Säulenstellung und Gewölbe erregen zwei Kuppelbauten, die von den bisher vorgestellten Schemata grundsätzlich abweichen: Der Rundsaal des sogenannten Kleinen Palastes oder Akademie (auch Apollotempel genannt)[32] und das Vestibül der 'Piazza d'Oro'. In ganz unterschiedlicher Weise wird hier versucht, beide Entwurfselemente zu verbinden, in beiden Fällen freilich bleibt die Säule Dekoration und ohne statische Funktion: Die Innenfassade in dem von Kähler vorgestellten Rundsaal des 'Kleinen Palastes' ist—darin dem Pantheon eng verwandt—in zwei Geschossen organisiert (Abb. 4a, c):[33] Im geschlossenen Erdgeschoß trägt eine der Wand vorgeblendete Ordnung schlanker Zweidrittelsäulen ein weit auskragendes Gebälk, das Obergeschoß ist als Fenstergadenzone ausgebildet,

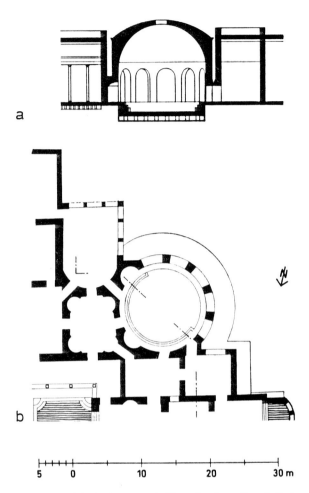

Abbildung 6.3. 'Heliocamino', Kuppelsaal; a. Grundriß; b. Rekonstruktionsversuch, Schnitt. a. Verf. nach Verduch,; b. Verduchi (Anm. 29)

die helles Tageslicht in den Saal fallen ließ.[34] Daß das Thema der Belichtung von Kuppelräumen die Architekten der Zeit intensiv beschäftigt hat, zeigt in der Nachfolge des augusteischen 'Merkurtempels' in Baiae am Golf von Neapel, bei dem Lichtöffnungen noch in der Kuppelzone liegen, dort exemplarisch

---

29. Zu dem Kuppelraum der 'Großen Thermen' s. H. Winnefeld (1895) *Die Villa des Hadrian bei Tivoli* (JdI Erg.H. 3) 136, Taf. 13 E'; zum 'Heliocamino' s. P. Verduchi (1975), in: *Ricerche sull'architettura di Villa Adriana* (QITA 8) 69ff.
30. Nicht nur aus statisch-konstruktiven Gründen wird man die Pfeilerform gewählt haben, sondern auch weil die als Verschluß notwendigen Fenster zwischen den Pfeilern ungleich einfacher montiert werden konnten als zwischen Säulen.
31. Wie die tonnengewölbten Räume mit eingestellten Frontkolonnaden an der 'Piazza d'Oro' sind die offenen Halbkuppelräume mit Frontkolonnaden ohne statische Funktion im Zusammenhang der Gewölbekonstruktion in unserem Zusammenhang von geringerem Interesse. Das Exedratriclinium des 'Canopus' ist von diesen das prominenteste Beispiel.

32. Die Bezeichnungen Accademia und Tempio di Apollo gehen auf Pläne und Beschreibungen von P. Ligorio und F. Contini zurück, vgl. Kähler 1950 (supra n. 20) 161 Anm. 19.
33. Kähler 1950 (supra n. 20) 75, 128, Taf. 12-13, vgl. Heilmeyer 1975 (supra n. 16) 335ff.
34. Kähler 1950 (supra n. 20) 128. Anders als beim Pantheon, dessen zweigeschossige Binnengliederung Heilmeyer 1975 (supra n. 16) 335ff., überzeugend aus der Fassadenarchitektur ableitet, ist hier die Wandgliederung nicht mehr nur dekorative Blendarchitektur, sondern über die Fenster tatsächlich Mittler zwischen innen und außen. E. Hansen (1960), (AnalRom, Suppl. 1) 48 f. Ähnlich auch der Annexbau am 'Venustempel', F. Rakob (1961), *RömMitt* (68) 114ff.

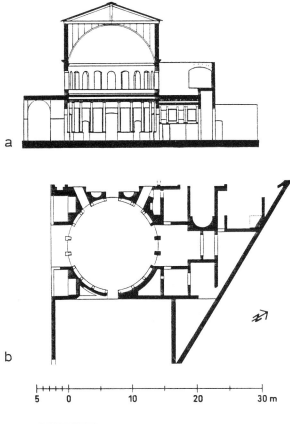

Abbildung 6.4. 'Akademie,' Kuppelsaal; a. Grundriß; b. Rekonstruktionsversuch, Schnitt; c. Innenansicht von Süden. a. Kähler/Verf., b. Kähler (Anm. 33), c. Verf.

der Rundbau des 'Venustempels' aus der 1. Hälfte des 2. Jhs.n.Chr., in bescheideneren Abmessungen auch der zentrale Kurvensaal der Kleinen Thermen in der Villa Hadriana. Zwar fehlt der Säulenunterbau, doch ist an dem Baianer Bau nach bisheriger Kenntnis zum ersten Mal ein massiv konstruierter Kuppelsaal über eine Fenstergadenzone belichtet worden; ein Schema, das für die spätantike Architektur von größter Bedeutung wird.[35] Kähler nimmt über dem Saal des 'Kleinen Palastes' eine Massivkuppel an, doch erscheint diese Lösung in Anlehnung an Rakobs Überlegungen zur 'Piazza d'Oro' auf Grund der verhältnismäßig schlanken Mauern als wenig wahrscheinlich.[36] Eher werden wir–wie möglicherweise auch über dem Zentrum der 'Piazza d'Oro'–mit einem hölzernen Dachstuhl und einer abgehängten Stuckkuppel zu rechnen haben (Abb. 4b).[37]

Ein anderer Weg wurde mit dem von C. F. Giuliani untersuchten Vestibül der 'Piazza d'Oro' beschritten.[38] Auf einem Nischenoktogon, dessen Ecken durch Säulen auf hohen Postamenten markiert waren, ruhte eine achtteilige Schirmkuppel (Abb. 5a-b). Die mit dieser Konstruktion durchaus vorhandene Möglichkeit, unter dem Kuppelfuß Lichtöffnungen oder gar große Aussichtsfenster einzufügen,[39] brauchte bei dem Vestibül nicht genutzt zu werden. Primäre Aufgabe dieses Gebäudes war es nicht, Rundumblick zu gewähren, sondern das Augenmerk des Eintretenden auf das Zentrum der 'Piazza d'Oro' zu kanalisieren. Der Innenraum des Vestibüls lebte jedoch von dem–wenn auch vorgespiegelten–Bild, die auch hier überaus schlanken Säulen trügen das Gewölbe. Eine perfekte Illusion: Der ruinöse Zustand des Gebäudes zeigt, daß die Kuppel ohne Säulen ausreichend Standfestigkeit besaß.[40] Doch weist diese Neuerung der hadrianischen Architektur, die über den Raum- und Konstruktionsgedanken des Pantheon entschieden hinausgeht, den Weg zu den verwandten Raumschöpfungen der Spätantike.

Ein zuvor angesprochenes Thema sei noch einmal aufgegriffen: Überwölbte Säulen- oder Pfeilerportiken kennen wir seit der spätrepublikanischen *caementicium*-Architektur des Fortuna-Heiligtums von Praeneste. Einige spätere, augusteische Beispiele waren oben genannt worden. In flavischer Zeit wurden die Portiken im Untergeschoß der Domus Augustana ge-

35. Vgl. zu diesem Fragenkomplex (supra n. 17): Rakob 1988, 1990; Rasch 1985, 1989; und ergänzend Rasch 1991: 358ff.

36. Zweifel an der von Kähler vorgeschlagenen Massivkuppel äußerte bereits Rakob 1988 (supra n. 17) 297 Anm. 101.

37. Vgl. die Überlegungen H. Bauers zur weit gespannten Überdeckung von Portiken und Exedren des Augustusforum s. o. Anm. 13.

38. C. F. Giuliani (1975), in: Ricerche sull'architettura di Villa Adriana, 9ff., vgl. Heilmeyer 1975 (supra n. 16) 342.

39. Vgl. hierzu Rasch 1985 (supra n. 17) 130.

40. s. Giuliani 1975 (supra n. 38) z.B. 10, Abb. 9.

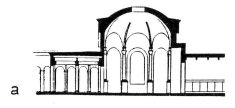

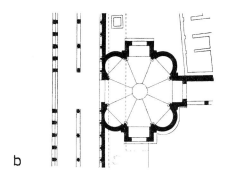

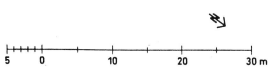

Abbildung 6.5. 'Piazza d'Oro', Vestibül; a. Grundriß; b. Rekonstruktionsversuch, Schnitt. a, b. Giuliani (Anm. 38)

baut. Über schlanken, aber eng stehenden Pfeilern mit ionischen Halbsäulen rekonstruierte G. Wataghin Cantino nach vorhandenen Spuren ein massives Tonnengewölbe (Abb. 6).[41] Dessen konstruktive Einzelheiten können nicht detailliert bestimmt werden, doch erscheint der Vorschlag nach Kenntnis etwa der Horrea Agrippiana wenig problematisch. Unzureichender ist die Ausgangslage für die Rekonstruktion des Obergeschosses. Die anscheinend auch hier nachzuweisende Massivtonne ist über den von Wataghin Cantino angenommenen Säulenarkaden ohne die Verwendung von Eisen kaum denkbar, zumal eine stabilisierende Attika nicht in Betracht gezogen ist.

Die Villa Hadriana nun bietet zu diesen konstruktiven Fragen aufschlußreiches Vergleichsmaterial. Zwei große Peristylanlagen der Villa waren mit überwölbten Portiken ausgestattet, das 'Teatro Marittimo' und die sogenannte Sala dei Pilastri Dorici (Abb. 7-8). Letztere gehörte zu dem nur zu einem geringen Teil erforschten Zentralbereich der Villa, der in un-

mittelbarer Nachbarschaft zum republikanischen Kern mit ganz unterschiedlichen Saalbauten und zugeordneten Gartenzonen repräsentativen Aufgaben diente.[42]

Die 'Sala dei Pilastri Dorici' ist der östliche Hofbereich eines Komplexes, der mit einem zwischengeschalteten Saal und einem westlichen, zweiten Gartenhof in axialer Anordnung eine dreiteilige Einheit bildet. Der große Triclinienbau an der 'Poikile' z.B. ist bei unterschiedlicher Detailausbildung nach demselben Schema entworfen.[43] Abwechslungsreichtum gilt als eines der Charakteristika der Villa, aber abgesehen von dem möglichen Wunsch, Gäste der Residenz mit immer neuen Architekturszenerien zu verblüffen oder vielleicht auch Besucher nach ihrem Rang in entsprechend abgestufter Umgebung empfangen zu können, vermutete B. Andreae sicher richtig einen ganz praktischen Grund für diese Vielfalt: Mehrere Besuchergruppen konnten so gleichzeitig nebeneinander zu Audienzen empfangen werden.[44] Daß nun auch für diesen Zweck nicht ein gleichförmiger Saal neben dem anderen entworfen wurde, liegt auf der Hand.

Die 'Sala dei Pilastri Dorici' variiert das Thema Peristylhof auf eine sehr originelle Weise (Abb. 7a-b). Extrem schlanke Pfeiler tuskanischer Ordnung–in dieser Form konstruktiv einer Säule entsprechend–trugen ein Tonnengewölbe aus *opus caementicium* und setzten damit eine Reihe fort, zu der einige ältere Parallelen schon vorgeführt wurden. Die nicht sicher belegte Form des oberen Peristyls der Domus Augustana und mögliche, aber ebenso wenig sicher nachgewiesene Beispiele der Thermenarchitektur (etwa in den Titusthermen von 60 n.Chr.) außer acht lassend, ist dies in der Villa Hadriana ein erster Peristylbau, bei dem Säulen oder säulenähnlich dimensionierte Stützen mit einem Massivgewölbe kombiniert waren.[45] Die entscheidende Neuerung dabei ist die Tatsache, daß anstelle einer Leichtkonstruktion (wie beim Augustusforum) *caementicium*-Gewölbe auf 'Säulen' ruhten, d.h. schwere Massivpfeiler, wie es sie noch das untere Peristyl der Domus Augustana aufweist, demnach zur Stabilisierung der Konstruktion nicht mehr notwendig erschienen.

Ein zweites Beispiel mit gleichem Konstruktionsprinzip ist in der Villa Hadriana mit der Inselvilla des 'Teatro Marittimo' erhalten (Abb. 8a-b). Auch hier trug die Kolonnade (ionischer Säulen) der rahmenden Ringportikus ein umlaufendes Tonnengewölbe.[46] Noch stärker spürbar als bei der 'Sala dei Pilastri Dorici' war hier eine perfekte Einheit von Plan und Aufriß gefunden worden: dem kreisrunden

41. Wataghin Cantino 1966 (supra n. 4) 37 (Untergeschoß) und 39 (Obergeschoß) dazu Taf. 9.1-2. Die Gewölbzonen zeichnen sich durch rauhe Bruchoberflächen an den Rückwänden der Portiken noch deutlich ab.
42. Kurz beschrieben nur bei Winnefeld 1895 (supra n. 29) 79ff. und S. Aurigemma (1961) *Villa Adriana*, 167ff.

43. Vgl. Kähler 1950 (supra n. 20) 55ff.
44. Vgl. Rahms 1989 (supra n. 1).
45. Eine frühere Variante in der freilich nicht völlig zweifelsfrei erscheinenden Kombination von Säulen und Gewölben könnte in der Basilica Ulpia vorliegen, vgl. o. Anm. 14.
46. Ueblacker 1985 (supra n. 2) 10f. Taf. 1, Beil. 21.

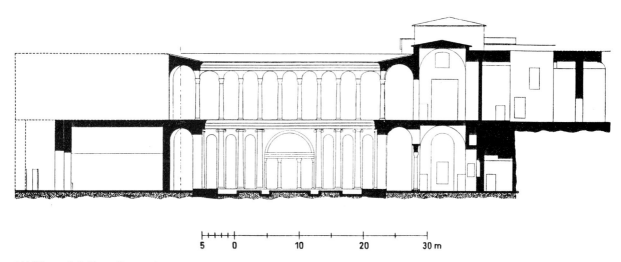

Abbildung 6.6. Rom, Domus Augustana, Rekonstruktionsversuch, Schnitt. Wataghin Cantino (Anm. 40)

Abbildung 6.7. 'Sala dei Pilastri Dorici', überwölbte Portikus; a. eisenverstärkte Architravkonstruktion; b. Rekonstruktionsversuch, Axonometrie. a. Verf., b. Olivier (Anm. 46)

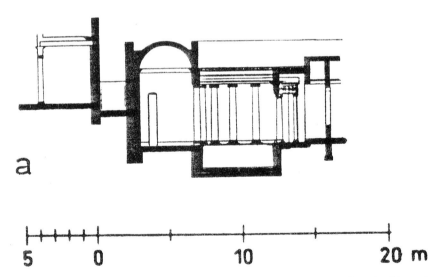

Abbildung 6.8. 'Teatro Marittimo', überwölbte Ringportikus; a. eisenverstärkte Architravkonstruktion; b. Rekonstruktionsversuch, Schnitt. a. Verf., b. nach Ueblacker (Anm. 45)

Grundriß mit der Krümmung der aufgehenden Wände antwortete die Wölbung der Decke, ein räumliches Gebilde, dessen Reiz durch das Spiel des unbegrenzt einfallenden Lichts und zusäztliche Spiegelreflexe des Ringgkanals noch erheblich gesteigert wurde. Nicht zuletzt muß auch der extreme Kontrast zwischen geschlossenen Wandflächen und lichten Kolonnaden ein erstrebter Effekt gewesen sein. Welchem von diesen beiden Bauten der Villa Hadriana die zeitliche Präferenz gehört, läßt sich noch nicht entscheiden. Bezeichnend ist es, daß einer dem privaten, der andere dem repräsentativen Bereich zugeordnet war. In beiden sollte offenbar dieses Raumerlebnis ermöglicht werden.

Waren die Baumeister nun, um dieses Ziel zu erreichen, einfach nur kühner geworden oder hatten sie ein anderes Konstruktionsprinzip gefunden? Die Gebälke der beiden Kolonnaden bestanden nicht aus monolithischen Werkstücken, sondern waren als scheitrechte, im Detail von der üblichen Methode abweichende Bögen konstruiert (Abb. 7b).[47] Auf den Stützen ruhten Werkstücke aus Travertin, dem Material, das in der stadtrömischen Architektur vor allem an Punkten hoher statischer Beanspruchung benutzt wurde. Die Travertinelemente sind mit geneigten Seitenflächen als Widerlager für senkrecht gestellte Ziegelplatten ausgebildet, aus denen der scheitrechte Bogen konstruiert war. Verkleidet mit Marmorplatten unterschied sich diese Konstruktion nur bei näherer Betrachtung von einem massiven Sturz oder Architrav. In einer Reihung von vielen Öffnungen ohne sonderlich massiv ausgebildete Endstützen wären die scheitrechten Bögen in herkömmlicher Art eine stark gefährdete Schwachstelle gewesen, die durch geringstes Ausweichen zum Einsturz der gesamten Dach- und Deckenkonstruktion geführt haben könnte. Diese Gefahr ist offensichtlich erkannt worden. Um die weit aufgelösten Kolonnaden zu einem in sich geschlossenen und damit stabilen statischen System zu machen, wurden die Kämpfersteine aus Travertin durch parallel gelegte Eisenbänder miteinander verbunden. Die Bänder selbst sind zwar verloren gegangen, doch haben sich in den Bettungskanälen an den Seitenflächen und in den Endlöchern an der Oberseite der Kämpfer Reste von Bleiverguß erhalten, mit dem wie bei der Klammer-Dübel-Technik verbleibende Hohlräume verfüllt wurden.[48] Die Konstruktion könnte in heutiger Terminologie als ein unterspannter scheitrechter Bogen bezeichnet werden. An den Auflagern, d.h. den Stützenköpfen waren auf diese Weise ausschließlich Ver-

tikallasten abzuführen, während die Gebälke wie Ringanker wirkten und auf diese Weise auch die Lasten aus den Gewölben aufnehmen konnten. Erst zusätzliches Einfügen von Eisenankern brachte dieser Konstruktion die erforderliche Standfestigkeit.

Ist man einmal auf dieses Konstruktionsdetail aufmerksam geworden, zeigt sich, daß ebenso die Architrave der Säulenapsiden der Annexbauten am 'Canopus' mit Eisenbändern zusammengehalten waren (Abb. 1c, 9).[49] Die Kombination von Säulen und Gewölbe erforderte also auch in diesem Falle zusätzliche Sicherungsmaßnahmen. Sie erscheinen umso notwendiger, als sich die Krümmung und Auskragung der Architrave auf Grund des kleinen Radius der Apsiden verstärkte. Zwar sind die entsprechenden Elemente verloren gegangen, doch muß man sicher bei der 'Lateinischen Bibliothek' und ebenso dem älteren Trikonchos-Bau sowie den Säulenapsiden der 'Piazza d'Oro' mit ähnlichen Hilfsmaßnahmen rechnen.

Nachzuweisen war diese Konstruktion ferner im Südsaal des 'Gartenstadions'.[50] Vor den Fensterpfeilern der Seitenwände dieses Gebäudes standen ionische Säulen, deren Gebälk ebenfalls mit Eisenbändern verstärkt war. Die skelettartig weit aufgelösten Wände mit ihren Kolonnaden trugen hier freilich kein Massivgewölbe, sondern ähnlich wie wir es bei den Portiken des Augustusforums kennengelernt hatten, wohl eher ein Scheingewölbe aus Stuck, das von einem hölzernen Dachstuhl abgehängt war.

Sehr ausgefeilte, bis dahin möglicherweise gar unbekannte Konstruktionsmethoden nutzten die Baumeister der Villa Hadriana, um bestimmte architektonische Zielvorstellungen in die Tat umzusetzen. Gestalterische Vielfalt und die Weiterentwicklung räumlicher Ideen, die das nach öffentlichen und privaten Aufgaben äußerst differenzierte Bauprogramm der Residenz charakterisieren, sind undenkbar ohne gleichzeitigen technologischen Fortschritt. Man darf vermuten, daß offiziellen Besuchern der Villa diese architektonischen Besonderheiten demonstrativ vorgeführt werden sollten, aber ebenso schätzte wohl auch Hadrian persönlich die Neuerungen, die er in seiner intimsten Umgebung, dem Refugium des 'Teatro Marittimo', wirkungsvoll einzusetzen wußte.

Die Villa erweist sich auf diese Weise auch in ihrer entwickelten Form noch als ein architektonisches Experimentierfeld, von dem innovative und in die Zukunft weisende Anregungen ausgingen.

---

47. Ueblacker 1985 (supra n. 2) 39f. vgl. ausführlich A. Olivier (1983), *MEFRA* (95) 940ff. und Hoffmann 1991 (supra n. 12) 101f.

48. A. Hoffmann (1980) *Das Gartenstadion in der Villa Hadriana* (Sonderschriften des DAI Rom, Bd. 4) 26 Anm. 146.

49. Aurigemma 1961 (supra n. 42) 100ff., Fig. 84, doch geht Aurigemma weder auf die Räume im einzelnen, noch auf Details der Konstruktion näher ein.

50. Hoffmann 1991 (supra n. 12) 26.

Abb. 6.9. 'Canopus', westlich flankierender Pavillon mit Säulenapsis, Reste der Gebälkkonstruktion. Verf.

Nach Angaben des Verf. wurden neu gezeichnet, umgezeichnet oder ergänzt von W. J. Brunner: Abb. 1a, c, 2a, 3a, 4a, 8b und von C. Haase: Abb. 1d, 2c.

7

THE ROMAN VILLA AS A LOCUS OF ART COLLECTIONS

Richard Neudecker

My concern on the following pages shall not be so much with pieces of art for art's sake but rather with the physical record of how Roman aristocrats created settings for their cultural self-understanding. They surely had fewer problems in handling their statues than we have in reconstructing their attitudes. After beginning with a search for "typical" attachments and *passepartouts*, scholars often get lost amid multiple meanings, finally taking refuge in supposed ambiguity. Surely, art in Roman villas had manifold aims, but we should try to define specific ideological and material contexts before getting lost in misty vagueness or mental labyrinths, which only reflect the modern scholar's methodological problems.[1]

In our day and age, Roman sculptures have their primary function as *objets d'art* in private and public art collections; they are bought, exhibited and viewed as such. But as soon as archaeologists try to interpret these same statues on the basis of the contexts in which they were originally found (and these are mainly the villas of the Roman upper classes), they arrive at widely varying reconstructions of how statues were evaluated and how they functioned in antiquity. This gave rise to the 19th-century polemic between L. Friedländer and K. F. Hermann (among others) as to whether these statues could have formed parts of authentic art collections.[2] The discussion

has remained open to the present day; there is now a tendency to interpret these works of art in terms of content, attributing to them all-embracing programs, conceived of by the person who commissioned them. On the other hand, there are archaeologists who claim to recognize a predominantly formal reception, who set out to turn these works into objects of a conscious "Kunstgeschmack." Views range from lofty appreciation of aesthetic sensitivity, to disdain for ostentatious display of high-luxury furniture, to derision toward decorative "Disneyland"-like kitsch.

Almost every view, of course, can be supported by appropriate quotations from literary sources. According to Lucian (*Zeux.* 5), the "idiotes" would see only the content, the educated only the form, and only real connoisseurs would see both. Contemporary designations for art collections include such terms as *delectationes*, *ornamentum*, and *voluptas*.[3] Vitruvius rates congruence between content and the statue's architectural environment as more important than quality,[4] and Lucian (*Dom.*) likewise introduces a program based on content. Juvenal (3.212ff.) mocks a situation in which, following a disastrous fire, the victim's friends supply him with money, furniture, books, a few "naked white figures" and *aliquid praeclarum Euphranoris et Policliti*. When perusing the relevant source collections,[5] one is struck by the fact that

1. For the invitation to develop one aspect of my former research, and for the opportunity to become acquainted with recent villa-research not strictly within traditional limits of so-called Kunstarchäologie, I want to express my deep thanks to Prof. A. Frazer. Footnotes are reduced to the most necessary ones; further references and more general background may be gathered from R. Neudecker (1988) *Die Skulpturenausstattung römischer Villen in Italien* (Mainz am Rhein).
2. L. Friedländer (1852) *Über den Kunstsinn der Römer in der Kaiserzeit*; K. F. Hermann (1856) *Über den Kunstsinn der Römer und deren Stellung in der Geschichte der alten Kunst*, reviewed by L. Friedländer (1856) in *Neue Jahrbücher für Philologie* (73) 391ff.; E. Bonaffé (1867) *Les collectionneurs de l'ancienne Rome*; H. Blümner (1873) in R. Virchow und F. v. Holtzendorff (Hrsg.), *Dilettanten, Kunstliebhaber und Kenner im Altertum* (Sammlung ge-

meinverständlicher wissenschaftlicher Vorträge 8) 281ff., 306ff.; A. Furtwängler (1899) *Über Kunstsammlungen in alter und neuer Zeit. Festrede gehalten in der öffentlichen Sitzung der Königlich-Bayerischen Akademie der Wissenschaften zu München*; T. Birt (1902) *Laienurtheil über bildende Kunst bei den Alten* (Marburger akademische Reden 7).
3. Varro, *Rust.* 1.2.10; 1.59.2; Cic., *Orat.* 132; 134; *Tusc.* 5.102; *Att.* 1.7; *Fin.* 2.107; 3.7–8; *QFr.* 3.1.3; Sen., *Dial.* 5.35.5; Tac., *Dial.* 22; Suet., *Tib.* 26; Dio. Chrys. 3.93, 30.28.
4. Vitr. 1.1.5; 1.2.7; 5.5–7.
5. H. Jucker (1950) *Vom Verhältnis der Römer zur bildenden Kunst der Griechen*; G. Becatti (1951) *Arte e gusto negli scrittori latini*; J. J. Pollitt (1966) *The art of Rome c. 753 B.C.–337 A.D. Sources and documents* (Englewood Cliffs, NJ).

these assessments are almost invariably associated with extra-artistic contexts or have been derived from such. The artistic sense of a Pollius Felix in the poems of Statius obtains an *otium cum dignitate* for him and at the same time underscores his high social position relative to the outside world;[6] likewise among the friends of Pliny the Younger, the *philokaloi*.[7] Vice versa, as Philostratus would have it, the collection of masterpiece-copies in the garden of Eucrates corresponds neither to his sense for art (which only spoils it), nor to his social standing.[8]

For this reason, I am convinced that we also must rely on the complete context, i.e., the cultural and architectural environment, if we want to avoid rigid schematicism and arrive at a reasonably historic evaluation. Particularly relevant is the question of whether there was a place for true art collections in Roman villas. I understand this as meaning the assembly of several *pièces d'art* according to specific artistic criteria, and not to mere enthusiasm for an individual masterpiece or for random viewing of art.

We do, of course, know of such "true" collections from literary sources. Caesar had a famous picture collection;[9] Petronius made his hero Encolpius visit such a private picture gallery;[10] *dactyliothecae* were highly appreciated, toreutic work was eagerly collected, exhibited and discussed;[11] Nero used an inherited glass collection for a special exhibition in a private theater.[12] But we learn nothing comparable about sculpture collections. The *statuae plurimae et antiquissimae et pulcherrimae* in the *horrea* of Domitius Tullus served only to make it possible for newly acquired villas to be furnished as quickly as possible.[13] Only collectors of *corinthia* and of paintings, especially those of Parrhasios, could distinguish themselves from the crowd of uncritical art-buyers.[14] Museum-like rooms were accordingly created for pictures, and would seem to have already become standard features, according to what Vitruvius tells us about villa design.[15] Hortensius, for instance, built a special pavilion for a high-priced picture by Kydias.[16] The absolute masterpieces of plastic art, on the other hand, were as far as possible carried about by their owners, as Brutus

did with his *Puer* by Strongylion,[17] or placed on the banqueting table, where they could be viewed more closely, touched or even sniffed. This undoubtedly referred to the greatly desired *corinthia* in the form of small bronzes.[18] Larger individual pieces were kept in intimate rooms with different functions, such as the bedroom in which Tiberius, in the wake of a Pergamene king, placed the *Apoxyomenos* for as long as he was allowed to keep it.[19] A replica of the classical ephebe type called Narcissus was found in an extremely private *cubiculum* of one of Tiberius' villas on the island of Capri.[20] Even a notorious miser purchased and then promptly mistook a statue for a burglar by night.[21] But no specific rooms were provided for extensive assemblages of statues. This purpose was served neither by the so-called *musaea*, as Lugli suspected,[22] nor by the so-called *glyptothecae*, for which B. Tamm wrongly expected that Vitruvius should have provided some prescription.[23]

In order to understand this distinct treatment of the sculpture park within the general reception of Greek art, we must return to the origins of Roman art-collecting and define its place within the social and cultural value system.

It is well known that the first Greek works of art found their way into Roman villas as simple pieces of loot.[24] This purely material appropriation of Greek cultural assets, often former possessions of Hellenistic rulers, was soon followed on the intellectual level by gradually acquired familiarity with Greek literature about art history.[25] One must expect such a transfer to be associated with a thorough shift in the significance of the art. *Otium* thereby became coupled with the cultivation of social prestige and, considering the wealth required for this purpose, could not be separated from luxury and magnificence. Enjoyment of art was based on such firmly established criteria as *veritas*, the canonized ranking order of the great masters, and the quasi-social hierarchy of type and material. This was supplemented by an emotional remembrance of the original places of cult and culture in Greece. In some cases the resulting sculpture collection may have been nothing but a facade;

6. Stat., *Silv.* 2.2.63–72; cf. 1.3.47ff., 3.1.93ff.
7. Pliny, *Ep.* 3.1.9, 3.7.7–9.
8. Philops. 18–20; cf. Philostr., *VA* 5.22.
9. Pliny, *NH* 35.26, 35.83.
10. Petron. 83ff., 104.
11. Hor., *Carm.* 4.8.1ff.; Petron. 50, 52, 73; Sen., *Dial.* 9.1.7–8, 12.11.3; Mart. 3.35, 8.6, 8.34, 8.50(51).1–2, 9.43.5–14, 9.44, 10.87.15f., 12.15.1–2; Stat., *Silv.* 4.6.20–30; Tac., *Dial.* 22; Suet., *Aug.* 70; Lucian, *Sat.* 33; SHA, *Lampr.Heliogab.* 23.4.
12. Pliny, *NH* 37.19; see also Sen., *Ep.* 123.8; Petron. 50.
13. Pliny, *Ep.* 8.18.11.
14. Pliny, *NH* 34.6 f.; Quint., *Inst.* 12.10.3.
15. Vitr. 1.2.7, 6.3.8, 6.4.2, 6.5.2, 6.7.3; see W. Ehlich (1978) *Altertum* (24) 167ff. On guided visits see Varro, *Rust.* 1.2.10; K. Lehmann (1941) *ArtB* (23) 16ff. on Philostr. Jun., *Imag.*
16. Pliny, *NH* 35.130.
17. Pliny, *NH* 34.82 and Mart. 14.171.

18. See for example Strab. 8.6.23; Acro: Hor., *Sat.* 1.4.28; Petron. 50, 52; Pliny, *NH* 34.48, 34.82; Pliny, *Ep.* 2.5.11, 3.1.9, 3.6.1–4. D. Emanuele (1989) *Phoenix* (43) 347ff. considers them to be cheap surrogates.
19. Pliny, *NH* 34.62. Cf. Pliny, *NH* 35.70 for paintings, Paus. 9.35.7 for Attalos.
20. A. Maiuri (1956) *Capri. Storia e monumenti*, 63ff. Abb. 33.
21. Lucian, *Gall.* 29.
22. G. Lugli (1938) in *Atti del IV° Congresso nazionale di studi romani 1935*, 156.
23. B. Tamm (1963) *Auditorium and Palatium* (Stockholm) 125.
24. M. Pape (1975) *Griechische Kunstwerke aus Kriegsbeute und ihre öffentliche Aufstellung in Rom*; G. Waurick (1975) *JRGZM* (22) 1ff.; see e.g., Polyb. 9.10.13 and *Or. frg.* 98 (Malcovati).
25. B. Schweitzer (1932) *Xenokrates von Athen*; F. Preißhofen und P. Zanker (1970–71) *DArch* (4–5) 100ff.

such a collection put together by a newly rich man is criticized by Apollonius of Tyana.[26] In other cases, however, a sculpture collection corresponded to an elevated self-estimation, e.g., Pollius Felix and Vindex.[27]

In order to avoid an excessively pejorative attitude towards our subject, let me remind you of Cardinal Albani. His enthusiasm culminated in the setting up of the first modern collector's villa, but Winckelmann, as the only expert charged with its assembly, also complained about the profane purposes which this museum served by night.[28]

The roots of Roman art reception may explain the manifold locations of the various types of art in the villa. While *pinacothecae* and small art, in keeping with the collection habits of Hellenistic rulers, occupied more or less fixed positions in the villa, major plastic art became inserted in a much wider architectural concept that—in the end—was to correspond to the

absorption of the entire Greek world, so that such *domini* were described as *Attici, Deliaci, Syri*, etc.[29] Just as villa architecture was made up of all the possible and supposedly Greek building forms, we meet sculptures in all parts of villas. In this way, each location was intended to underscore some particular aspect, including—ultimately—pure contemplation of art. But bearing in mind both the conception and the reception, one can hardly expect strict spatial and temporal distinction between furniture and collection.[30] This thesis must be tested against villa ensembles that have either been preserved or handed down to us in literature.

The *Horti* of Rome were—and still are—considered the quintessence of villa luxury.[31] That they were also appropriate places for viewing art is demonstrated by (among other things) the inventory lists to be found in the books of Pliny, e.g., the list of statues in the garden of Asinius Pollio.[32] Alternatively (though not

Figure 7.1. Campana-relief Musée du Louvre Cp 3832. Foto M. Chuzeville.

26. Philostr., *VA* 5.22.
27. See Stat., *Silv.* 2.2, 4.6.
28. See S. Röttgen (1982) in *Forschungen zur Villa Albani*, 156.
29. Cic., *Verr.* 3.9, 5.12.7; *Orat.* 132.
30. In fact, Roman *domini* knew well enough that their villa gardens little resembled a real Greek *gymnasion.* Cicero's academia must have looked quite different from the original. The objects of Roman *otium* pleasures, be they works of art, books, or even ideas, were always Greek in the end; but in handling them the *domini* consciously changed them—if not to say perverted them—into highly valued items of their own cultural life. Juv. 8.100–104 (cf. Hor., *Epist.* 2.1.93–98; Cic., *Verr.* 4.132–134) gives a fine example by tracing back Roman art collecting to the

Greeks—of the classical age, so as to prevent any collision with contemporary realities. In this sense "Greek" was always a fiction. For further discussion see Wallace-Hadrill (this volume); also P. Boyancé and L. P. Wilkinson (1956) in *L'influence grecque sur la poésie latine de Catulle à Ovide* (Fondation Hardt, Entretiens 2) and N. Petrochilos (1974) *Roman attitudes to the Greeks*, 63ff., 197ff.
31. See P. Grimal (1969) *Les jardins romains*² (Paris); id. (1986) in M. Cima and E. La Rocca (eds.), *Le tranquille dimore degli dei. La residenza imperiale degli Horti Lamiani* (Venice).
32. Pliny, *NH* 36.23–25, 36.33 f. See L. Urlichs (1861)*AZ* (19) 143f.; D. Detlefsen (1905) *JdI* (20) 113ff.; cf. inventory lists, G. Nicole (1913) in *Mélanges Holleaux*, 145ff.

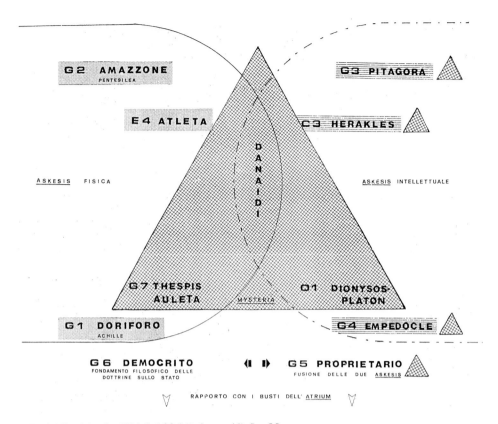

Figure 7.2. Villa dei Papiri, after Wojcik 1986 (infra n. 41) fig. 89c.

exclusively), Pliny offers an interpretation of these same pieces that was surely not an original idea of his age: in terms of content, he held that these statues reflected the character of the temperamental Pollio.[33] Their official name, *monumenta*, clearly points to the origin of these statues as part of Roman war booty. Last but not least, the greater part of the subjects, namely *Maenades, Thyiadae, Sileni, Centauri Nymphas gerentes, Appiades, Hermerotes* and a Dirke group, satisfied the emotional longing for a mythological garden landscape of the *aurea aetas*. Visitors versed in art may have considered the *monumenta* of Asinius Pollio a museum, but the collection doubtless had not been conceived as such.

We are thoroughly well-informed about the way in which Cicero and Verres, an otherwise highly contrasting pair, handled their sculptures. Yet modern evaluations tend to differ very widely.[34] Cicero showed great interest when he was little more than 30 years of age, especially concerning thematic rela-

tionships between the subjects and his own personality. When he desired *quam plurimas*, he really refers to sculptural furnishing.[35] It is a matter of course that he regarded his book collection as more important. But as a 50-year-old, he confessed that—among all the various types of art—he would at the very most collect pictures.[36] Verres, on the other hand, was an enthusiast, perhaps even a fanatic, the whole of his life. His refusal to forego a precious little bronze would eventually cost him his head while in exile at Marseilles.[37] His truly active interest in toreutics in Sicily strikingly resembles the hobby of King Agathocles.[38] His criteria for appropriating major sculptural works, on the other hand, were determined by the ennobling value of the artists' ranking. He literally stuffed his villa in Rome with Greek originals, though he never lived there.[39] Thus, though belatedly, he imitated the violent ap-propriation of art by earlier, aristocratic *triumphatores*.

The effect produced by such crowded porticos is

33. See RE II.2 1589ff., 1600f., s.v. "Asinius" 24 (Groebe). Different views: J. André (1949) *La vie et l'oeuvre d'Asinius Pollio*, 119ff.; J. J. Pollitt (1978) *TAPA* (108) 188.
34. See W. Goehling *De Ciceronis artis aestimatione*, quoted by G. Showerman (1904) *AJPh* (25) 306ff.; W. Echinger (1951) *Ciceros Stellung zur Kunst*, 82–117; H. Bardon (1960) in *Studi in onore di L. Castiglioni* 1, 25ff.; J. Ferguson et al. (1962) *Cicero and the arts. Studies in Cicero*, 129ff.; A. Desmouliez (1962) *Cicéron et son goût*, 589ff.; Pollitt 1978 (supra n. 33) 162; for Verres, see, e.g,

R. Heidenreich (1972) *AA* , 579; Bardon 1960 (supra) 34; G. Zimmer (1989) *Gymnasium* (96) 493ff.
35. Cic., *Att.* 1.4.3 (66 B.C.).
36. Cic., *Fam.* 7.23.3 (58 B.C.).
37. Pliny, *NH* 34.6.
38. Cic., *Verr.* 4.54; Diod. 20.63.
39. Cic., *Verr.* 1.51; cf. Suet., *Iul.* 46 for the Horti Caesaris.
40. C. C. Vermeule (1967) *BMusFA* (65) 182.

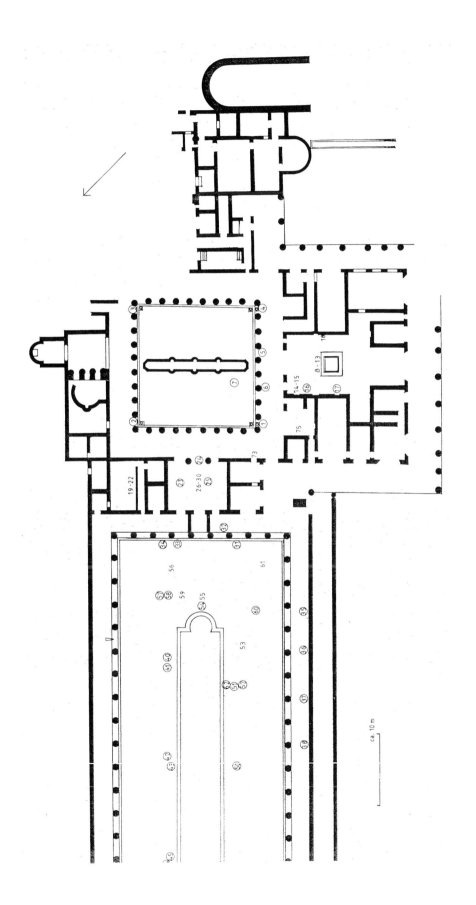

Figure 7.3. Villa dei Papiri, drawn after Comparetti and De Petra 1883 (infra n. 41).

Figure 7.4. Herm bust of Doryphoros M. N. Napoli inv. 4855. Foto DAI Rom Inst. Neg. 64.1804.

Figure 7.5. Herm bust of 'Amazone' M. N. Napoli inv. 4899. Foto DAI Rom Inst. Neg. 85.1031.

demonstrated by a series of Campana reliefs (Fig. 7.1).[40] Statues of athletes, which not only copied famous masterpieces but also defined the portico as *gymnasion*, were arranged side by side with Dionysian hermai from garden landscapes and magnificent marble vessels from the votive inventories of sanctuaries. What at first sight seems to be a closed collection thus proves to be a subtle combination of symbolic evocation and luxurious furnishing.

The best known and richest series of sculptures is that of the Villa dei Papiri near Herculaneum. Not only has it been preserved almost completely, but it is even believed that we can identify its owner or, at least, deduce his intellectual identity from his library. The multiplicity of modern interpretations is therefore all the more surprising.[41] It has been described as an art collection ever since the time of its discovery. This is probably why its architecture served as a model for the Getty Museum.[42] Pandermalis, Sauron, and Wojcik, on the other hand, interpret the collec-

tion as a *Gesamtprogramm* fixed with regard to content. Their methods are essentially the same: seen from a bird's-eye view at a height of about 50 m, the names of the sculptures (or proposals for such names) are combined into a network, even over considerable distances, and this network is somehow supposed to be confirmed by the geometric figures resulting from the connecting lines (Fig. 7.2). It is thus overlooked that not only the design, but also—and above all—the reception, must depend on the everyday (and less frequent) use of the various *loci*. Quintilian even uses such a passing through rooms and perception of the statues placed there as a comparison for mnemotechnics.[43] I should like to pick out a few of these loci and ensembles in order to examine the question of collector activity and intent (Fig. 7.3).[44]

Each visitor probably had to walk through some part of the small peristyle. At the two western corners, arranged on hermai pillars, there stood replicas

41. See D. Comparetti and G. De Petra (1883) *La villa ercolanese dei Pisoni. I suoi monumenti e la sua biblioteca* (Turin); L. Friedländer (1910) *Darstellungen aus der Sittengeschichte Roms in der Zeit von August bis zum Ausgang der Antonine* 8, III 38ff., 93; T. Lorenz (1965) *Galerien von griechischen Philosophen- und Dichterbildnissen bei den Römern*, 10ff.; D. Pandermalis (1971) "Zum Programm der Statuenausstattung in der Villa dei Papiri," *AthMitt* (86) 173ff.; P. Zanker (1979) in F. Zevi (ed.), *Pompei 79* (Naples) 198ff.; G. Sauron (1980) *MEFRA* (92) 277ff.; M. Gi-

gante (1985) *CronErcol* (15) 5ff.; M. R. Wojcik (1986) *La Villa dei papiri ad Ercolano* (Rome), reviewed in *Gnomon* 61 (1989) 59ff.; see also *La Villa dei papiri* (*CronErcol* suppl. 2, 1983).
42. See N. Neuerburg (1975) *Herculaneum to Malibu. A Companion to the Visit of the J. Paul Getty Museum Building.*
43. Quint., *Inst.* 11.2.20.
44. Numbers in the plan correspond to my catalogue numbers; see supra, n. 1.

Figure 7.6. Bust of intellectual(?) M. N. Napoli inv. 5607. Foto DAI Rom Inst. Neg. 85.928.

Figure 7.7. Bust of intellectual(?) M. N. Napoli inv. 5623. Foto DAI Rom Inst. Neg. 85.914.

Figure 7.8. Bust of unknown man M. N. Napoli inv. 5588. Foto DAI Rom Inst. Neg. 85.890.

Figure 7.9. Bust of Thespis M. N. Napoli inv. 5598. Foto DAI Rom Inst. Neg. 85.961.

Figure 7.10. Bust of Ptolemaios II M. N. Napoli inv. 5600. Foto DAI Rom Inst. Neg. 85.939.

Figure 7.11. Bust of Antiochos IV M. N. Napoli inv. 5596. Foto DAI Rom Inst. Neg. 85.950.

of the heads of the Polyclitan Doryphoros (1), and a classical girl type (2) (Figs. 7.4 and 7.5). The former—and, according to J. Frel, also the latter[45]— bears the signature of the Athenian copyist Apollonos, which can be understood as publicity for his workshop. Both pieces must have been readily recognized as citations of Greek masterpieces. The identification of the remaining five bronze busts (3–7) was undoubtedly more difficult. We do not know any of the intellectuals (Figs. 7.6 and 7.7), the identification of the so-called Hellenistic ruler (Fig. 7.8) is extremely hypothetical—he may even be an athlete—and we can be certain only about the Alexandrian music-star Thespis (Fig. 7.9). Even if a program of content may have been intended, this gap makes it impossible for us to pinpoint it. All the heads could never be seen in a single glance, but as the visitor passed in front of or behind them, he would indeed realize that he found himself in the presence of masterpieces (with quality seals) cast in costly bronze, of Greek cultural personalities and possibly even rulers. Detailed examination and contemplation was impossible, above all in the case of the two masterpieces if—as seems like-

ly—these really faced towards the garden and were provided with a fountain basin. Qualitatively, moreover, they are inferior to the other bronzes. The overall impression clearly aims at introducing the visitor into a cultural environment that is defined as Greek and corresponds to the social and intellectual standing of the host. Artistic value is an accessory, and the offering is by no means museum-like.

The goal of a visitor could have been one of two rooms adjacent to the peristyle. A shining statue of Athena (24), arranged between columns on the west side, specially marks an entrance to a room that I will discuss in greater detail below. Upon arrival in the atrium, however, the visitor would have recognized the continuation of the ruler portrait motif, although the heads (16–17), were here placed in wall-niches. Unfortunately, we do not yet know the height of these niches above the floor. But there can be no doubt that this was not an appropriate place for contemplating art, and it may even have been difficult to identify the heads reliably as those of Ptolemy II and Antiochus IV (Figs. 7.10 and 7.11). More emphasis was placed on the elevated atmosphere of an *aula ba-*

---

45. J. Frel (1988) *RStPomp* (2) 267f.

Figure 7.12. Statuette of flute playing satyr M. N. Napoli inv. 5296. Foto DAI Rom Inst. Neg. 85.1496.

Figure 7.13. Statuette of flute playing satyr M. N. Napoli inv. 5296, detail. Foto DAI Rom Inst. Neg. 69.699.

silike, which conveyed a feeling of aristocratic life. (We know the antecedents—a similar portrait gallery from the floating palace of Ptolemy IV.)[46] Yet another element associates this atrium with the imitated status of a Hellenistic ruler, namely a series of precious small bronzes that were put on view here. Two statuettes of satyrs (14–15) with thyrsus and flute must have stood against the wall, possibly on elegant abaci (Figs. 7.12 and 7.13). Collector passion and a feeling for art have always been closely associated with such *corinthia*. In keeping with their significance, we consistently find them in specific places: on precious side tables and large banqueting tables, in treasuries and cupboards.[47] Here again, Roman collectors were surely not unaware of a kind of chronological distortion in attributing these *corinthia* to 5th century masters and the costly material they were made of to the destruction of Corinth in 146 B.C.

What seems surprising at first sight is the third set of objects displayed in the atrium: 11, possibly 15, small Dionysian bronze figures (8–13) surrounded the impluvium as if it were a garden pond (Figs. 7.14–7.16). Their quality is poor in both execution and invention. Strictly speaking, we have variations of only three types. E. Bartman has given us a sensitive interpretation of similar sets of mirror replicas, considering them to be the expression of refined artistic criteria of *varietas et dispositio*.[48] However, the excavation reports of the Villa dei Papiri seem to exclude any symmetrical arrangement. Thus we may rather look back to the characteristics of this thematic genre, namely desire for multiplicity, for variation in external features, and for the small format which optically enlarges the distance from the beholder. This is exactly in keeping with the spectrum of meaning found in literary descriptions. There we can see just

46. Ath. 5.204e–206c; cf. Ath. 5.196a–197c and Pliny, *NH* 35.4–5. See Pandermalis 1971 (supra n. 41) 187. For "royal halls," see Hor., *Carm.* 2.18; Strab. 5.2.5, 5.3.12; Vitr. 5.7.9, 6.5.2.
47. For cupboards, see *NSc* (1907) 556f.; *NSc* (1929) 404ff.; *AA*

(1930) 396. For tables, see supra, n. 18. For treasuries, see Petron. 73.
48. E. Bartman (1988) "*Decor et duplicatio*: pendants in Roman sculptural display," *AJA* (92) 211–225. See Varro, *Ling.* 9.33.46 and E. Lefèvre (1977) *Gymnasium* (84) 533ff.

Figure 7.14. Bronze statues of Dionysiac boys M. N. Napoli inv. 5028/5030. Fotos DAI Rom Inst. Neg. 39.172, 39.173.

Figure 7.15. Statue of Silen M. N. Napoli inv. 5007. Foto DAI Rom Inst. Neg. 85.1469.

how popular this sculpture genre was in villa *otium*, where a Dionysian-bucolic setting was used to evoke current concepts of happiness which were dream-like or, at least, consciously unreal.[49] The portion of private life thereby affected usually was spent resting on the *clinae* of dining rooms or in rooms intended for enjoying a view. Here just such a room was situated immediately after the atrium, where the eyes could sweep south to the horizon of the sea, and back to the central part of the atrium, which in this setting fulfills an entirely different function. Contemplation was collective and from a distance, never in detail.

The peristyle was in every sense a constitutive element of Roman villa architecture. It is well known how intimately emotional and intellectual memories and stimuli were associated with this architectural form. One need only think of sanctuaries and similar large public buildings, or of the gymnasium as a place of Greek culture par excellence: the inner room was taken up by a garden, which recalls the temenos gardens and evokes sacral-idyllic landscapes, ultimately even *paradeisoi*. What is here conveyed by architectural language had a parallel in the display of

Figure 7.16. Statue of boy with vase M. N. Napoli inv. 5029. Foto DAI Rom Inst. Neg. 85.1475.

49. See L. Beaujeu (1955) *La religion romaine à l'apogée de l'Empire*, 80ff., 109; E. Dwyer (1982) *Pompeian domestic sculpture* (Rome) 123ff.; J. Raeder (1983) *Die statuarische Ausstattung der Villa Hadriana bei Tivoli*, 293ff.; cf. Catull. 64.384–396.

Figure 7.17. Statues of five "Dancers" M. N. Napoli inv. 5604–5605, 5619–5621. Foto DAI Rom Inst. Neg. 83.2142.

Figure 7.18. Statue of a "Dancer," detail of inv. 5621. Foto DAI Rom Inst. Neg. 83.1785.

Figure 7.19. Statue of a "Dancer," detail of inv. 5620. Foto DAI Rom Inst. Neg. 85.542.

statues of athletes, poets and thinkers, Dionysian and bucolic figures, hunting animals, etc., all pointing in the same direction.[50] Out of this variegated fabric of sculptural ensembles, I will pick out a few that seem to come closest to a predominantly aesthetic form of art reception.

Karl Weber found four of the five female "dancers" (35–39) at regular intervals in front of the rear wall of the south portico (Figs. 7.17–7.19). I deem Sgobbo's highly ingenious reconstruction of their presumed locations to be mistaken.[51] He suspects that they originally stood in or at the edge of the small *piscina*. They were found, so he holds, in a state of storage prior to their final removal. However, such bay-like enlargements of *piscinae*, for which there are numerous examples, were not an invention for accommodating statues, but for breeding fish.[52] What remains unclear, above all, is how the 'dancers' could have stood there: if above the semicircles, we should expect solid bases instead of hollow spaces; arguing from the dimensions (35–41 cm for the bases, 59 cm for the niches according to Sgobbo) they must have stood in the water. But even for this subject one can hardly justify a footbath. Their hypothetical identification as Danaidae, moreover, would not presuppose any water at all, for the Danaidae in the porticos of the Apollo sanctuary on the Palatine, the classical model, surely all stood on dry land. However, precisely this reference to the sanctuary of Apollo, as Zanker has pointed out,[53] would provide a good explanation for an original location in the south portico of the villa. And even if a visitor could not concretely recall the Apollo sanctuary, a Roman art tourist, irrespective of whether he had visited Sicily, Knidos, Delphi or Samos, would in any case be familiar with the image of the massed and often rather similar votive statues in the *stoai* of the *temenoi*.[54] That this evocation was intentional is made clear by the emphatically precious appearance of the bronze statues with their rich inlay work.[55] A similar effect, though closer to reality, must have been produced by the original votive statues that, looted from the sanctuaries to which they belonged, stood side by side in the porticos of Verres' villas. In Herculaneum, where no art looting was involved, the same effect appears artificially arranged. Only in their totality, therefore, do these statues suggest a symbolic art collection and a privatization of the famous public museums.[56]

While such galleries must therefore be regarded as vehicles for claims to nobility, effective contemplation of art would have been visualized right from the start in the case of another group in the Villa dei Papiri. Let us continue to consider the "temenos garden." Plutarch tells us graphically, unconsciously exposing some trivialities, how Roman art tourists moved in Greek sanctuaries as if they were public museums.[57] Indeed, even Virgil makes Aeneas behave in Carthage like an educated Roman on his Grand Tour.[58] In the Villa dei Papiri we find two pairs of bronze busts (57, 58, 60, 61) arranged on pillars on the narrow east side of the garden. In the northern corner are an Apollo by the side of a lady, probably Artemis; two busts of Heracles reside in the other corner (Figs. 7.20–7.23). Wojcik's claim to recognize relations between their contents can neither be confirmed nor rejected.[59] This arrangement of four heads appeals rather to our knowledge of the history of art, and therefore necessarily also to that of Roman beholders, the sourcebooks being more or less the same. In the case of the northern pair, a markedly "archaic" Apollo stands in sharp counterpoint to a late classical work of art, so that we here may compare phases of style that could be interpreted even with respect to the gods that they represent. In the other corner, the Heracles by Polyclitus is placed opposite one by Skopas, so that the contrast might raise the question as to which period represented the god more appropriately. These epochs of style were familiar to educated Romans, if only from their textbooks of rhetoric, as was also the method of direct comparison. One ought to compare the lives of two personalities, so Plutarch tells us, in just the same way as one would compare two works of art.[60] The owner must have known that these four pieces lent themselves to such a discussion and must have planned the arrangement. We may therefore rightfully speak of them as a small art gallery; but once again a neutral museum environment is lacking, replaced by the

---

50. Cf., e.g., K. M. Swoboda (1919) *Römische und romanische Paläste* 35; K. Schefold (1954) in *Neue Beiträge zur Klassischen Altertumswissenschaft. Festschrift B. Schweitzer* 301; H. Lauter (1968) *AA* 626ff.; B. S. Ridgway (1971) *Hesperia* (40) 338ff.; Zanker 1979 (supra n. 41) 201; H. v. Hesberg (1980) *RömMitt* (87) 271; Sauron 1980 (supra n. 41) 290ff.
51. I. Sgobbo (1971) *RendNap* (46) 51ff., 115ff.
52. See A. G. McKay (1975) *Houses, villas and palaces in the Roman world* (London) 53.
53. Zanker 1979 (supra n. 41) 199; id. (1983) in *Città e architettura nella Roma imperiale* (*AnalRom* suppl. 10) 27ff.
54. Strab. 14.1.14; Pliny, *NH* 36.20; Plut., *Mor.* 394–402B, 818D; for further sources see Friedländer 1910 (supra n. 41) I 389ff.;

cf. Ridgway 1971 (supra n. 50).
55. See W. Trillmich (1973) *JdI* (88) 256ff.
56. Cf. Cic., *Verr.* 4.126; Cic., *Tusc.* 5.102; Pliny, *NH* 36.27. For "museums," see D. E. Strong (1973) in *Archaeological theory and practice. Essays presented to W. F. Grimes*, 247ff.; R. Chevallier (1989) *Cahiers de l'Académie d'architecture*, 104ff.
57. See, e.g., Plut., *Mor.* 394–402B; *Aetna* 594.
58. Verg., *Aen.* 1.494f.
59. Wojcik 1986 (supra n. 41) 87ff. I cannot follow her combinations.
60. Plut., *Mor.* 243C. See also Dio. Chrys. 12.53; Plut., *Mor.* 575B.

*Figure 7.20. Bust of archaistic Apollo M. N. Napoli inv.
5608. Foto DAI Rom Inst. Neg. 85.1039.*

*Figure 7.21. Bust of Artemis M. N. Napoli inv. 5592. Foto
DAI Rom Inst. Neg. 85.1013.*

*Figure 7.22. Bust of Polyclitan Heracles M. N. Napoli inv.
5610. Foto DAI Rom Inst. Neg. 85.1018.*

*Figure 7.23. Bust of Heracles by Scopas M. N. Napoli inv.
5594. Foto DAI Rom Inst. Neg. 85.900.*

pseudo-temenos, which A. Rauveret recently described—appropriately so—as a "lieu de mémoire privilégié."[61]

Different considerations apply in the case of works of art put on display individually, for which locations seem to have been defined more specifically. We are led to this conclusion by the description of a unpreserved statue base with the remnants of a Greek artist's inscription inlaid in bronze from the area of the library.[62] It is surely not a matter of chance that in Pergamon the royal library was associated with a small statue gallery.[63]

Back in the small peristyle the gilded statue of Athena Promachos (24), as *insigne*, draws attention to

the so-called tablinum (Fig. 7.24), where practically all the family portraits of the villa were found. This is probably the same kind of room as that in which Brutus, the murderer of Caesar, had his family trees affixed. He called it his "Parthenon" and thus marked it as sacred,[64] though as a typical representative of phillaconism,[65] he can hardly be expected to have had a personal liking for Athens. That a replica of the Herculanean Promachos was found on the Acropolis at Athens, perhaps even the original, seems to confirm this association.[66] In any case, the *dominus* consciously put a private *sacrarium* on par with a renowned temple. Perhaps people even recalled that the Greek temple, and particularly the Parthenon,

Figure 7.24. Statue of archaistic Athena M. N. Napoli inv. 6607. Foto DAI Rom Inst. Neg. 83.2119.

61. A. Raveret (1987) in *Pline l'Ancien, témoin de son temps* (Conventus Pliniani internationalis Namneti 22–26 Oct. 1985 habiti acta) 431ff. See also Philostr., *VA* 5.22. For a similar arrangement in Pompeii, see Zanker 1979 (supra n. 41) 182f.
62. Comparetti and De Petra 1883 (supra n. 41) cat. 1096.
63. E. V. Hansen (1971) *The Attalids of Pergamon*, 316ff., 353ff., 366ff.; V. M. Strocka (1981) *Gymnasium* (88) 298ff.

64. Cic., *Att.* 13.40.
65. Cic., *Att.* 15.9.
66. See M. Brouskare (1986) in *Archaische und klassische griechische Plastik* (Akten des internationalen Kolloquiums vom 22.–25. April in Athen 2) 77ff., but also M. Fullerton (1989) *AA*, 57ff. Cf. Aristid., *Or.* 1.354; Livy 45.27.11.

was not only a temple, but also a treasury. It does not matter how precise may have been a person's recollections of a general kind or of his own years of study in Athens,[67] but a sacral room as the recipient of the most treasured votives would have been familiar. It is therefore in this sense that one must understand the collocation of the bronze head (30c) of a young man in a refined and eclectic mixture of styles and of a late classical athlete's head (26) in the "Parthenon" of the Villa dei Papiri (Figs. 7.25 and 7.26). As such works increase in number, the *sacrarium*, which always remains such, will increasingly assume the character of a museum, e.g., the private *sacellum* of Heius, which in Cicero's days had long since become the famous private museum of Messina, and which Cicero himself, given the Caryatids to be found there, immediately associated with the recollection of the Acropolis at Athens.[68]

The Villa dei Papiri may well give us an idea of how all the costly and refined works of marble and bronze could also be understood as works of art within a wider frame of architectural environments and intellectual climates. The possibilities of combination were variegated; nevertheless, they were well-defined. In the end, sculptures were always intended to promote the prestige of the villa owner and to stimulate his own enjoyment. A personal contemplation of art would, most likely, be directed toward individual pieces, but, in most cases, it was directed not toward sculpture but toward other types of art. True collector activity was overlaid or codetermined by symbolic value judgments, and therefore never required a canonization of specific museum rooms. This may perhaps be one of the reasons for the somewhat unclear distinction between copies and originals in Roman art.

There remains one aspect of the modern definition of an art collector that I have omitted, namely the manner in which he acquires his pieces, which always provides a great deal of insight. At this crucial point, we might be able to see most clearly both his zeal and his intention. We shall become more certain in our assessment of the Villa dei Papiri as soon as we are able to identify the groups of workshops concerned, and the placement of the works they created for that villa.[69]

Figure 7.25. Bust of youth M. N. Napoli inv. 5633. Foto DAI Rom Inst. Neg. 85.1003.

Figure 7.26. Bust of youth M. N. Napoli inv. 5614. Foto DAI Rom Inst. Neg. 85.1009.

67. See Cic., *Brut.* 245, 307, 312, 315f.; for Romans as ephebes in Athens see, e.g., IG 2² (1916) no. 1008 line 128.
68. See Zimmer 1989 (supra n. 34).
69. Apart from the above quoted works on single sculptures (Frel, Pandermalis, Trillmich, Zanker) see also L. Forti (1959) *RendNap* (34) 63ff.; B. S. Ridgway (1967) *Antike Plastik* (7) 60; V. Kruse-Berdolt (1975) *Kopienkritische Untersuchungen zu den Porträts des Epikur, Metrodor und Hermarch*, passim.

8

PROSPECTS OF PATRONAGE: REALISM AND *ROMANITAS* IN THE ARCHITECTURAL VISTAS OF THE 2ND STYLE

Ann Kuttner

The Roman villa was a phenomenon whose dimensional cooordinates were both social and material. The material dimension had two aspects: the lands in which the villa was situated as locus of agricultural activity, and the house constructed for the residence of the land's *dominus* or *domina*,[1] the villa owner, occasional or otherwise. A productive estate could exist without any form of an elaborated owner's residence, as in the case of *latifundia* holdings; a villa-style residence could exist without a substantial estate behind it, for residence in a pleasing extra-urban landscape (e.g., some shore and suburban villas). Here the term *villa* is applied to an owner's residence whose planned construction lifts it above the level of a simple farmhouse, and which is situated on an active estate, mono-crop or otherwise. This paper interprets some decorative habits of the villa owner; any functioning villa had a sizable population, but the choice of its architectural and esthetic dispositions had no more to do with the workers than did any other major dispositions on the estate.

The striking thing about the developed Roman villa, from the Republican period on, is the combination of working farm and fine residence, a context that fused the persona of farmer with that of a *civis* with urban rights and responsibilities (and predilections). Romans did not worry about fusing such multiple identities, but simply assumed that in any individual of means they would co-exist—however schizophrenically—as complementary aspects of personality. Such a "collage" attitude governed the disposition of elite careers, whether over a long span or over the course of a single day; an individual was expected to switch both abruptly and gracefully among the characters of soldier and magistrate, political patron and *amicus*, legal prosecutor and legal defender, staunchly Roman man of action and Philhellenic litterateur, orator and dinner host. An identity as rural landowner might indeed be held up as a virtuous reproach to a life of urban dissipation or over-ambition. However, at least for the governing classes, to foreswear one's urban identity could be held equally blameworthy, as one can see in the text traditions on aristocrats such as Lucullus and Tiberius, who withdrew in pique from public life in too absolute a fashion. For a paradigm of the Roman demand for a balanced collage of personal roles, Lucullus' reshaping of Epicurean ethics is a most striking exemplum: what in the Greek world was a philosophy of withdrawal from public life was promulgated by the Late Republican

---

1. In this paper I will use *dominus* to define the persona of one controlling the material frameworks of the family enterprise; when active patrons, women seem to have conducted themselves in the Republic after patterns for *otium* and *negotium* set by male citizens, rather than evolving any distinctively female form of conduct. Women were often of course engaged in the active disposition of estates. Cornelia, the mother of the Gracchi, is a good example of the widowed mother taking over the functions of a male head of family; Cicero's letters show also

how married women like his wife Terentia could act as independent partners in estate administration on behalf of the corporate enterprise of the individual Roman gens, just as Fulvia and Octavia were to act for their husband Antony at roughly the same period. And married women could autonomously control their own properties and slave *familiae*, Livia's holdings at Primaporta (and presumably her house on the Palatine next to Augustus') were her own responsibility.

poet as a way of life in symbiosis with the actvities of a noble (Memmius) actively engaged in the great imperialistic enterprise of the 1st century B.C.

Other contributors to this project look at the material constructions of the villa to understand the conceptual underpinnings of the villa estate and the mentalities of villa owners. They all delineate the deep involvement of self on the part of the landowning class in its estates, and the expression of social identity in the forms of the architecturally developed villa residence.[2] Villa house plans themselves articulate family and class identities in their traditional division into the *pars rustica* and the *pars urbana*, physical spheres that are coterminous but absolutely distinct, occupied by sharply distinct classes and the locus of very distinct activities and modes of life. The *dominus* might supervise and even help out in the *pars rustica* with the estate's productive activities. But the *pars urbana* was for the sole residence of the *dominus*' family, and the layout of its rooms bears out the evidence of its appellation—the *dominus* lived in his quarters as one would live in the city. It's the *pars urbana* that gets the art—the decorations and architecture that served convivial activities, and that provided both esthetic and (as in the bath or built *ambulatio*) physical pleasures. That provision of social pleasures as an expected function of the villa is what linked it most closely to the culture of the city,[3] and it is what makes relevant those papers in this volume that examine the place of the visual arts in the Roman *villa* and its activities.

I will examine a decorative fashion of fine villas in the latter part of the exuberant formative period of the Roman "great house," that is, during the Late Republic from about 80–20 B.C. At this time wall-painting ateliers developed in Latium and Campania a fairly coherent system of trompe l'oeil representation, characterized by the almost ubiquitous presence of fictive architecture as primary subject or frame, which we call the 2nd (Pompeian) Style. The development of the great urban or country house around Rome is part of a Hellenistic trend more general in the Mediterranean, and the architectural roots of the Roman villa in Hellenistic Greek and Italian palaces and in fine house construction are well documented.[4] The articulation in the Late Republic and early Empire of a distinctively Roman language for magnificent domestic architecture, from a mixed Italian and East Greek inheritance, is one of the most interesting chapters in Roman cultural history.[5] The appreciation and interpretation of 2nd Style wall painting are deeply implicated in this phase of Roman culture. The styles of the Central Italian workshops have been shown to have affinities to both Italian and East Mediterranean source architecture and painting styles. This style of wall decoration clearly has affinities in the Greek-speaking Mediterranean. Its Central Italian variant is just as clearly the product of a close-knit, self-referential workshop tradition; thus, just as with Roman portraiture of the 2nd–1st century B.C., it is legitimate to discuss these products of a larger tradition as a distinctive, Roman artistic class.[6] In the context of this volume's theme, I want to look at the systems of architectural painting that so dominate the corpus of 2nd Style interiors.[7]

My purpose is not to provide a survey of architectural motifs,[8] or to set up developmental chronologies, or to list comprehensively examples of 2nd Style

2. See A. Wallace-Hadrill, "The Social Structure of the Roman House," *PBSR* 66 (1988) 43–97; J. Clarke, "Space and Ritual in Domus, Villa and Insula, 100 B.C.–A.D. 250," ch. 1 in *The Houses of Roman Italy 100 B.C. –A.D. 250: Ritual, Space ,and Decoration* (Berkeley 1991); T. P. Wiseman, "*Conspicui postes tectaque digna deo*: The Public Image of Aristocratic and Imperial Houses in the Late Republic and Early Empire," *L'urbs: Espace urbain et histoire (Ier siècle av. J.C. —IIer siècle ap. J.C.), CEFR* 98 (1987) 393–413.
3. A good introduction is R. Ling, "The Arts of Living," in *The Oxford History of the Classical World: The Roman World* (1986/1988) 308–337.
4. The best discussion is by E. La Rocca, "Il lusso come espressione di potere," pp. 3–52 in *Le tranquille dimore degli dei. La residenza imperiale degli horti Lamiani. Roma, maggio-settembre 1986. Campidoglio, Palazzo dei Conservatori,* M. Cima and E. La Rocca eds. (Vicenza 1986).
5. On the arts in general in Hellenistic Italy and the formation of Republican visual culture, see: "Hellenismus," in *Mittelitalien. Kolloquium in Göttingen . . . 1974,* P. Zanker ed., Abh. Gtt. (1976); *Ricerche di pittura ellenistica. Lettura e interpretazione della produzione pittorica dal Iv. secolo A.C. all'ellenismo (Quaderni dei Dial. d'Arch.* 1; Rome 1985); *L'art décoratif à Rome la fin de la République et au début du Principat, CEFR* 55 (1981); *Kaiser Augustus und die verlorene Republik.* (Berlin 1988).

6. This conclusion emerges even from the most recent, polemically "anti-Roman" work on 2nd Style architectural wall painting, R. A. Tybout's *Aedificiorum figurae. Untersuchungen zu den Architekturdarstellungen des frühen Zweiten Stils* (Amsterdam 1989).
7. Wall-painting styles seem to have been fairly consistent throughout the region; this mitigates the problem that accidents of preservation mean that much extant painting comes from townhouses in Pompeii, and occasionally from Rome. For a bibliography to civic architecture and individual houses at Pompeii, refer to L. Richardson, Jr., *Pompeii: An Architectural History* (Baltimore 1988). For public monuments at Rome, see: (for ancient sources) S. B. Platner and T. Ashby, *A Topographical Dictionary of Ancient Rome* (London 1929), and, for basic references and illustrations, E. Nash, *Pictorial Dictionary of Ancient Rome,* vols. 1 and 2, 2nd ed. (London 1968).
8. See Tybout (supra n. 6); J. Engemann, *Architekturdarstellungen des frühen zweiten Stils. Illusionistische römische Wandmalerei der ersten Phase und ihre Vorbilder in den realen Architektur, RM-EH* 12 (1967); W. Ehrhardt, *Stilgeschichtliche Untersuchungen an römischen Wandmalereien der späten Republik bis zur Zeit Neros* (1987); B. Wesenberg, "Römische Wandmalerei am Ausgang der Republik: der Zweite pompejanische Stil," *Gymnasium* 92 (1985) 470–488; K. Fittschen, n. 15.

painting.[9] A number of essays and handbooks[10] can do that for the curious reader. Several villas in particular—the Villa of P. Fannius Synistor at Boscoreale;[11] the Villa dei Misteri at Pompeii,[12] and the 2nd Style rooms of the great residence at Oplontis[13]—make a good introduction to their range and character.[14] I want to address instead some more slippery conceptual problems: What is architectural painting doing in 2nd Style country houses? What did it represent literally and figuratively for the patron and viewer? What tastes might it have satisfied in Republican culture—the taste for the obtrusively Greek or that for a cultured *Romanitas*? This kind of study cannot explain the inner workings of an estate, or its economic relations to the world about it. What it can do is examine some of the cultural habits of the landowning class and, by extension, illuminate some of the concepts and values animating any landowner's social choices, esthetic options included.[15] The points made here are suggested for general application; in this restricted essay more than a limited number of illustrative examples would be superfluous.

The great painted rooms of 2nd Style houses, diverse in content, consistently use highly realistic, often trompe l'oeil styles of representation. Not just their framing architecture, but also their other subjects raise much-debated questions about imitation, synthesis, and creation in Roman art. Sometimes Hellenistic palace painting does seem to have supplied some prototypes, as in the figural paintings copied for the great salon at Boscoreale (villa of P. Fannius Synistor), which arranges elements of an Antigonid royal cycle from Macedon. At other times, the aim is to represent a Roman physical world, most notably in the genre of realistic landscape architecture depictions, as in the Garden Room of Livia's villa at Primaporta,[16] the "poetry pavilion" on Maecenas' suburban estate at the edge of Rome[17] or in room (M) at Boscoreale at the center of the side walls and on the end wall.[18] Painterly realism is applied to evoke real objects in an arrangement plausible to contemporary Romans, often an ephemeral arrangement like the hanging of garlands, the placement of bowls of fruit on ledges, or the installation of masks, painted tablets (*pinakes*), or sculpture.

Plainly, the architectural vistas and frames of the 2nd Style intend to display the qualities of both plausibility and palpability, shared by depictions of Roman subjects such as gardens and garlanded rooms, though with a somewhat fantastic extension of forms and materials. But do they replicate Roman or Greek Hellenistic architecture? The air of sumptuousness conveyed by the architectures of the great dining and reception rooms of this style does seem part of a Hellenistic culture of civic and regal magnificence, which in Late Republican Italy is translated to private construction. As in the development of the domestic painting and sculpture collection, 2nd Style wall painting can be seen to document the effects of the Roman conquest of the Eastern Mediterranean

9. The best comprehensive survey of the period up to the eruption of Vesuvius is A. Barbet's *La peinture murale romaine. Les styles décoratifs Pompiens* (Paris 1985)—ch. 2 covers the 2nd Style; the review of this by E. W. Leach in *AJA* 91 (1987) 342–344 surveys analytical trends. Barbet's isometric house plans, which map all areas of painted decor, are especially useful. See also the bibliographic article by H. Mielsch, "Wandmalerei der Prinzipätszeit," *ANRW* II 12.2 (1980) 157–264.
10. See R. Ling, *Roman Painting* (Cambridge 1990); Clarke (supra n. 1) 41ff.; H. G. Beyen, *Die pompeijanische Wanddekoration vom zweiten bis zum vierten Stil*, vols. 1 and 2 (The Hague 1938/1950). Illustrations and chronological surveys: D. Strong, *Roman Art*, 2nd ed. (Pelican Books 1988); B. Andreae, *The Art of Rome* (New York 1977); R. Bianchi Bandinelli, *Rome. The Center of Power: Roman Art to A.D. 200* (New York 1970); the chapter by J. Liversidge in *A Handbook of Roman Art: A Comprehensive Survey of All the Arts of the Roman World*, M. Henig, ed. (Ithaca 1983); E. Simon, *Augustus. Kunst und Leben um die Zeitenwende* (Mainz 1986) 182–210. Painting is discussed in any survey of Pompeii: cf. T. Kraus and L. von Matt, *Pompeii and Herculaneum: The Living Cities of the Dead* (New York 1975); A. Claridge and J. B. Ward-Perkins, *Pompeii A.D. 79*, vols. 1 and 2 (1979). Much from the Bay of Naples ended up in the Naples Museum; see *Le Collezioni di Museo Nazionale di Napoli I. I mosaici, le pitture, gli oggetti di uso quotidiano, gli argenti, le terracotte invetriate, i vetri, i cristalli, gli avori* (Rome 1986); M. Borda, *La Pittura Romana* (1958); the numerous books on paintings from Pompeii by K. Schefold.
11. See M. L. Anderson, *Pompeian Frescoes in the Metropolitan Museum of Art* (New York 1987; = *MMAB* 1987/88); B. Andreae in *Kaiser Augustus* (supra n. 5) 278–282; K. Fittschen and H. Borbein in *Neue Forschungen in Pompeji*, B. Andreae and H. Kyrieleis, eds. (Recklinghausen 1975).

12. Clarke (supra n. 1) 94–111; A. Maiuri, *La Villa dei Misteri* I-II (Rome 1931).
13. See Clarke (supra n. 1) 113–123; A. de Franciscis, *The Pompeian Wall Paintings in the Roman Villa of Oplontis* (Heidelberg 1975); id., "La Villa romana di Oplontis," *Neue Forschungen in Pompeji* (1975) 9–38.
14. See also: the late 2nd Style House of Augustus on the Palatine in Rome, G. Carettoni, *Das Haus des Augustus auf dem Palatin* (Mainz 1983), and in *Kaiser Augustus* (supra n. 5) 287–290; the transitional 2nd to 3rd Style suburban villa of Agrippa at Rome, under the Villa Farnesina, *Museo Nazionale Romano. Le Pitture* II.1 *Le Decorazioni della Villa Romana della Farnesina*, I. Bragantini and M. de Vos, eds. (Rome 1982).
15. This author is engaged in writing a monograph on the great figure-painted rooms of the 2nd Style house, to which this essay is ancillary. A paradigmatic discussion of the 2nd Style as a cultural phenomenon remains K. Fittschen, "Zur Herkunft und Entstehung des 2. Stils. Probleme und Argumente," *Hellenismus in Mittelitalien* (1976) 539–563.
16. G. Calci and G. Messineo, *La Villa di Livia a Primaporta* (1984); M. Gabriel, *Livia's Garden Room at Primaporta* (1955); R. Förtsch, "Ein *Aurea Aetas* Schema," *RM* 96 (1989) 333–345; D. Strong (1988) sv. figs. 47–48.
17. Garden painting: see Barbet (supra n. 9) 126–127, 136–139, 164–165 (garden rooms); known paintings tabulated in H. Eschebach et al., *Die Stabianer Thermen in Pompeii* (Berlin 1979) 92. The Auditorium of Maecenas: M. Cima in *Tranquille dimore* (supra n. 4) 43, 45, figs. 22–23, 29; M. de Vos, "Funzione e decorazione dell' Auditorium de Mecenate," *Roma capitale 1870-1911. L'archeologia in Roma tra sterro e scavo*, G. Sartorio and L. Quilici, eds. (1983) 231–247.
18. M. L. Anderson, see n. 11.

upon the conquerors.[19] Much of the literature on 2nd Style architectural painting has focused on its postulated character as an imitation of Greek, rich architecture; those who look for the mentalité to be read in the *floruit* of this style, take it for a transcription, either literal or imagined, of (Greek) palace architectures, executed for a proudly conquering or wistfully covetous clientele.[20] But an air of sumptuousness is one thing; strict iconographic derivation is another! Recent research, indeed, has begun to show just how closely some of the seemingly more extravagant features of 2nd Style walls corresponded to the actual deployment of metal and glass inlays in the wealthier suburban villas of Rome.[21] Although those fashions themselves had roots in Italian and East Mediterranean royal decor, the fact remains that the wall paintings did refer to practices observable in the actual commissions of those at the very pinnacle of the Roman state. These sumptuous visions are often of architectural arrangements, which must have seemed authorized by contemporary Roman practice, in the eyes of their Roman patrons—certainly these architectural iconographies fused Eastern Mediterranean and Roman traditions, but the Roman side of the equation needs to be stressed.

First of all, any 2nd Style room, when viewed (as it ought) as a whole, appealed to deeply ingrained habits of viewing set by an Italian, not Greek, esthetic. Most rooms were arranged with mirror-image side walls framing the end opposite the door, an arrangement to which the painted architectural frames were crucial; the resulting A/B/A pattern echoed the typical arrangement of rooms in A/B/A suites in the larger plan; the Etrusco-Italian character of trilobate interior systems (e.g., *tablinum* and *alae*) is too well known to need explication. The mirror-image architectures on side walls set up a series of transverse axes marking stages through which a viewer progressed, as she moved down the length of a room on the main axis, toward the central set-piece. This strategy, one of penetration through a series of lateral axes, marks

Roman complex planning from the great Sanctuary of Fortuna at Praeneste (c. 150–100 B.C.)[22] to the Forum of Augustus (2 B.C.)[23] and beyond.

Sometimes the painted room presented a sequence of individual panels within the encircling frame, each of which provided an architectural vista with its own vanishing point. Such panel sequences could be fully appreciated only if the viewer stopped to face each framed image head-on, then turned to move forward again to the next stopping point opposite the next panel. This kind of progression, with its scheduled *voltes-face*, was that expected of the series of temples that accreted in Roman civic precincts, typically in a straight row of facades aligned along a single plane parallel to a path; for the effect, a modern visitor can still look along the temple series at the Largo Argentina.[24] Vitruvius (4.5.2) even supplies that very rare form of ancient evidence, a text on spectator response: he describes how temples were arranged along the public roads (*circum vias publicas*) so passersby could stop, face the temple and utter a prayer, then move along to the next facade (*respicere et in conspectu salutationes facere*). If, as it seems, the architectural rooms of the 2nd Style were constructed at very basic levels to evoke Roman modes of response to architecture, then the architectural details of those rooms were likely also to have a Roman flavor.

As for the "message" of 2nd Style architectural iconography, two theses have dominated interpretation. I do not find either one plausible. One school holds that these architectures had an overt theatrical quality;[25] I discuss below the relation of these paintings to ancient scene paintings. The architecture represented does not itself seem to have any overt connection with what we know of prior or contemporary theater-backdrop construction; the wall articulated by columns was too widely used in Republican and Hellenistic architecture to signify the theatrical as such. The "theatrical" school sets much store by the common depiction of masks as secondary ornaments

19. For the Roman digestion of Hellenistic material culture, in its broad social context, see E. Gruen, *Culture and National Identity in Republican Rome* (Ithaca 1992) ch. 6–7.
20. Fittschen, La Rocca, and others are notable exponents of this view, often put forth also to account for the demise of the 2nd Style. On the 2nd Style as a sublimation (out of poverty or modesty) of *luxuria*, see M. Torelli (36–43) and P. Zanker (35–40) in *Kaiser Augustus* (supra n. 5) 23–48; below p. xx and n. xx.
21. See M. Cima in *Tranquille dimore* (supra n. 4) 105ff. at 124–127.
22. F. Sear, *Roman Architecture* (Ithaca 1982) 26f., fig. 12; F. Coarelli, *I santuari del Lazio* (1975) 35ff., Tybout (supra n. 6) fig. 14—in these, edit out the *monopteros* above (see n. 4); H. Lauter, "Bemerkungen zur spaethellenistischen Baukunst in Mittelitalien," *JdI* 94 (1979) 390–359 at 390ff.; F. Rakob, "Die Rotunda in Palästrina. Mit einer Bauaufnahme und Rekonstruktion von Martin Kleibrink," *RM* 97 (1990) 61–92.
23. Sear (supra n. 22) 65f.; J. B. Ward-Perkins, *Roman Imperial Architecture* (Penguin Books 1981) 30f.; P. Zanker, *Forum Augus-*

tum. Das Bildprogramm (Tübingen 1973); J. Ganzert and V. Kockel in *Kaiser Augustus* (supra n. 5) 149–200, plans figs. 51–52, p. 87.
24. The only good Greek parallel I know for this kind of alignment is the treasury sequence at Olympia. The Roman habit is reflected also in the common ordering of facades of varied building types flush with one another to line fora.
25. This approach is generated by the cryptic pronouncement of Vitruvius 7.5.2 that walls of what we call the 2nd Style might depict *scaenarum frontes tragico aut comico seu satyrico more*. For a potent expression of this view, see especially the work of E. W. Leach, "Patrons, Painters and Patterns: the Anonymity of Romano-Campanian Painting and the Transition from the Second to the Third Style," *Literacy and Artistic Patronage in Ancient Rome*, B. K. Gold, ed. (Austin 1982) 135–187; *The Rhetoric of Space. Literary and Artistic Representations of Landscape in Republican and Augustan Rome* (Princeton 1988) 214–219. See the excellent discussions of Vitruvius and of the general problem by Tybout (supra n. 6) 82–88 and 187–213.

propped on or hanging from 2nd Style frames. Such ornament is typical of Greco-Roman house decoration, however, from the middle Hellenistic period through the Italian Masonry Style period, when floor mosaics constitute the zone of figure decoration in houses; I cannot see that they make these architectures a theater any more than the typical fruit-and-game still-lives make 2nd Style walls into markets. A vague Dionysiac air of felicity and culture, conveyed by these masks, does not equate with overt, primary reference to the theater. Both architecture and figure painting became in the late 2nd, 3rd, and 4th Styles subjects for (fictive) framed panels rather than life-size frieze elements; it seems to me significant that none of these later "paintings" of architecture show anything like a theater.

The other dominant interpretation holds that over the *floruit* of the 2nd Style (more than 50 years) painted architecture substituted for a desired but unavailable solid architecture, which could only be afforded by the wealthiest patrons or by Eastern kings. An unstated corollary of this view is that the veneers of the Masonry Style, which dominated the Mediterranean East and West for at least two centuries, signified in the same way—plainly, a false sociological reading. Concomitantly, the shift to the 3rd Style early in the reign of Augustus is taken as a conscious reaction to Republican luxury seen as decadent.[26] Yet it is plain that Augustus took 2nd Style architectural painting as a symbol of the best Roman Republican *mores* in his attempt to style himself *renovator* of the Republican institutions of family and state. We could hardly have a clearer document for the perceived *Romanitas* of 1st-century B.C. wall painting than the decoration of the Ara Pacis (13–9 B.C.)—the altar enclosure's exterior celebrates the *domus Augusti* in its persons, the interior is modeled in the style of a 2nd Style *domus*' rooms in format, pilaster details, and garland decoration.[27]

It seems as if modern Western viewers find disturbing the intensity of the 2nd Style esthetic, and unthinkingly equate austerity of design with moral virtue, conditioned by a century when the Bauhaus esthetic has trickled down to the middle-class parlor. It is bad cultural anthropology to dismiss the 2nd Style as in the recent query of an influential Romanist,

"Who would really want to sleep in a room like the cubiculum from Bosocreale or in the Villa of the Mysteries?"; one wonders if he would similarly attribute "neurotic obsession" to the Quattrocento patrons of the Italian Renaissance, whose *studioli* and reception rooms exhibit an identical esthetic?[28] No modern critic would postulate that garlands, theatrical masks, and religious emblems painted on a wall stood in for something the owner couldn't buy, or thought would be too splashy to "really" put up; no one would say that Romans painted gardens on walls because they couldn't or were too embarassed to actually have them. No more does 2nd Style architecture of the same period act crudely as material subsitutes! The thesis of a cheaper makeshift cannot account for the staying power of this decorative fashion for more than four decades, employed (to judge by the elaboration of villa plans) at social levels extending up to the wealthiest of patrons.

Periods of trompe l'oeil realism must indeed be related to deep cultural attitudes toward a dominant culture of materialistic display, as in Holland in its ages of mercantile expansion. However, such images are not generated only by a simplistic reflex to substitute for desired objects. Hyper-realist styles can appeal in and of themselves; the Greco-Roman fascination with surface realism as a criterion of artistic success in painting and in sculpture is well known. Anyone who lived through the 1980's in Europe or North America is well placed to appreciate the congruence of wealth, display culture, and a taste for decorating interiors with *faux* veneers and architectural elements of all kinds, valued not least for their charm as imitations. When one looks about at Hellenistic and Republican visual culture in general, one finds a fascination with the visual *jeu d'esprit* constituted by illusionistic replication, made available by advancements in artistic technique that were valued for their own sake. No one postulates what we might call the "realism of envy" for the weapons-pile parapets with which the 2nd-century Attalids framed the citadel Temple of Athena,[29] for the fictive trophies of the San Omobono triumphal monument in Republican Rome,[30] or for the edibles of Hellenistic and Roman *xenia* still-lives. 2nd Style architectural illusions cannot be excerpted from this broader visual culture.

26. This is a typical reading of the 2nd Style, which comes up often to explain the switch to the quieter 3rd Style as an Augustan moral reaction to the extravagances of the Republic—another thesis I find implausible, given that Augustus' own Ara Pacis has walls formatted in imitation of 2nd Style walls. For recent, overly authoritative expressions of this view, see M. Torelli in *Kaiser Augustus* (supra n. 5) 36f., B. Andreae in the same volume at 277f.; P. Zanker *The Power of Images in the Age of Augustus* (Ann Arbor 1988): "The next style of wall-painting . . . shows clearly how in Augustan times the old style was perceived as a mere show of extravagance and self-deception" (28); it flourished when "the ambitious but naive Roman" (25) felt "an almost pathological need for excesses of pleasure and exhibition-

ism"; "The imagined version of the walls took the place of richly decorated interiors . . . " (28).
27. It is striking that the 2nd Style remains from Rome are so scanty and yet provide such clear parallels: see the Odyssey Landscape pilasters and capitals (ca. 40 B.C., n. 10), the format and garland ornament of the "golden frieze" room in the House of Livia (ca. 30 B.C., n. 69), and the slatted wood constructions of the Room of the Masks in the House of Augustus (ca. 30 B.C., n. 14).
28. P. Zanker, *Kaiser Augustus* (supra n. 5) 28.
29. W. Radt *Pergamon*. Geschichte und Bauten. Funde und Erforschung einer antiken Metropole (Cologne 1988) 181 fig. 68.
30. Strong (supra n. 10) p. 48, fig. 17.

Although I disagree with the conclusions of the two schools outlined above, I do feel that they have a legitimate aim in asking what 2nd Style architecture signifies. These fictions must have served some end in Roman villa and house schemes, or, rephrased in Roman terms, they must have fitted the principle of *decorum*, and been seen as appropriate to the *dominus'* cultivated life in the *pars urbana*. Like other typical aspects of villa construction and decoration, this genre will have served to embody the status and taste of its patrons. The library at a villa showed a *dominus* to be a man of learning; its decorative statues showed him to be (if not himself a general who won his own booty) a man of high culture. 2nd Style architectural painting attributed to the *dominus* a lively and refined architectural imagination, and a status of power and wealth as a builder in *potentia* of public as well as private construction. The exuberant development of this genre over a period of at least two generations reflects, at an appropriate interval, the well-documented explosion of architectural patronage from after 150 B.C. in the cities and sanctuaries of Roman Italy. It coincides, with even less time lag, with the rapid evolution of the great houses and villas of Roman and Romanized nobility. In this period both public and private identity are bound up to a phenomenal degree with architectural patronage, from the highest echelons of society down through what we would call a middle class.

The extent and function of public architectural patronage in Republican Italy, as the paramount expression of individual and clan achievement, is now well understood in outline and detail (thanks most of all to Filippo Coarelli[31]). The assumption of an active interest in architecture, and of a developed architectural sensibility, are documented by contemporary sources both visual and textual. The Romans added something entirely new to the canons of Hellenistic art, when they began in the Late Republic to make graphic images of *known* buildings and constructions, in the context of depicting a building as a *monumen-*

tum to the individual of rank who had put it up or restored it. This is the series of numismatic images that began in 75 B.C. with a depiction of the Temple of Jupiter Libertas[32] and that surely reflects like much other numismatic imagery a graphic tradion executed on a larger scale.[33] Contemporary rhetorical exercises recommended as an *ars memoria* the imaginative construction or reminiscences of individual buildings, of typical house plans, and of urban landscapes, made up in the imagination from familiar elements; forensic oratory, like satirical drama, manipulated the itinerary of real buildings in Rome as a standard dramatic device.[34] As for houses and villas, Vitruvius wrote in the latter part of the century, under Augustus, for a class of patrons whom he knew took a keen and (often unfortunately!) direct interest in the planning and construction of their own houses (6.praef.6-7). Earlier in the 1st century B.C., Lucretius had already expected his educated readers to be confirmed Do-It-Yourself addicts. That philosophical poet compared the devastating results of bad logical premises to a house-building scenario: he appealed to his audience's common knowledge of what happens if one makes little mistakes in the measurements for new foundations, which result by roof level in a completely crooked house (4.511f.). Architectural metaphors and imagery—drawn often from villa and house iconography—dominate the poetry of Lucretius and of Vergil over the course of the 1st century B.C.,[35] in a way that is new to the Greek poetic tradition. These authors' confident appeal to a taste for architectural recollection, construction, and fantasy aptly mirrors the taste for architectural imagery on the walls of contemporary houses.[36]

What about the graphic culture, the artistic resources that made possible the elaborate perspectives of this genre of 2nd Style painting? Many scholars (especially those reconstructing ancient theatrical arts) assert that these architectures mimic scene paintings, for we have some evidence that plausibly illusionistic architectural backdrops occasionally fig-

31. See F. Coarelli, "Architettura e arti figurative in Roma 150–50 a.c.," *Hellenismus in Mittelitalien* (1976) 38–51; "Architettura sacra e architettura privata nella tarda Repubblica," *Architecture et societ* (1983) 191–217; and *I santuari del Lazio in eta repubblicana* (Rome 1988).
32. M. H. Crawford, *Roman Republican Coinage* I-II (Cambridge 1974) no. 391.
33. For numismatic evidence, see: G. Fuchs, *Architekturdarstellungen auf römischen Münzen der Republik und frühen Kaiserzeit* I-II (AMUGS 1; Berlin 1969); cf. J. P. C. Kent, *Roman Coins* (New York 1978) nos. 65 (57 B.C.), 66, 68 pl. 18, 75 pl. 19, 83 pl. 22, 100 pl. 27, etc. Much other numismatic imagery is symbiotic with monumental art forms like sculpture, historical relief, and painting; this is certainly the case with portraits, divine images, depictions of battle, and civic ceremonies. Roman historical paintings (typically made for triumphs) characteristically documented man-made as well as natural landscapes.
34. These texts are discussed in Leach (supra n. 25) 73–78; see esp. Cicero, *De inventione rhetorica* 1.38, the *Auctor ad Herennium* 3.16.29 and 3.17.30, and Quintilian, *Inst.* 11.2.17-22.
35. This author is preparing an article on Vergil's architectural imagery. Three examples can document this Vergilian image system in the Aeneid: Book 2's Ilioupersis, where the ravages inflicted on the *domus* of Priam are imaged as the rape of a screaming house, 11.486ff.; the house of Hades in Book 6.271ff., where Orcus becomes the guard dog at the vestibule, across the atrium iron chambers, which parody womens' cubicula, hold the Furies and Discord, and in the peristyle garden grows the Tree of Dreams; Book 12.470ff., where Juturna, driving through the Trojan ranks, is compared to a dark swallow darting through the halls of a rich house, whirring through colonnades and over garden tanks.
36. Leach (supra n. 25) is broadly interested in landscape depictions in painting and in texts (principally poetry) in the period of the 2nd and 3rd Styles; however, this monograph is not interested, as I am, in systematically cataloguing the deployment of architectural imagery by authors of the 1st century B.C., to distinguish descriptions of man-made from natural landscape elements, and to work with media other than painting.

ured in stage presentations.[37] These two genres, the extant domestic paintings and the lost *scaenographiae*, must have been related; however, they are more likely to have been parallel developments than imitations, one of the other. The domestic wall paintings develop in a way that is too self-consistent, and too obviously rooted in the non-theatric Masonry (or 1st) Style, to be viewed as products of an active class of scene painters taking private commissions between shows. Do they then paint images of the carved backdrops of Roman theaters? Again, there is no evidence that the conformation of the Roman stage as it existed in the 1st century B.C. was the seminal influence on 2nd Style painting.[38] If the wall paintings were intended to reproduce the spectacular effects of even temporary theaters, one would expect to see something of the great colored *velae* (colored cloth awnings) and constructions covered with gold, silver, or ivory (cf. Val. Max. 2.4.5-6)—none of which appear.[39] As well, it seems now that when painted backdrops were used in theaters they consisted of narrow panels mounted on rotating prismatic stands at either end of the long stage platform—hardly a source for the format of an entire 2nd Style wall.[40]

2nd Style walls and the productions at Roman spectacles should rather be grouped together as manifestations of a culture that enjoyed graphic and low relief architectural fictions.[41] Relevant here is a vogue evident on 1st-century B.C. tombs for covering a large structure with a linear (low-relief and paint) depiction of an elaborated facade, often with statues and garlands.[42] As with painting, this decorative system seemingly was felt to be charming in itself, rather than used in default of the means for actual

construction. Given the textual report of elaborate perspectives possible to Hellenistic artists, and the occasional perspectives of townscapes encountered in 2nd Style painting, which do employ varied angles of vision, it is worth noting that images of buildings in the more elaborate vistas tend toward a flat head-on view. This is in marked contrast to the angled views of similar buildings inserted into narrative contexts, in sacro-idyllic friezes[43] and in mythological panels, which avoid any head-on views even when such a motif might attractively silhouette a figure group.[44]

In 2nd Style images of buildings one seems to be looking at an elaborate model for an elevation. Here, Vitruvius' instructions for architectural draftsmanship come to mind. He recommends that any architect must be able to come up with a *dispositio* for the shape and appearance of a noble building with all its decorative appurtenances (1.1.4-5): the *species* of a building, which includes its *ornamenta*, make up an *erecta frontis imago*, a picture of the facade of a building set upright and properly drawn in the proportions of the projected work (1.2.2). This art of drawing a proper *dispositio* must be rooted in theoretical sciences inherited from the Greeks—perspective, optics, chiaroscuro, etc.; however, as Vitruvius documents, these Greek arts had become current Roman practice by the 1st century B.C. Although no such "blueprints" survive, I would suggest that this lost genre (rather than scene painting) is most likely to have supplied the technical armory for those specialists draughting 2nd Style schemata.[45] The single-point, head-on views of buildings and architecturally limited spaces in 2nd Style frames, like the facade

37. Cf. A. Little, *Roman Perspective Painting and the Ancient Stage* (Maine 1971). For the ancient evidence, see J. J. Pollitt, *The Ancient View of Greek Art* (New Haven 1974) 230–241 (*skenographia*), 66–71 (Vitruvius); id., *The Art of Rome c. 753 B.C.–A.D. 337: Sources and Documents* (Cambridge 1966/83) 52, 84, 87–88, 127–129. According to Valerius Maximus (2.4.6, a section on the chronology of innovations in staging and theater design), painted backdrops were first used to any extent in a Roman theater by Clodius Pulcher, evidently the consul of 92 *b.c.*, in his earlier aedileship: *Cl. Pulcher scenam varietate colorem adumbravit, vacuis ante pictura tabulis extentam.* Valerius does not name the subjects of these paintings.
38. This is not to deny overt reference to theater *scaenae* in Roman wall painting—it plainly features in 4th Style painting; cf., recently, E. Moormann, "Rappresentazioni teatrali su scaenae frontes di quarto stile a Pompeii," *PompHercStab* 1 (1983) 73–117.
39. 2nd Style ceilings were decorated in pale or partly colored stucco, or with painted imitations of such stucco work, whose format imitated elaborately beamed and coffered carved (wooden) ceilings; see Ling (supra n. 10) 42f.
40. On these *periaktoi*, and Roman stage fronts, see Tybout (supra n. 6) 82f., 189f.; at 199f. he makes the plausible suggestion that influence from theater painting should be seen, if at all, in the narrow upright panels with the roofs of a townscape, which

occur a few times in the 2nd Style repertoire.
41. The view of Tybout (supra n. 6) is also that this fashion served an intellectual taste for calculated optical effects, in both real and painted facades.
42. On the round tomb on the Via Appia at milestone 6, and the monopteros tomb at Aquileia: W. von Sydow, "Eine Grabrotunde an der Via Appia Antica," *JdI* 92 (1977) 241–321, at 298–299 discussing 2nd Style painting. M. Bergmann asserts an autonomous development at Alexandria, "Perspektivische Malerei in Stein: einige alexandrinische Architekturmotive," in H. Büsing and F. Hiller, eds., *Bathron. Beiträge zur Architektur und verwandten Kunsten . . . H. Drerup* (Saarbrücken 1988) 59–77.
43. A monograph on landscape views of temples, sacred groves, and shrines by E. Bergmann is forthcoming from Princeton Uniersity Press.
44. As architecture does in historical relief of the 1st century A.D. and after. By contrast, 1st-century B.C. decorative and state reliefs use small, elevated, three-quarter building vignettes, as do contemporary paintings; examples include the Grimani Reliefs (Simon [supra n. 10] fig. 163) and the Ara Pacis Aeneas panel.
45. On 2nd Style workshop practice, and the division of labor between architecture and figure painters, see Clarke (supra n. 1) 45f., and cf. 57f.

imagines of real buildings, which feature in commemorative relief by the early 1st century A.D.,[46] are perhaps best thought of as *dispositiones* for decorative ends.

Such a link to real architectural practice would help to clarify the problem of artistic transmission between house painting and building practice. For the often-noted correspondence between painting and real architectures contrasts markedly with the observed absence of such coherence in another image system beloved of wall painters; there is little correlation between the painted representation of statues, on the one hand, and the actual record of preferred statue types and their installation on the other.[47] Although there are occasional attempts to mimic the programmatic installation of sculpture, these too are rare.[48] The chance for an architect's staff and a painting workshop to associate with one another existed because wall painting in Roman villas and houses seems to have been executed as a phase in the construction of the house itself; that the two could be more than casually linked is implied by Vitruvius' inclusion of the choice of colors and subjects for wall painting in the section of his treatise on house construction.

This raises the question of correspondence between painted image and contemporary architectural practice. To what extent did a spectator expect such images to be "real"?[49] It is clear that many of these walls do extend from a base of plausible detail and structure into a slightly fantastic realm. This should not surprise any cultural historian; literature and figural representation in the Hellenistic centuries typically used "surface realism" not as an end but as a means toward the plausible evocation of those non-real subjects we call "mythological." In architectural representation, the exact line where mimicry leaves off and fantastic recombination begins is problematic only in that scholars mine 2nd Style images to reconstruct lost building habits and to assign the source cultures for those habits. (A parallel case is that of

the relation between the tomb facades of 4th–3rd century B.C. Macedon and the lost corpus of Hellenistic palace facades.)

As it happens, we have a parallel genre of architectural representation, which exhibits a similar evocation of known forms to provide a plausible frame for a fantastic creation that still commands willing belief. These are Vergil's poetic ekphrases, composed toward the end of the 2nd Style's *floruit*, for which we know the actual architectural referents. One can compare the imaginary "Precinct of Augustus," elaborated in the Georgics (3.2), with both the real Forum of Augustus, which it took as a starting point,[50] and the more documentary paean to the same complex written by Ovid (*Fast.* 5.550-96) when the precinct was dedicated in 2 B.C. after decades of work. Similarly, we know to compare the set piece at the end of the Shield ekphrasis in Aeneid 8 (718ff.) to the actual Augustan complex on the Palatine. One can easily see that the rich veneers and jeweled surfaces of 2nd Style architectures expand with gusto according to the decorative predilections of the richer nobles, documented for us by the deceptively snide comments of their like-minded contemporaries.[51] A project well worth undertaking would be a comparison of the strategies and vocabulary of 2nd Style architecture painting to the strategies of Golden Age architectural ekphrasis, annalistic and poetic.

Now I want to address further the Roman character of the specific architectural forms employed in 2nd Style vistas, and not just the fictitious house interiors far more widely accepted as versions of Roman realities. How far did the general *Romanitas* of the architectonic convention as such extend to its more prominent motifs?

In the main, the broad formats of 2nd Style architectures visibly evolve from Italian architectural decoration of the late 2nd century B.C., that is, from the painted and molded stucco schemes of the so-called 1st Pompeian Style, better called the Masonry Style (as it it is now known to have been current around

46. See, e.g., the Palatine facade represented on the Augustan base at Sorrento, which seems to copy paintings or reliefs from the capital: T. Hölscher in *Kaiser Augustus* (supra n. 5) 376, no. 208d; and the early Tiberian relief cycle at the Villa Medici in Rome, showing the Temples of Mars Ultor and of Cybele, Strong (supra n. 10) fig. 57; Hölscher, ibid. 378–379, nos. 209–210.
47. E. Moormann, *La pittura parietale romana come fonte di conoscenza per la scultura antica* (Assen 1988). It is striking to see just how little correspondence there is between the statues in wall painting, and the types known from marble and bronze statuary both large and small, including such *opera nobiliora* as the Polykleitan athletes.
48. A good 2nd Style case is that of the philosopher statues in apsidal *aediculae* depicted in the house Pompeii VI.ins. occ. 41; M. de Vos in *Tranquille dimore* (supra n. 4) 68–69, figs. 43–44.

49. Vitruvius' carping (7.5.1 f.) about the fantastic extension of the plausible only highlights the popularity of the phenomenon.
50. While the precinct was dedicated only in 2 B.C., plans for its portico surround and program will have been much circulated in the intervening decades between the vowing of the Temple of Mars Ultor and the final dedication. Vergil's statue program in particular is plainly a fantasy elaborating on the core themes of the real program.
51. For some key sources see Pollitt (supra n. 37) 81–84. To snarl at *luxuria* was a *topos* of Republican rhetoric; although these pronouncements are often swallowed whole-sale by modern historians, in fact they document the wide-spread desire for and prevalence of rich and colorful decoration, and the avid interest of the Republican upper class in the exact details of the houses of their friends and rivals.

the Hellenistic Mediterranean, documented in the Greek world from the 4th century B.C.).[52] At Pompeii, note for instance how the molded ashlar patterns and elaborate stucco moldings of, for example, the *atrium* of the House of Sallust, a well-preserved 1st Style house,[53] turn up in a purely two-dimensional painted rendering as the "back wall" of the *oecus* of the House of the Silver Wedding. The articulation of the wall, as in the later *oecus*, by fictive column screens derives also from three-dimensional systems, both public and private; note the stucco decorations of the grand vestibule (*fauces*) of the House of the Faun, and the applied column and ashlar systems lining the walls of the Basilica of Pompeii behind screening colonnades. Vitruvius knew what we call the Masonry Style—indeed he recommended its typical black/yellow/red color scheme—and he attributed the use of heavy applied stucco cornices to those he called "the ancients" (7.3.3), warning against their tendency to fall upon peoples' heads. (This kind of testimony makes one wonder if one reason why early 2nd Style patterns caught on was because of their practicality—no more crumbling moldings or chipped plaster edges!)

As Engemann[54] showed long ago, many key elements in the 2nd Style vocabulary were distinctively Roman, and were to be explained by the refraction of real architectural experience.[55] For instance, he juxtaposed the motif of the arcade (painted at Villa dei Misteri in *cub.* 16) with real arcades, like those in the House of Fortuna. On this wall at the Villa dei Misteri, the systems of socle plinths and of entablatures and the impression of an arcuated lintel zone match the three-dimensional arrangement of the Corinthian *oecus* in the House of the Silver Wedding. Obvious though such juxtapositions seem, it is worth pointing out how they depict Roman patrons and artists, continually feeding their experience of villa and house forms back into the repertoire of painted walls. Like Vitruvius' comments on old-time painting

fashions, they show Romans aware of their own decorative traditions, enjoying and refining upon them with at least some degree of self-consciousness. This process prefigures the great explosion of retrospective interest in the accumulated fashions of the previous century and more, which occurs in the later 1st century A.D. (under the modern rubric of the 4th Style).

Other standard wall-painting motifs turn up in Italian public construction between 150 B.C. and the end of the 1st century. The late 2nd-century forum basilica at Praeneste, though battered, shows evidence of richly colored articulated interiors.[56] The Temple of Apollo Sosianus in Rome (19 B.C.) shows that sumptuous columns, fantastic capitals, and articulated wall screens with decorative aediculae are what a Roman noble built as a matter of course by the end of the century.[57] To explore the symbiosis between Italian-source architectures and wall painting, an interesting case motif is that of the caryatid entablatures (e.g., in the Boscoreale dining room) and caryatid herms (e.g., in the House of the Criptoportico) popular in the 2nd Style and also in 3rd Style upper-wall zones. As domestic motifs these are prefigured by the terracotta caryatid series employed in late Hellenistic Sicilian houses. These in turn domesticate a theme from Sicilian palace and theater decoration,[58] which is picked up in the 2nd-century B.C. Latium at Praeneste, where such a caryatid attic graced the "screen wall" facade before the theatrical cavea crowning the sanctuary.[59] The domesticated Roman wall-painting motif thus has sources in both Sicilian house decoration and Latin public architecture. In turn, the painted motif emerges in force in Augustan public construction at Rome of the later 1st century, in the caryatid galleries of Agrippa's Pantheon (Pliny, *NH* 36.38), the Forum of Augustus,[60] and the Basilica Aemilia.[61]

It makes a large difference to our idea of the *dominus'* self-conception if we believe that he painted

52. Barbet (supra n. 9) chap. 1; I. Baldassare, "Pittura parietale e mosaico pavimentale dal IV. al II. sec. a.C.," *Ricerche di pittura ellenistica* (Rome 1985) 203ff.; V. Bruno, "Antecedents of the Pompeian First Style," *AJA* 73 (1969) 305–317; A. Laidlaw, "A Reconstruction of the First Style Decoration in the Alexander Exedra of the House of the Faun," *Neue Forschungen* (supra n. 11) 39ff.; in the "triclinium" of the Francois Tomb at Vulci: C. Blanck et al., *Malerei der Etrusker in Zeichnungen des 19. Jh.s* (Mainz 1988).
53. Pompeii VI.2.4. Richardson (supra n. 7) 108–111; T. Kraus (1974) (supra n. 10), fig. 292.
54. See n. 8.
55. Cf. B. Wesenberg, "Attische Saulenbasen in der Wanddekoration des 2. pompejanischen Stils," *Bathron* (supra n. 42) 407–420.
56. Lauter (supra n. 22) 436ff.
57. Sear (supra n. 22) 64–65; E. La Rocca, *Amazzonomachia. Le sculture frontonale del tempio di Apollo Sosiano* (Rome 1985) 83–96, fig. 15. Equally rich will have been the elevation of the earlier Temple of Venus Genetrix constructed by Julius Caesar, known only in plan. For a survey of the articulated wall schemes (esp.

the "aedicula style") of 1st-century B.C. Roman architecture, see U.-W. Gans, "Die Quellbezirk von Nîmes. Zur Datierung und zum Stil seiner Bauten," *RM* 97 (1990) 93–125 s.v. the Nîmes colonnaded hall at 98ff. Cf. also Lauter (supra n. 22) s.v. the forum and sanctuary architecture at Praeneste, 416f. and 436f.; and Tybout (supra n. 6) pls. 104–106, fig. 15.
58. On the Centuripe house's terracotta Dionysiac figures, and its prototypes in Sicilian public construction (Monte Iato theater, Hieron's yacht *Syrakosia*) see R. J. A. Wilson, "Roman Architecture in a Greek World: the Example of Sicily," *Architecture and Architectural Sculpture in the Roman Empire*, M. Henig, ed. (Oxford 1990) 66–90 at 70–71.
59. Lauter (supra n. 22) 398–400.
60. Most recently, V. Kockel in *Kaiser Augustus* (supra n. 5) 190f., figs. 82–85.
61. The Parthian caryatid figures of the Basilica's Augustan phase, quoted by the Dacians of Trajan's Forum, are still not well known; see R. M. Schneider, *Bunte Barbaren. Orientalstatuen aus farbigem Marmor in der römischen Republik* (Mainz 1986) 98ff. at 115f.; id., "Kolossale Dakerstatuen aus grünem Porphyr," *RM* 97 (1990) 235–260 at 259 on attic caryatids in the imperial fora.

his living quarters to approximate, as much as possible, Greek rather than Italian forms. Naturally, Italy in general and Rome in particular were in dialogue throughout the Hellenistic period about developments in Greece, Asia Minor, Syria, and Egypt, and architectural motifs on Roman soil may often have originated somewhere else in the Hellenistic *koine*. The point is that, once assimilated into the Roman visual sphere, such elements when perpetuated are not likely to have been perceived as significantly foreign. As Hans Lauter pointed out in a key article, the Roman assimilation and transformation of the Eastern Hellenistic architectural repertoire took place in the period 150–90 B.C. The 2nd Style came into being afterward, ca. 100–20 B.C. Although this painted repertoire continued to respond to Hellenistic fashions from the East as well as the West, and to incorporate exotica, much in its terms of reference will have seemed something "we Romans do" rather than something "those Greeks do." The 2nd and 1st centuries B.C. were also a period when Romans began broadly to distinguish Italian culture as a whole from Eastern Greek culture, and the role of Sicilian architectures as a model is certainly significantly underrated in critical discussion of the Roman experience. What seems to us direct influence from Alexandria may often have come to a more northerly Italian audience, filtered through South Italy and Sicily.[62]

A striking Roman conceptual innovation within the Hellenistic oikoumene is the introduction of the architectural prospect, a Roman innovation in interior decoration schemes. Coexisting with images of wall veneers and shallow views into adjacent rooms we find true prospects, through foreground elaborated screens onto separate buildings and deep porticoes. Although this motif is foreshadowed in Hellenistic figure scenes by the occasional interposition of a par-

tition wall in the background, the Roman examples are far more detailed and comprehensible. Typically in 2nd Style rooms, the several modes of prospect screen and articulated wall are used concurrently. (In publications, corner shots of decorated rooms are welcome because they show how these differing zones abutted one another, and document what an actual occupant of a room would experience more accurately than cropped shots of single zones.[63]) The Roman esthetics of the painted prospect, or *Durchblick*, a staged view through door/gate/wall, have been well explored.[64] The esthetics of the painted prospects were embedded in a conscious habit of architectural patronage, for the staged view and the considered prospect were carefully considered factors both in the location of fine villas and in the determination of sites for windows and room types within the villa itself.[65]

It is in these prospects that the cultivated *urbanitas* or the *pars urbana* strikes home most forcefully. Here, in the midst of the well-loved Italian countryside, what a Republican Roman patron was most likely to put on his walls was not some image evocative of the rural landscape, but rather images for the most part of the completely artificial, man-made terrain of villa suite and sun-drenched portico. As far as we can tell, the decorations of 2nd Style country houses were not markedly different from the decorations of townhouses in Rome.[66] Apart from the very early Casa dei Grifi,[67] and the cropped wall holding the Odyssey Landscapes,[68] 2nd Style walls are not well preserved from the capital. The same holds true for painting in the 3rd and 4th Styles. Mostly, extrinsic political factors saw to the preservation or entombment of those palace and suburban estate constructions that document late 2nd, 3rd and 4th Style painting in the capital, as at the imperial properties of Livia,[69] Augustus,[70]

---

62. E.g., the state galley of Hiero II of Syracuse (306–215 B.C.), a gift to the Alexandrian court, was an eclectic floating palace that in fact inspired Ptolemy IV's better-known galleon (Ath. 5.208), that paradigm of Hellenistic luxury architecture. This is not the occasion to try to synthesize what is known about West Hellenistic developments—but someone should. Pergamon and Macedon, as court centers plainly influential on Republican culture, similarly tend to be ignored for Alexandria.

63. Such documentation is rare; a self-conscious exception is made by Clarke (supra n. 1).

64. A. Borbein, "Zur Deutung von Scherwand und Durchblick auf den Wandgemälden des 2. Pompejanischen Stils," *Neue Forschungen* (supra n. 11) 61–75; W. Ehrhardt, "Bild und Ausblick in Wandbemalungen Zweiten Stils," *AntK* 34.1 (1991) 28–65; Tybout (supra n. 6) esp. conclusion; B. Wesenberg "Zur asymmetrischen Perspektive in der Wanddekoration des 2. pompejanischen Stils," *MarbWPr* (1968) 102–109; cf. Leach (supra n. 25) 100–107. Cf. W. Macdonald, *The Architecture of the Roman Empire* II: *An Urban Appraisal* (New Haven 1986) on the staging of framed vistas in urban contexts by means of gates and arches.

65. Cf. E. Bergmann, "Painted Perspectives of a Villa Visit: Landscape as Status and Metaphor," *Roman Art in the Private Sphere*, E. Gazda, ed. (Ann Arbor 1990) 49–70.

66. I. Jacopi, "Sistemi decorativi di II Stile a Roma," *Roma repub-*

blicana dal 270 a.C. all' eta augustea (Rome 1987) 65–76. For the symbiotic relation between villa and townhouse design at Pompeii, see P. Zanker, "Die Villa als Vorbild der späten pompejanischen Wohngeschmacks," *JdI* 94 (1979) 460–523.

67. G. Rizzo, *Le pitture della Casa dei Grifi* (Monumenti della pittura antica scoperta in Italia III, Roma I 1936); Tybout (supra n. 6) 373–375; color angle shot, F. Coarelli, *Guida archeologica di Roma* (Rome 1974) at 160; Strong (supra n. 10) s.v. fig. 25.

68. B. Andreae in *Kaiser Augustus* (supra n. 5) 282–285, no. 132; Simon (supra n. 10) s.v. fig. 283; color ill., O. Dalton, *Art treasures of the Vatican Library* (Rome 1969).

69. G. Rizzo, *Le pitture della "Casa di Livia"* (Monumenti della pittura antica III, Roma II 1936); Simon (supra n. 10) s.v. figs. 244, 246, 248, col. pl. 29.2.

70. See n. 14; Simon (supra n. 10) s.v. figs. 240–241, col. pl. 28, 29.1.

71. For the remains of the 4th Style from the Domus Aurea and Domus Transitoria, see N. Dacos, *La découverte de la Domus Aurea et la formation des grotesques à renaissance* (London 1969); M. de Vos, "Nerone, Seneca, Fabullo e la Domus Transitoria al Pala-tino," *Gli Orti Farnesiani sul Palatino* (Rome 1990) 58–86.

72. G. Rizzo, *Le pitture dell' Aula Isiaca di Caligola* (Monumenti della pittura antica III, Roma II 1936); Simon (supra n. 10) s.v. fig. 243.

73. See n. 14.

and Nero,[71] and at the Aula Isiaca,[72] Villa Farnesina[73] (of Agrippa), and the Horti Lamiani (which became an imperial estate).[74] What is preserved indicates that 2nd and 3rd Style wall painting in the countryside of Etruria,[75] Latium,[76] and Campania was not substantially different from what was executed in the cramped confines of the capital city. (Floor mosaics and stucco from within and without the city show the same coherence of format and styles.)

Because the architectural prospects as such seem to have a distinctively Late Republican flavor, it is worth looking more closely at two elements that figure in most "prospect" panels: the arcuated pediment elevated on columns as a frame for the prospect, as if the spectator looked out from a kind of pavilion or porticus rather than from a walled room; and the round shrine seen through that frame. More than any other single feature, the prospect screens and temple complexes of the developed 2nd Style have been appropriated by those scholars who wish to use the 2nd Style as an illustrated handbook of (lost) Hellenistic "baroque" architectural forms.[77] The wall screens and decorative broken gables of 2nd Style painting, for instance, are often compared to the late Hellenistic Palazzo delle Colonne at Ptolemais, an exemplary monument of the "Alexandrian baroque";[78] yet exterior colonnade screens are known for Roman theater-set construction at the turn of the 1st century B.C., interior colonnade screens (freestanding or applied) typified Latin basilica and nymphaeum construction by the same century, and half-gable systems were freely employed at Praeneste before 100 B.C. Similarly the baroque architectures of

temples and tombs at the Roman client-state of Petra are products of the late 1st century B.C., when the 2nd Style was already mutating into the 3rd Style; their decorative pediment series (broken and lunette pediments especially) are predated by Italian constructions in the Roman sphere.[79]

The arcuated pediment has proved especially problematic, because it is so typical of later imperial "baroque" architecture and is so popular in the East. Generally illustrated by the facade of the little 2nd-century A.D. Temple of Hadrian at Ephesos, it is documented in Syria for the early 1st century A.D.[80] As with painted arcades, an arch form should alert us to seek Western as well as East Greek sources. In fact, by the early 1st century A.D. in the West, this motif was already circulating as a fully developed *dispositio* suitable for low-relief paraphrase on state monuments. It is applied to the short ends of the great Tiberian Arch at Orange, in Gaul,[81] where the illusion is that we see one end of a *porticus* from the outside. By 2 B.C. in Rome itself, at the Forum Augustum, the side aisle vistas terminated in *exedrae* set in arcuated molding and pilaster frames under a pedimented and vaulted roof;[82] this gives an illusionistic version of the view from within an Orange-style porticus or pavilion.[83] And prototypes for the Ephesos Hadrian temple seem to have been available in the West by A.D. 16, when a piece of military finery made for an officer of the Rhine Legions (the "Sheath of Tiberius") depicts such an arcuated lintel on a shrine of Divus Augustus.[84] The real chronology of the extant examples suggests that the transmission of the arcuated pediment as a favored facade type may have run from

74. For the Auditorium of Maecenas on this property see n. xx; for other remains, M. Cima, "Pavone e Pocta. Due frammenti di pittura parietale dell' Esquilino," *Le tranquille dimore* (supra n. 4) 67–75.

75. Best known is the villa at Settefinestre: Tybout (supra n. 6) pl. 73.2; A. Carandini, ed., *Settefinestre. Una villa schiavistica nell' Etruria romana* I–II (Modena 1985) at I. 47, 82f., 215f., 223f., and II. 77–86, 101–102. For a public building, see the Capitolium at Brescia, *Atti del convegno internazionale del Capitolium e per il 150. anniversario della sua scoperta* (Brescia 1975). For 2nd Style painting reflected in late Etruscan chamber tombs, see: A. Laidlaw, "The Tomb of Montefiore: A New Roman Tomb Painted in the Second Style," *Archaeology* 17 (1964) 33–42 (cf. Tybout [supra] pl. 73.1); S. Steingräber, "Die Tomba dei Festoni in Tarquinia und die Deckenmalereien der jüngeren etruskischen Kammergräber," *JdI* 103 (1988) 217–245.

76. For Primaporta, cf. Calci and Messino (supra n. 16), plus: P. A. Gianfrotta, "Villa sulla Via Tiberina," *Arch. Laziale* 2 (1979) 86–90, another 2nd Style house here. The Campanian villa at Boscotrecase has always been taken to show the work of painters working under direct court patronage; see P. H. von Blanckenhagen, *The Paintings from Boscotrecase* (Mainz 1991); cf. now the new Latin villa at Castel del Guido: M. R. Sanzi di Mino, "Le pitture della villa di Castel di Guido," *Arch. Laziale* 10 (1990) 143–153; *Invisibilia. Rivedere i capolavori, vedere i progette* (Roma, Pal. delle Esposizioni 19 feb.–12 apr., 1992) 110–111.

77. Chief spokesman here is M. Lyttelton, *Baroque Architecture in Classical Art* (London 1974), whose chronologies and assertions have still not been put aside. And see the thrust of Tybout (supra n. 6) on 2nd Style architectural painting.

78. H. P. Lauter, "Ptolemais in Libyen. Ein Beitrag zur Baukunst Alexandriens," *JdI* 86 (1971) 149–178.

79. For Pompeii, basilica and tribunal ca. 120–100 B.C.: Richardson (supra n. 7) 95–99; Tybout (supra n. 6) 223, pl. 106.1. (Cf. the multi-aisled interior colonnades of the 2nd-century Forum basilicas of Republican Rome, known roughly in plan.) Praeneste, Forum basilica nymphaeum (it held the famous Nile mosaic in the apse), 150–100 B.C.: Lauter (supra n. 22) 442f.; Tybout (supra): fig. 15; G. Gullini, "Architettura italica ed ellemismo alessandrino," *Alessandria e il mondo ellenistico-romano. Studi in onore di Achille Adriani* III (Rome 1984) 527–592. Castel Gandolfo basilica nymphaeum, 100–50 B.C.: Tybout (supra): 246 and n. 878, pls. 104–105. Rome, Temple of Apollo Sosianus interior screens and pediments, ca. 19 B.C.: see n. 57. Petra: Tybout (supra): pl. 78.2, pl. 101; cf. n. 96.

80. Cf. Tybout (supra n. 6) 254. His pl. 108.3 is an Alexandrian grave relief of the "late 1st century b.c.," a poor-quality stele of generic Early Imperial type.

81. Its presence here was noted recently by Macdonald (supra n. 64) 82, fig. 76.

82. See the architectural drawings by H. Bauer in *Kaiser Augustus* (supra n. 5) 187–188, figs. 78–91.

83. Although the triangle of the gabled roof was concealed from within by the arc of barrel-vaulting, in cross section the resemblance to 2nd Style screens is striking; the *dispositio* is now clear in palimpsest on the right back wall of the Forum Augustum precinct. Zanker (supra n. 23) figs. 10–11.

84. Most recently, E. Künzl in *Kaiser Augustus* (supra n. 5) 558–559, no. 383.

West to East, as did other architectural conventions. (Recent scholarship has begun to delineate the process of Roman influence on the architectural forms and arrangements of the old Greek world in the course of the 2nd and 1st centuries B.C., a process accelerated by the imposition of autocratic rule by Augustus.[85])

I have just treated two isolated motifs tied to the world of Roman commemorative and civic architecture. My exploration of 2nd Style rooms began by discussing their broad formats; I turn now to the arranged relationship between individual architectural motifs, taking the case of that beloved 2nd Style subject, the round shrine with a circular colonnade. Because round colonnaded buildings were rare forms in the Hellenistic world,[86] it is hard to see how their prominence in 2nd Style painting can have been meant to give an East Mediterranean flavor as such! Their prominence in wall painting is partly a function of the painters' tendency to develop an autonomous decorative vocabulary, but we can still consider just how the sight of so many round colonnaded shrines could have struck a Roman audience.

Walled behind its columns such a shrine is termed a *tholos*,[87] unwalled a *monopteros*. The latter may have been a Hellenistic invention but the evidence does not favor its frequent use.[88] It was, however, a form beloved of Roman patrons; its presence in the geographic area of the Eastern Hellenistic world seems a product of strong Roman influence and eventual

domination.[89] A good juxtaposition is that of a wall of the Corinthian *oecus* of the House of the Labyrinth, or from Oplontis (*cub.* 15) with the Early Imperial tomb facade at Petra called the Khazneh.[90] The Petra facade, with its round shrine and statues,[91] are plainly a frozen simulacrum lovingly modeled after a Western architectural reality. That Western reality is documented not only by the *dispositiones* of Republican wall painting but by the Western class of commemorative *monopteroi* with statues. These were used for tombs in Late Hellenistic Sicily[92] and in the Roman West, especially Italy and Gaul[93] (i.e., the Monument of the Julii at S. Remy);[94] they were employed too for big commemorative monuments such as the colossal Augustan trophy pile of 14 B.C. at La Turbie.[95] The political situation of Petra in this period as a Roman client-state also supports the notion that patrons here are likely to have imitated Western forms.[96]

Round temples, *tholoi*, were a subject for classical architectural treatment from the 4th century B.C. on in Greece, but they remained rare compared to rectangular temples, and their deployment calls for comment in any one case. (The evidence suggests that *tholoi* may have been primarily a mainland Greek form, connected often to hero cults.) For Rome and Latium, the situation was different[97]—after all, one of the oldest shrines in the Forum Romanum was the round temple of Vesta, and the burst of Late Republican temple building takes readily to the round form, as at Tivoli and in the Forum Boarium. These

85. See the symposium volume: S. Macready and F. H. Thompson, eds., *Roman Architecture in the Greek World* (London 1987).

86. H. Lauter, *Die Architektur des Hellenismus* (1986) 176f.; he includes all round forms in this section, not just those with colonnades.

87. On the Greek tholos, see F. Seiler, *Die griechische Tholos. Untersuchungen zur Entwicklung, Typologie und Funktion kunstmäßiger Rundbauten* (Mainz 1986).

88. The 4th-century Choregic Monument of Lysikrates in Athens is often cited to document the Greek origin of the *monopteros*, cf. Seiler (supra n. 87) 138, 146. However, that it is a miniaturized simulacrum of a walled *tholos* is made clear by the tripod frieze crowning the *naos*, which disappears behind the encircling columns. This miniature *tholos* was built by first putting up columns and then slotting slabs between them; this does not mean, however, that it was meant to represent a *monopteros*, which requires a similar technique of slotting wall slabs between pillars, as employed for the gallery zone of the 3rd-century Arsinoeion at Samothrace. The next oldest candidate is the building at Pergamon, not after 150 B.C.; ibid. 141–142.

89. On the monopteros: see Seiler (supra n. 87) 135–147; V. Kockel, *Die Grabbauten vor dem Herkulanischen Tor in Pompeji* (Mainz 1983) 31f.; W. Dinsmoor, "The Monopteros in the Athenian Agora," *Hesperia* 43 (1974) 412–447.

90. Tybout (supra n. 6) pls. 101–102; bibl. Seiler (supra n. 87) 139, fig. 66.; cf. the Deit tomb, Sear (supra n. 22) fig. 168.

91. The fictive statue group in the *monopteros*, a portrait flanked by dancing Amazons, is widely ignored. The tiptoe twirling Amazons quote late 1st-century B.C. Roman neo-Attic and eclectic statuary fashions; a good parallel is the Augustan iconography of the state Lares as twin dancers with flared skirts. The group's format, a portrait flanked by symbolic secondary statues, is also more a Roman than a Greek Hellenistic conception; cf. the Villa dei Misteri red salon corner group (ca. 50 B.C.) of a Roman

bride flanked by Amor statues. The flanking Dioscuri of the lower "temple" facade seem to quote Roman installations also; cf. the Forum temple of Concord (ded. A.D. 12).

92. On the early 3rd-century b.c. Marsala tomb: see bibl. Seiler (supra n. 87) 139; von Sydow (supra n. 42) 310; J. Fedak, *Monumental Tombs of the Hellenistic Age: A Study of Selected Tombs from the Pre-Classical to the Early Imperial Era* (Toronto 1990) 180–181.

93. See von Sydow (supra n. 42) 304f., citing late 1st century B.C. and Augustan examples at Rome (his illusionistic Via Appia tomb), Aquileia, Altino, etc., with some Eastern examples of the same period; Kockel (supra n. 89) 33f., nn. 276–277. Fedak (supra n. 92) does not address this type.

94. Cf. Ward-Perkins (supra n. 23) fig. 146, Macdonald (supra n. 64) fig. 86.

95. R. Bedon, R. Chevallier, and M. Pinon, *Architecture et urbanisme en Gaule romaine* I. *L'architecture et la ville* (Paris 1988) 174–188; Ward-Perkins (supra n. 23) 171–172.

96. Most recently on the Khazneh and Petra, see J. Mackenzie, *The Architecture of Petra* (London 1990), who maintains with many that Petra shows influence from Ptolemaic Alexandria, whose capital and palace have left little or no architectural remains. Given the lack of Alexandrian parallels, the strong Western evidence for a taste for round statue-framing shrines, and the sociopolitical context, I do not feel comfortable with the often-proposed "Alexandrian prototype" school of thought. Royal art and architecture in the Augustan client-kingdoms of Juba II in North Africa and Herod in Judaea show a similar tendency to mimic Roman elite forms, save that at Petra we have the products of a broader court circle, where Cherchel and the Herodian palaces demonstrate an autocrat's taste.

97. Cf. also the fondness of Roman patrons for round garden-pavilions, as in the aviary of Varro or the *diaeta* of the Gardens of Maecenas (supra n. 4).

forms seem to be tied to no particular cultic function either, in contrast with East Greek practice. The famous round marble temple by the Tiber in the Forum Boarium[98] (ca. 100 B.C.) was designed by a Greek architect of Asia Minor, but the frame of the project—a round temple in an urban setting—seems the terms of the Roman patron, without good parallels in its architect's homeland (see below).

In decorative as well as funerary contexts round shrines were a favored frame for a particular statue, and this is reflected in the tendency in Roman painting and stucco to delineate carefully the presence of such figures. Ptolemy IV had used a round shrine to house an Aphrodite statue on his celebrated boat (Athenaeus 5.204), but the expanded taste for such constructions came later. The round shrine for the Cnidian Venus seems to have been a Roman-era construction; Caesar installed such a shrine on his Roman *horti* in the mid-1st century B.C.;[99] in the central Roman Venus Genetrix panel of the Boscoreale reception room, a round temple stands to Venus' right like a kind of identifying attribute,[100] and other painted *tholoi* often contain a Venus statue. I have already outlined above the distinctive tendency of Western tombs to use round "shrines" to house funerary statues; in the 2nd century *monopteroi* were already used for other ends not paralleled in the East, as at Pompeii for a sanctuary fountain or at Praeneste to cover a sacred pit (see below). With regard to round colonnaded shrines, I would suggest that once again we are dealing with a form that has East Mediterranean roots, to be sure, but one that was assimilated readily in the Roman Late Republic, and used with a distinctively Roman freedom of deployment.

Note also that *monopteroi/tholoi* in 2nd Style architectural painting always occur as part of a set "constellation," consisting of a discrete monument centrally located in a monumental portico and viewed on axis, in a calculated prospect of structures seen through and above one another.[101] If we are to decide what sort of reminiscences the individual elements of

portico and shrine were meant to provoke, we must consider these putative complexes as such.[102] Whatever the Hellenistic roots of such arrangements, by 100 B.C. at the latest—before the earliest Italian examples of the 2nd Style—they must have seemed triumphantly Roman, once triumphant ex-generals had multiplied temple and portico complexes throughout the Campus Martius at Rome and at great sanctuaries all around Latium.[103] It is easy to see the derivation of simple wall articulation schemes in the 2nd Style from three-dimensional conventions for interior decoration; in the House of the Griffins in Rome (ca. 100 B.C.), our earliest 2nd Style room,[104] the design of interior columns before colored ashlar blocks clearly mimics arrangements of free-standing columns observable in the typical withdrawing or reception room called a Corinthian *oecus*. Similarly, the arrangement of elements in the *monopteros* scheme draws on actual forms of architectural arrangement and siting, this time in the public sphere, where round walled shrines always stood in close visual relationship to porticoes and colonnades. The *monopteros* prospects at the architectural *cubiculum* at Boscoreale, for instance, were made by and for persons familiar with arrangements like those in Pompeii at the Triangular Forum, with its 2nd-century B.C. fountainhouse *monopteros* viewed against a columnar screen or facade.[105] This effect was taken up again for the mid-Julio-Claudian kiosk of the *Macellum* porticoes set on axis with an imperial ruler temple.[106] In the later 2nd century it seems to have been available to the Praeneste architects as a natural esthetic solution to the problem of marking a sacred spot in front of the colonnades of the lower sanctuary terrace: a *monopteros* is what they put over the holy cleft by the right-hand terrace exedra.[107] A parallel case for siting and representation can be made for round temples, which might also be placed to be viewed next to the peripteral colonnades of a conventional podium temple, in spaces more loosely framed; this effect too is replicated in painted images. By 100 B.C. *tholoi* had accret-

---

98. F. Coarelli, *Il Foro Boario dalle origini alla fine della repubblica* (Rome 1988) 84f., map p. 8, figs. 18–19. See also n. 31, 108.
99. Cf. La Rocca (supra n. 4) 20, fig. 18.
100. B. Andreae in *Kaiser Augustus* (supra n. 5) figs. at 276–277, 279.
101. Cf. Tybout (supra n. 6) pls. 18–19 (Villa dei Misteri); 27, 29, 31 (Boscoreale); 45, 47 (Oplontis); 59–60 (Pompeii, House of the Labyrinth). Pl. 78.1 shows a fragmentary round shrine from Alexandria at Grave 1 (room 3) of Mustapha Pascha: there is no evidence of its framing context; I feel that the date of this grave is too widely debated to be useful, and the Latin-Campnaian workshop tradition is autonomous enough (as Tybout himself describes) to stand alone.
102. One curious feature of these prospects is that the shrines illustrated are often lifted up, by unexplained means, to tower over precinct gates. In this respect they illustrate the un-rational satisfaction of the esthetic impulse toward making monuments and temples visible that so governed Roman public construction; cf. compare here Macdonald's discussion of "Visibil-

ity" (supra n. 64) 133–142.
103. See the bibl. for Coarelli (supra n. 22).
104. See n. 67.
105. Richardson (supra n. 7) 70–71; the still unpublished *monopteros*, see Seiler (supra n. 87) 139, n. 573. Nice drawn reconstructions of the shrine in relation to the temple on this *forum* are in *Pompéi. Travaux et envois des architectes français au xix.e siècle. Institut Français de Naples . . . 1981* (Naples 1981) 48, fig. 41; 77, fig. 47 (Weichhardt).
106. Richardson (supra n. 7) 198f; plan, Ward-Perkins (supra n. 23) fig. 88.
107. Coarelli (supra n. 22) 50, fig. 15. Earlier reconstructions attributed a *monopteros* to the sanctuary's crowning point, and that version is unfortunately the most widely reproduced, esp. in English handbook versions (see n. 22). This structure was, rather, an enclosed domed rotunda opening off the curved portico at the top of the "theater" cavea, not visible from any lower point in the complex; see most recently Rakob (supra n. 22) figs. 6, 13, 19–24.

ed by deliberate planning next to the podium temples of the Forum Boarium in Rome[108] and on the acropolis at Tibur;[109] that such a juxtaposition was savored is documented by its role as a painted subject in 2nd Style monumental landscapes, e.g., the central Venus panel of the Boscoreale salon[110] (40s B.C.) and the late 2nd Style vista (Naples inv. 8594).[111]

The round building and portico constellations of the 2nd Style, then, or the temple groupings of other panels, seem to correspond to Roman public building habits as much as to the arrangements of Hellenistic palaces. The 1st-century taste for *monopteroi* and the esthetics of their siting is documented, finally, by projects of Augustus, a Late Republican noblemen reared in 2nd Style interiors who had the power and wealth to do whatever he would like as an architectural patron. In Rome, Augustus ornamented the porticoed terraces of the Capitoline Hill itself with a baldachino shrine for one of his most important cultic commissions; this *monopteros* shrine of Mars Ultor upon his coinage[112] must be imagined in the kind of grand porticoes seen in the Oplontis *triclinium.* In Athens, he wanted to impose a monument of imperial and personal authority on the iconic center of Greek visual culture; the Temple of Rome and Augustus was inserted as a *monopteros* shrine on axis with the Parthenon facade, silhouetted against its colonnades.[113] One could even suggest that these Augustan commissions were the result of conditioning by the habits of 2nd Style painting, the decors in which Augustus and his circle will have been raised.

This essay has traversed between matrix sensibility, broad structure, and case details to explore the signifying qualities of 2nd Style architectural villa decoration. Simply put, I suggest that these images were made for patrons who liked to look at buildings and to see themselves as builders. A Roman esthetic, a Roman structure, animates these architectonic constellations. The magnificence of their simulated veneers was appropriated originally from the Hellenistic East, but that atmosphere of magnificence was rapidly absorbed into the Roman obsession with rank and *decorum;* hence Vitruvius' explicit statement that the fineness of material employed in a building reflects praise directly upon the owner and patron of a

building (*De Arch.* 6.8.9). Taken together, the fictive architectural arrangements of the 2nd Style and their simulated materials combine to flatter their *dominus* by setting him in a frame with overtones of public as well as private architecture. This frame both attributes and satisfies an architectural sensibility, a category of the imagination documented broadly in 1st century B.C. representation, visual and textual. These painted frames confer on their living inhabitants the putative status of a great builder, not only of Lucullan villas but also of civic monuments to military and political achievement.

Perhaps the most urbane elements of the 2nd Style suites of the *pars urbana* in a villa will have been the class of vista motifs, prospects onto a familiar world of public architecture, exuberantly breathing out *Romanitas* in their spatial esthetics and architectural iconography. Sometimes—often—2nd Style architectures expanded on house construction itself, commenting in the sphere of otium on the physical trappings of *otium.* But the villa residence, though superficially removed from the urban townhouse, was also a sphere in which the *civis Romanus* and the magisterial class of the Italian towns retained a public as well as a private identity. Lucretius, indeed, mocked at the end of Book III of his Epicurean epic the unhappy and unstable *civis* who dashed madly back and forth between his villa and his townhouse, because in either place he would be consumed by thoughts of the other; Cicero, a little more balanced, used the refreshment of rural seclusion to retire to his library to write, in the intervals of estate management, about the politics, religion, institutions, and great men of the *urbs.* Just so, the owner of the Boscoreale villa seated in his small salon could pass at will, with a flick of the eye, from the jumbled cliffs of a multistory townscape to portico precinct to villa *hortus* and grotto, each the stage for a different *persona.* All his choices were framed in the solid painted architectures that he would have seen in his urban dwelling, as here amid his vineyards. The architectures of the Late Republican house can seem alien to a Cato-and-cabbages rusticity. They were in fact a thoroughly decorous vestment for a Roman country life precisely *because* they imported the values of the well-to-do and

---

108. For the conjunction of the Corinthian T. Heracles Victor (n. 98) and the earlier Ionic T. Portunus, see: Nash (supra n. 7) s.v.; Coarelli (supra n. 22) 280, 285–286; Sear (supra n. 22) fig. 9.
109. Coarelli (supra n. 22) 85 f., ca. 120–90 B.C.; a Corinthian *tholos* and its terrace were added next to the older Doric podium temple in the course of the late 2nd-century remodeling of the city.
110. See n. 11.
111. From Pompeii VI.ins. occ.; col. pl. at p. 40 (no. 36) in *Collezioni del Museo Nazionale di Napoli* (1986); Beyen 1938/50 (supra n. 10) 8f.; Tybout (supra n. 6) pl. 66.
112. E.g., the shrine for Augustus' patron deity Mars Ultor on the Capitol, dedicated 12 May 20 B.C. (when it held the returned Parthian standards): aureus 18–19 B.C. *RIC* I.2 43 no. 28, C.

H. V. Sutherland, *Roman History and Coinage 44 B.C.–A.D. 69* (Oxford 1987) 4–5; denarius 18 B.C., *RIC* I.2 49 no. 119, Sutherland (supra) 15–16, Zanker (supra n. 26) 108, fig. 89; cistophoros 19/18 B.C. *RIC* I.2 82 no. 507, W. Trillmich in *Kaiser Augustus* (supra n. 5) 514–515, no. 341. On this Eastern issue the shrine is given walls. See Fuchs (1975) [1969 (supra n.33)] 38, pl. 5f, nos. 65–74.
113. J. Travlos, *Pictorial Dictionary of Ancient Athens* (1971/90) s.v., 494–497, figs. 624–627; D. J. Geagan, "Roman Athens: Some aspects of life and culture. I. 86 B.C.–A.D. 267" *ANRW* II.7.1 (1979) 371–437 at 382, 420–421. W. Binder, *Der Roma-Augustus Monopteros auf der Akropolis in Athen und sein typologischer Ort* (1976) locates the shrine beside the Erechtheion; if so, this would resemble the Republican constellation of podium temple and *tholos.*

accomplished citizen to that countryside so revered by Romans as the nurse of civic virtue. The framing architectures and architectural vistas of the 2nd Style appealed to an ethic, that of building and making, which *could* transfer from city to country. Economically, the goal for any estate may have been to achieve self-suffiency and sever dependence on the city or other individuals; by contrast, the *dominus* cultivated and enjoyed an artistic culture that explicitly bridged the gap between his different worlds and different selves.

List of Figures